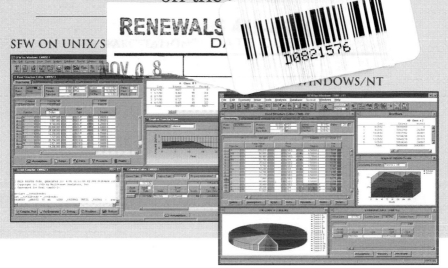

Perspectives on Interest Rate Risk Management for Money Managers and Traders

Edited by

Frank J. Fabozzi, CFA
Adjunct Professor of Finance
School of Management
Yale University

Published by Frank J. Fabozzi Associates

ISBN: 1-883249-29-5

Printed in the United States of America

Table of Contents

Contributing Authors

Oren Cheyette	BARRA, Inc.
Kenneth B. Dunn	Miller Anderson & Sherrerd, LLP
Frank J. Fabozzi	Yale University
H. Gifford Fong	Gifford Fong Associates
Teri Geske	Capital Management Sciences
Bennett W. Golub	BlackRock Financial Management, Inc.
Benjamin J. Gord	Miller Anderson & Sherrerd, LLP
Ronald N. Kahn	BARRA, Inc.
Gunnar Klinkhammer	Capital Management Sciences
Michele A. Kreisler	Miller Anderson & Sherrerd, LLP
Wai Lee	J.P. Morgan Investment Management Inc.
Jingxi Liu	Capital Market Risk Advisors, Inc.
Biao Lu	
Michael Minnich	Capital Market Risk Advisors, Inc.
Wesley Phoa	Capital Management Sciences
Shrikant Ramamurthy	Prudential Securities Incorporated
Robert R. Reitano	John Hancock Mutual Life Insurance Company
Scott F. Richard	Miller Anderson & Sherrerd, LLP
Roberto M. Sella	Miller Anderson & Sherrerd, LLP
Leo M. Tilman	BlackRock Financial Management, Inc.
Oldrich A. Vasicek	Gifford Fong Associates
Ram Willner	PIMCO
Richard B. Worley	Miller Anderson & Sherrerd, LLP

Chapter 1

Interest Rate Models

Oren Cheyette, Ph.D.
Manager, Fixed Income Research
BARRA, Inc.

INTRODUCTION

An interest rate model is a probabilistic description of the future evolution of interest rates. Based on today's information, future interest rates are uncertain: an interest rate model is a characterization of that uncertainty. Quantitative analysis of securities with rate dependent cash flows requires application of such a model in order to find the present value of the uncertainty. Since all fixed-income securities other than option-free bonds have interest rate sensitive cash flows, this matters to most fixed-income portfolio managers, as well as to traders and users of interest rate derivatives.

For security valuation and risk estimation one wants to use only models that are arbitrage free and matched to the currently observed term structure of interest rates. "Arbitrage free" means just that if one values the same cash flows in two different ways, one should get the same result. For example, a 10-year bond putable at par by the holder in 5 years can also be viewed as a 5-year bond with an option of the holder to extend the maturity for another 5 years. An arbitrage-free model will produce the same value for the structure viewed either way. This is also known as the *law of one price*. The term structure matching condition means that when a default-free straight bond is valued according to the model, the result should be the same as if the bond's cash flows are simply discounted according to the current default-free term structure. A model that fails to satisfy either of these conditions cannot be trusted for general problems, though it may be usable in some limited context.

For equity derivatives, lognormality of prices (leading to the Black-Scholes formula for calls and puts) is the standard starting point for option calculations. In the fixed-income market, unfortunately, there is no equally natural and simple assumption. Wall Street dealers routinely use a multiplicity of models based on widely varying assumptions in different markets. For example, an options desk most likely uses a version of the Black formula to value interest rate caps and floors. This use assumes a lognormal distribution of bond prices (since, e.g., a caplet is a put on a 3-month discount bond), which in turn implies a normal distribution of interest rates. A few feet away, the mortgage desk may use a lognormal interest rate model to evaluate their passthrough and CMO effective durations.

1

It may seem that one's major concern in choosing an interest rate model should be the accuracy with which it represents the empirical volatility of the term structure of rates, and its ability to fit market prices of vanilla derivatives such as at-the-money caps and swaptions. These are clearly important criteria, but they are not decisive. The first criterion is hard to pin down, depending strongly on what historical period one chooses to examine. The second criterion is easy to satisfy for most commonly used models, by the simple (though unappealing) expedient of permitting predicted future volatility to be time dependent. So, while important, this concern doesn't really do much to narrow the choices.

A critical issue in selecting an interest rate model is, instead, ease of application. For some models it is difficult or impossible to provide efficient valuation algorithms for all securities of interest to a typical investor. Given that one would like to analyze all assets using the same underlying assumptions, this is a significant problem. At the same time, one would prefer not to stray too far from economic reasonableness — such as by using the Black-Scholes formula to value callable bonds. These considerations lead to a fairly narrow menu of choices among the known interest rate models.

The organization of this chapter is as follows. In the next section I provide a (brief) discussion of the principles of valuation algorithms. This will give a context for many of the points made in the third section, which provides an overview of the various characteristics that differentiate interest rate models. Finally, in the fourth section I describe the empirical evidence on interest rate dynamics and provide a quantitative comparison of a family of models that closely match those in common use. I have tried to emphasize those issues that are primarily of interest for application of the models in practical settings. There is little point in having the theoretically ideal model if it can't actually be implemented as part of a valuation algorithm.

VALUATION

Valuation algorithms for rate dependent contingent claims are usually based on a risk neutral formula, which states that the present value of an uncertain cash flow at time T is given by the average over all interest rate scenarios of the scenario cash flow divided by the scenario value at time T of a money market investment of $1 today.[1] More formally, the value of a security is given by the expectation (average) over interest rate scenarios

$$P = E\left[\sum_i \frac{C_i}{M_i}\right]$$

(1)

where C_i is the security's cash flows and M_i is the money market account value at time t_i in each scenario, calculated by assuming continual reinvestment at the prevailing short rate.

---

[1] The money market account is the *numeraire*.

The probability weights used in the average are chosen so that the expected rate of return on any security over the next instant is the same, namely the short rate. These are the so-called "risk neutral" probability weights: they would be the true weights if investors were indifferent to bearing interest rate risk. In that case, investors would demand no excess return relative to a (riskless) money market account in order to hold risky positions — hence equation (1).

It is important to emphasize that the valuation formula is not dependent on any *assumption* of risk neutrality. Assets are valued by equation (1) *as if* the market were indifferent to interest rate risk *and* the correct discount factor for a future cash flow were the inverse of the money market return. Both statements are false for the real world, but the errors are offsetting: a valuation formula based on probabilities implying a nonzero market price of interest rate risk and the corresponding scenario discount factors would give the same value.

There are two approaches to computing the average in equation (1): by direct brute force evaluation, or indirectly by solving a related differential equation. The brute force method is usually called the Monte Carlo method. It consists of generating a large number of possible interest rate scenarios based on the interest rate model, computing the cash flows and money market values in each one, and averaging. Properly speaking, only path generation based on random numbers is a Monte Carlo method. There are other scenario methods — e.g., complete sampling of a tree — that do not depend on the use of random numbers. Given sufficient computer resources, the scenario method can tackle essentially any type of security.[2]

A variety of schemes are known for choosing scenario sample paths efficiently, but none of them are even remotely as fast and accurate as the second technique. In certain cases (discussed in more detail in the next section) the average in equation (1) obeys a partial differential equation — like the one derived by Black and Scholes for equity options — for which there exist fast and accurate numerical solution methods, or in special cases even analytical solutions. This happens only for interest rate models of a particular type, and then only for certain security types, such as caps, floors, swaptions, and options on bonds. For securities such as mortgage passthroughs, CMOs, and index amortizing swaps, simulation methods are the only alternative.

MODEL TAXONOMY

The last two decades have seen the development of a tremendous profusion of models for valuation of interest rate sensitive securities. In order to better understand these models, it is helpful to recognize a number of features that characterize and distinguish them. These are features of particular relevance to practitioners wishing to implement valuation algorithms, as they render some

---

[2] This is true even for American options. For a review see P. Boyle, M. Broadie, and P. Glasserman, "Monte Carlo Methods for Security Pricing," working paper, 1995, to appear in the *Journal of Economic Dynamics and Control*.

models completely unsuitable for certain asset types.[3] The following subsections enumerate some of the major dimensions of variation among the different models.

One Versus Multi-Factor

In many cases, the value of an interest rate contingent claim depends, effectively, on the prices of many underlying assets. For example, while the payoff of a caplet depends only on the reset date value of a zero coupon bond maturing at the payment date (valued based on, say, 3-month LIBOR), the payoff to an option on a coupon bond depends on the exercise date values of all of the bond's remaining interest and principal payments. Valuation of such an option is in principle an inherently multi-dimensional problem.

Fortunately, in practice these values are highly correlated. The degree of correlation can be quantified by examining the covariance matrix of changes in spot rates of different maturities. A principal component analysis of the covariance matrix decomposes the motion of the spot curve into independent (uncorrelated) components. The largest principal component describes a common shift of all interest rates in the same direction. The next leading components are a twist, with short rates moving one way and long rates the other, and a "butterfly" motion, with short and long rates moving one way, and intermediate rates the other. Based on analysis of weekly data from the Federal Reserve H15 series of benchmark Treasury yields from 1983 through 1995, the shift component accounts for 84% of the total variance of spot rates, while twist and butterfly account for 11% and 4%, leaving about 1% for all remaining principal components.

The shift factor alone explains a large fraction of the overall movement of spot rates. As a result, valuation can be reduced to a one factor problem in many instances with little loss of accuracy. Only securities whose payoffs are primarily sensitive to the shape of the spot curve rather than its overall level (such as dual index floaters, which depend on the difference between a long and a short rate) will not be modeled well with this approach.

In principle it is straightforward to move from a one-factor model to a multi-factor one. In practice, though, implementations of multi-factor valuation models are complicated and slow, and require estimation of many more volatility parameters than are needed for one-factor models, so there is substantial benefit to using a one-factor model when possible. The remainder of this chapter will focus on one-factor models.

Exogenous Versus Endogenous Term Structure

The first interest rate models were not constructed so as to fit an arbitrary initial term structure. Instead, with a view towards analytical simplicity, the Vasicek[4]

---

[3] There is, unfortunately, a version of Murphy's law applicable to interest rate models, which states that the computational tractability of a model is inversely proportional to its economic realism.
[4] O. Vasicek, "An Equilibrium Characterization of the Term Structure," *Journal of Financial Economics* (November 1977).

and Cox-Ingersoll-Ross[5] (CIR) models contain a few constant parameters that define an endogenously specified term structure. That is, the initial spot curve is given by an analytical formula in terms of the model parameters. These are sometimes also called "equilibrium" models, as they posit yield curves derived from an assumption of economic equilibrium based on a given market price of risk and other parameters governing collective expectations.

For *dynamically* reasonable choices of the parameters — values that give plausible long-run interest rate distributions and option prices — the term structures achievable in these models have far too little curvature to accurately represent typical empirical spot rate curves. This is because the mean reversion parameter, governing the rate at which the short rate reverts towards the long-run mean, also governs the volatility of long-term rates relative to the volatility of the short rate — the "term structure of volatility." To achieve the observed level of long-rate volatility (or to price options on long-term securities well) requires that there be relatively little mean reversion, but this implies low curvature yield curves. This problem can be partially solved by moving to a multi-factor framework — but at a significant cost as discussed earlier. These models are therefore not particularly useful as the basis for valuation algorithms — they simply have too few degrees of freedom to faithfully represent real markets.

To be used for valuation, a model must be "calibrated" to the initial spot rate curve. That is, the model structure must accommodate an exogenously determined spot rate curve, typically given by fitting to bond prices, or sometimes to futures prices and swap rates. All models in common use are of this type.

There is a "trick" invented by Dybvig that converts an endogenous model to a calibrated exogenous one.[6] The trick can be viewed as splitting the nominal interest rate into two parts: the stochastic part modeled endogenously, and a non stochastic drift term, which compensates for the mismatch of the endogenous term structure and the observed one. (BARRA uses this technique to modify the CIR model to match the observed term structure in its fixed income analytics.) The price of this method is that the volatility function is no longer a simple function of the nominal interest rate, because the nominal rate is not the one that governs the level of volatility.

Short Rate Versus Yield Curve

The risk neutral valuation formula requires that one know the sequence of short rates for each scenario, so an interest rate model must provide this information. For this reason, many interest rate models are simply models of the stochastic evolution of the short rate. A second reason for the desirability of such models is that

---

[5] J.C. Cox, J.E. Ingersoll, Jr., and S.A. Ross, "A Theory of the Term Structure of Interest Rates," *Econometrica* (March 1985).

[6] P. Dybvig, "Bond and Bond Option Pricing Based on the Current Term Structure," working paper, 1989, forthcoming in *Mathematics of Derivative Securities*, M. A. H. Dempster and S. Pliska, (eds.), Cambridge University Press.

they have the *Markov property*, meaning that the evolution of the short rate at each instant depends only on its current value — not on how it got there. The practical significance of this is that, as alluded to in the previous section, the valuation problem for many types of assets can be reduced to solving a partial differential equation, for which there exist efficient analytical and numerical techniques. To be amenable to this calculation technique, a security's cash flow at time t must depend only on the state of affairs at that time, not on how the evolution occurred prior to t, or it must be equivalent to a portfolio of such securities (for example, a callable bond is a position long a straight bond and short a call option).

Short-rate models have two parts. One specifies the average rate of change ("drift") of the short rate at each instant; the other specifies the instantaneous volatility of the short rate. The conventional notation for this is

$$dr(t) = \mu(r, t)dt + \sigma(r, t)dz(t) \tag{2}$$

The left-hand side of this equation is the change in the short rate over the next instant. The first term on the right is the drift multiplied by the size of the time step. The second is the volatility multiplied by a normally distributed random increment. For most models, the drift component must be determined through a numerical technique to match the initial spot rate curve, while for a small number of models there exists an analytical relationship. In general, there exists a no-arbi-trage relationship linking the initial forward rate curve, the volatility $\sigma(r,t)$, the market price of interest rate risk, and the drift term $\mu(r,t)$. However, since typically one must solve for the drift numerically, this relationship plays no role in model construction. Differences between models arise from different dependences of the drift and volatility terms on the short rate.

For assets whose cash flows don't depend on the interest rate history, the expectation formula (1) for present value obeys the Feynman-Kac equation

$$\frac{1}{2}\sigma^2 P_{rr} + (\mu - \lambda)P_r + P_t - rP + c = 0 \tag{3}$$

where, for example, P_r denotes the partial derivative of P with respect to r, c is the payment rate of the security, and λ, which can be time and rate dependent, is the market price of interest rate risk.

The terms in this equation can be understood as follows. In the absence of uncertainty ($\sigma = 0$), the equation involves four terms. The last three assert that the value of the security increases at the risk-free rate (rP), and decreases by the amount of any payments (c). The term $(\mu - \lambda)P_r$ accounts for change in value due to the change in the term structure with time, as rates move up the forward curve. In the absence of uncertainty it is easy to express $(\mu - \lambda)$ in terms of the initial forward rates. In the presence of uncertainty this term depends on the volatility as well, and we also have the first term, which is the main source of the complexity of valuation models.

The Vasicek and CIR models are models of the short rate. Both have the same form for the drift term, namely a tendency for the short rate to rise when it is below the long-term mean, and fall when it is above. That is, the short-rate drift has the form $\mu = \kappa(\theta - r)$, where r is the short rate and κ and θ are the mean reversion and long-term rate constants. The two models differ in the rate dependence of the volatility: it is constant (when expressed as points per year) in the Vasicek model, and proportional to the square root of the short rate in the CIR model.

The Dybvig-adjusted Vasicek model is the mean reverting generalization of the Ho-Lee model,[7] also known as the mean reverting Gaussian (MRG) model or the Hull-White model.[8] The MRG model has particularly simple analytical expressions for values of many assets — in particular, bonds and European options on bonds. Like the original Vasicek model, it permits the occurrence of negative interest rates with positive probability. However, for typical initial spot curves and volatility parameters, the probability of negative rates is quite small.

Other popular models of this type are the Black-Derman-Toy[9] (BDT) and Black-Karasinski[10] (BK) models, in which the volatility is proportional to the short rate, so that the ratio of volatility to rate level is constant. For these models, unlike the MRG and Dybvig-adjusted CIR models, the drift term is not simple. These models require numerical fitting to the initial interest rate and volatility term structures. The drift term is therefore not known analytically. In the BDT model, the short-rate volatility is also linked to the mean reversion strength (which is also generally time dependent) in such a way that — in the usual situation where long rates are less volatile than the short rate — the short-rate volatility decreases in the future. This feature is undesirable: one doesn't want to link the observation that the long end of the curve has relatively low volatility to a forecast that in the future the short rate will become less volatile. This problem motivated the development of the BK model in which mean reversion and volatility are delinked.

All of these models are explicit models of the short rate alone. It happens that in the Vasicek and CIR models (with or without the Dybvig adjustment) it is possible to express the entire forward curve as a function of the current short rate through fairly simple analytical formulas. This is not possible in the BDT and BK models, or generally in other models of short-rate dynamics, other than by highly inefficient numerical techniques. Indeed, it is possible to show that the only short-rate models consistent with an arbitrary initial term structure for which one can find the whole forward curve analytically are in a class that includes the MRG and Dybvig-adjusted CIR models as special cases, namely where the short-rate volatility has the form[11]

---

[7] T.S.Y. Ho and S.B. Lee, "Term Structure Movements and Pricing Interest Rate Contingent Claims," *Journal of Finance* (December 1986); and, J. Hull and A. White, "Pricing Interest Rate Derivative Securities," *The Review of Financial Studies*, 3:4 (1990).

[8] This model was also derived in F. Jamshidian, "The One-Factor Gaussian Interest Rate Model: Theory and Implementation," Merrill Lynch working paper, 1988.

[9] F. Black, E. Derman and W. Toy, "A One Factor Model of Interest Rates and its Application to Treasury Bond Options," *Financial Analysts Journal* (January/February 1990).

[10] F. Black and P. Karasinski, "Bond and Option Prices when Short Rates are Lognormal," *Financial Analysts Journal* (July/August 1992).

[11] A. Jeffrey, "Single Factor Heath-Jarrow-Morton Term Structure Models Based on Markov Spot Interest Rate Dynamics," *Journal of Financial and Quantitative Analysis*, 30:4 (December 1995).

$$\sigma(r, t) = \sqrt{\sigma_1(t) + \sigma_2(t)r}.$$

While valuation of certain assets (e.g., callable bonds) does not require knowledge of longer rates, there are broad asset classes that do. For example, mortgage pre-payment models are typically driven off a long-term Treasury par yield, such as the 10-year rate. Therefore a generic short-rate model such as BDT or BK is unsuitable if one seeks to analyze a variety of assets in a common interest rate framework.

An alternative approach to interest rate modeling is to specify the dynam-ics of the entire term structure. The volatility of the term structure is then given by some specified function, which most generally could be a function of time, matu-rity, and spot rates. A special case of this approach (in a discrete time framework) is the Ho-Lee model mentioned earlier, for which the term structure of volatility is a parallel shift of the spot rate curve, whose magnitude is independent of time and the level of rates. A completely general continuous time, multi-factor framework for constructing such models was given by Heath, Jarrow and Morton (HJM).[12]

It is sometimes said that all interest rate models are HJM models. This is technically true: in principle, every arbitrage-free model of the term structure can be described in their framework. In practice, however, it is impossible to do this analytically for most short-rate Markov models. The only ones for which it is pos-sible are those in the MRG-CIR family described earlier. The BDT and BK mod-els, for instance, cannot be translated to the HJM framework other than by impracticable numerical means. To put a model in HJM form, one must know the term structure of volatility at all times, and this is generally not possible for short-rate Markov models.

If feasible, the HJM approach is clearly very attractive, since one knows now not just the short rate but also all longer rates as well. In addition, HJM mod-els are very "natural," in the sense that the basic inputs to the model are the initial term structure of interest rates and a term structure of interest rate volatility for each independent motion of the yield curve.

The reason for the qualification in the last paragraph is that a generic HJM model requires keeping track of a potentially enormous amount of informa-tion. The HJM framework imposes no structure other than the requirement of no-arbitrage on the dynamics of the term structure. Each forward rate of fixed matu-rity evolves separately, so that one must keep track of each one separately. Since there are an infinite number of distinct forward rates, this can be difficult. This difficulty occurs even in a one factor HJM model, for which there is only one source of random movement of the term structure. A general HJM model does not have the Markov property that leads to valuation formulas expressed as solutions to partial differential equations. This makes it impossible to accurately value interest rate options without using huge amounts of computer time, since one is forced to use simulation methods.

---

[12] D. Heath, R. Jarrow, and A. Morton, "Bond Pricing and the Term Structure of Interest Rates: A New Methodology for Contingent Claims Valuation," *Econometrica*, 60:1 (January 1992).

In practice a simulation algorithm breaks the evolution of the term structure up into discrete time steps, so one need keep track of and simulate only forward rates for the finite set of simulation times. Still, this can be a large number (e.g., 360 or more for a mortgage passthrough), and this computational burden, combined with the inefficiency of simulation methods has prevented general HJM models from coming into more widespread use.

Some applications require simulation methods because the assets' structures (e.g., mortgage-backed securities) are not compatible with differential equation methods. For applications where one is solely interested in modeling such assets, there exists a class of HJM models that significantly simplify the forward rate calculations.[13] The simplest version of such models, the "two state Markov model," permits an arbitrary dependence of short-rate volatility on both time and the level of interest rates, while the ratio of forward-rate volatility to short-rate volatility is solely a function of term. That is, the volatility of $f(t,T)$, the term T forward rate at time t takes the form

$$\sigma_f(r, t, T) = \sigma(r, t)e^{-\int_t^T k(u)du} \tag{4}$$

where $\sigma(r,t) = \sigma_f(r,t,t)$ is the short-rate volatility and $k(t)$ determines the mean reversion rate or equivalently, the rate of decrease of forward rate volatility with term. The evolution of all forward rates in this model can be described in terms of two state variables: the short rate (or any other forward or spot rate), and the slope of the forward curve at the origin. The second variable can be expressed in terms of the total variance experienced by a forward rate of fixed maturity by the time it has become the short rate. The stochastic evolution equations for the two state variables can be written as

$$d\tilde{r}(t) = (V(t) - k(t)\tilde{r})dt + \sigma(r, t)dz(t)$$

$$V_t(t) = \sigma^2(r, t) - 2k(t)V(t) \tag{5}$$

where $\tilde{r}(t) \equiv r(t) - f(0, t)$ is the deviation of the short rate from the initial forward rate curve. The state variable $V(t)$ has initial value $V(0)=0$; its evolution equation is non-stochastic and can be integrated to give

$$V(t) = \int_0^t \sigma_f^2(r, s, t)ds = \int_0^t \sigma^2(r, s)e^{-2\int_s^t k(u)du} ds \tag{6}$$

---

[13] O. Cheyette, "Term Structure Dynamics and Mortgage Valuation," *Journal of Fixed Income* (March 1992). The two state Markov model was also described in P. Ritchken and L. Sankarasubramanian, "Volatility Structure of Forward Rates and the Dynamics of the Term Structure," *Mathematical Finance*, 5(1) (1995), pp. 55-72.

In terms of these state variables, the forward curve is given by

$$f(t, T) = f(0, T) + \phi(t, T)\left(\tilde{r} + V(t)\int_t^T \phi(t, s)ds\right) \tag{7}$$

where

$$\phi(t, T) = \sigma_f(r, t, T)/\sigma_f(r, t, t) = e^{\displaystyle -\int_t^T k(s)ds}$$

is a deterministic function.

Instead of having to keep track of hundreds of forward rates, one need only model the evolution of the two state variables. Path independent asset prices also obey a partial differential equation in this model, so it appears possible at least in principle to use more efficient numerical methods. The equation, analogous to equation (3), is

$$\frac{1}{2}\sigma^2 P_{\tilde{r}\tilde{r}} + (V - k\tilde{r})P_{\tilde{r}} + (\sigma^2 - 2kV)P_V + P_t - rP + c = 0. \tag{8}$$

Unlike equation (3), for which one must use the equation itself applied to bonds to solve for the coefficient $\mu - \lambda$, here the coefficient functions are all known in terms of the initial data: the short-rate volatility and the initial forward curve. This simplification has come at the price of adding a dimension, as we now have to contend also with a term involving the first derivative with respect to V, and so the equation is much more difficult to solve efficiently by standard techniques.

In the special case where $\sigma(r,t)$ is independent of r, this model is the MRG model mentioned earlier. In this case, V is a deterministic function of t, so the P_V term disappears from equation (8), leaving a two dimensional equation that has analytical solutions for European options on bonds, and straightforward numerical techniques for valuing American bond options. Since bond prices are lognormally distributed in this model, it should be no surprise that the formula for options on pure discount bounds (PDBs) looks much like the Black-Scholes formula. The value of a call with strike price K, exercise date t on a PDB maturing at time T is given by

$$C = P(T)N(h_1) - KP(t)N(h_2), \tag{9}$$

where

$$h_1 = \frac{k}{(1 - e^{-k(T-t)})\sqrt{V(t)}}\ln\frac{P(T)}{KP(t)} + \frac{\sqrt{V(t)}(1 - e^{-k(T-t)})}{2k},$$

$$h_2 = h_1 - \frac{\sqrt{V(t)}(1 - e^{-k(T-t)})}{k},$$

$N(x)$ is the Gaussian distribution, and $P(t)$ and $P(T)$ are prices of PDBs maturing at t and T. (The put value can be obtained by put-call parity.) Options on coupon bonds can be valued by adding up a portfolio of options on PDBs, one for each coupon or principal payment after the exercise date, with strike prices such that they are all at-the-money at the same value of the short rate. The Dybvig-adjusted CIR model has similar formulas for bond options, involving the non-central χ^2 distribution instead of the Gaussian one.

If $\sigma(r,t)$ depends on r, the model becomes similar to some other standard models. For example, $\sigma(r,t)=a\sqrt{r}$ has the same rate dependence as the CIR model, while choosing $\sigma(r,t)=br$ gives a model similar to BK, though in each case the drift and term structure of volatility are different.

Unless one has some short- or long-term view on trends in short-rate volatility, it is most natural to choose $\sigma(r,t)$ to be time independent, and similarly $k(u)$ to be constant. This is equivalent to saying that the shape of the volatility term structure — though not necessarily its magnitude — should be constant over time. (Otherwise, as in the BDT model, one is imposing an undesirable linkage between today's shape of the forward rate volatility curve and future volatility curves.) In that case, the term structure of forward-rate volatility is exponentially decreasing with maturity, and the integrals in equations (6) and (7) can be computed, giving for the forward curve

$$f(t, T) = f(0, T) + e^{-k(T-t)}\left(\tilde{r} + V(t)\,\frac{1 - e^{-k(T-t)}}{k}\right). \tag{10}$$

Finally, if the volatility is assumed rate independent as well, the integral expression for $V(t)$ can be evaluated to give

$$V(t) = \sigma^2\,\frac{1 - e^{-2kt}}{2k}\,, \tag{11}$$

and we obtain the forward curves of the MRG model.

Empirically, neither the historical volatility nor the implied volatility falls off so neatly. Instead, volatility typically increases with term out to between 1 and 3 years, then drops off. The two state Markov model cannot accommodate this behavior, except by imposing a forecast of increasing then decreasing short-rate volatility, or a short run of negative mean reversion. There is, however, an extension of the model that permits modeling of humped or other more complicated volatility curves, at the cost of introducing additional state variables.[14] With five state variables, for example, it is possible to model the dominant volatility term structure of the U.S. Treasury spot curve very accurately.

Recently, a model of bond price dynamics was devised[15] that does not fit the dichotomy of this section, for the simple reason that it is not a model of interest

---

[14] O. Cheyette, "Markov Representation of the HJM Model," working paper, 1995.
[15] B. Flesaker and L. P. Hughston, "Positive Interest," *Risk Magazine* (January 1996) and "Dynamic Models for Yield Curve Evolution," working paper (January 1996).

rates, but is instead a model of discount factors (PDB prices). Rather than using a valuation formula based on risk-neutral rate movements and a money-market numeraire, the model is based on another probability distribution and numeraire with many nice properties. The developers of the model call their approach the "positive interest" framework, since it has the attractive feature that all models in the framework have positive interest rates at all times. In addition, the interest rate process is guaranteed not to explode. Like the HJM approach, this model is really a framework for constructing specific models, as it imposes no structure other than that dictated by the requirements of arbitrage freedom, calibration, and positivity of rates. Unfortunately, the only published model based on this approach (the "rational lognormal model"[16]) suffers from some fairly serious financial defects.[17] First, interest rates are bounded below at a level that approaches the forward rate curve, so floors with strikes below the bound are valued at zero, as are long calls on bonds with low but nonzero coupons. Second, the short-rate volatility decreases over time and eventually approaches zero. So, while the model provides closed form solutions for many types of derivatives, its defects seem to render it unusable.

EMPIRICAL AND NUMERICAL CONSIDERATIONS

Given the profusion of models, it is reasonable to ask whether there are empirical or other considerations that can help motivate a choice of one model for applications. One might take the view that one should use whichever model is most convenient for the particular problem at hand — e.g., BDT or BK for bonds with embedded options, Black model for caps and floors, a two state Markov model for mortgages, and a ten state, two factor Markov-HJM model for dual index amortizing floaters. The obvious problem with this approach is that it can't be used to find hedging relationships or relative value between assets valued according to the different models. I take as a given, then, that we seek models that can be used effectively for valuation of most asset types with minimum compromise of financial reasonableness. The choice will likely depend on how many and what kinds of assets one needs to value. A trader of vanilla options may be less concerned about cross-market consistency issues than a manager of portfolios of callable bonds and mortgage-backed securities.

The major empirical consideration — and one that has produced a large amount of inconclusive research — is the assumed dependence of volatility on the level of interest rates. Different researchers have reported various evidence that volatility is best explained (1) as a power of the short rate[18] ($\sigma \propto r\gamma$) — with γ so large that models with this volatility have rates running off to infinity with high

[16] Ibid.

[17] O. Cheyette and L. Goldberg, unpublished note, and L. Goldberg, "An Examination of the Rational Lognormal Model," working paper, 1996.

[18] K.C. Chan, G.A. Karolyi, F.A. Longstaff, and A.B. Sanders, "An Empirical Comparison of Alternative Models of the Short Rate," *Journal of Finance* 47:3 (1992).

probability ("explosions"), (2) by a GARCH model with very long (possibly infinite) persistence,[19] (3) by some combination of GARCH with a power law dependence on rates,[20] (4) by none of the above.[21] All of this work has been in the context of short-rate Markov models.

Here I will present some fairly straightforward evidence in favor of choice (4) based on analysis of movements of the whole term structure of spot rates, rather than just short rates, from U.S. Treasury yields over the period 1977 to early 1996.

The result is that the market appears to be well described by "eras" with very different rate dependences of volatility, possibly coinciding with periods of different Federal Reserve policies. Since all the models in common use have a power law dependence of volatility on rates, I attempted to determine the best fit to the exponent (γ) relating the two. My purpose here is not so much to provide another entrant in this already crowded field, but rather to suggest that there may be no simple answer to the empirical question. No model with constant parameters seems to do a very good job. A surprising result, given the degree to which the market for interest rate derivatives has exploded and the widespread use of lognormal models, is that the period since 1987 is best modeled by a nearly *normal* model of interest rate volatility.

The data used in the analysis consisted of spot rate curves derived from the Federal Reserve H15 series of weekly average benchmark yields. The benchmark yields are given as semiannually compounded yields of hypothetical par bonds with fixed maturities ranging from 3 months to 30 years, derived by interpolation from actively traded issues. The data cover the period from early 1977, when a 30-year bond was first issued, through March of 1996. The spot curves are represented as continuous, piecewise linear functions, constructed by a root finding procedure to exactly match the given yields, assumed to be yields of par bonds. (This is similar to the conventional bootstrapping method.) The two data points surrounding the 1987 crash were excluded: the short and intermediate markets moved by around ten standard deviations during the crash, and this extreme event would have had a significant skewing effect on the analysis.

A parsimonious representation of the spot curve dynamics is given by the two state Markov model with constant mean reversion k and volatility that is time independent and proportional to a power of the short rate: $\sigma(r)=\beta r^\gamma$. In this case, the term structure of spot rate volatility, given by integrating equation (4), is

$$\sigma(r_t)v(T) = \beta r_t^\gamma \frac{1-e^{-kT}}{kT} \tag{12}$$

where T is the maturity and r_t is the time t short rate. The time t weekly change in the spot rate curve is then given by the change due to the passage of time ("rolling

[19] See R.J. Brenner, R.H. Harjes, and K.F. Kroner, "Another Look at Alternative Models of the Short-Term Interest Rate," University of Arizona working paper (1993), and references therein.
[20] Ibid.
[21] Y. Aït-Sahalia, "Testing Continuous Time Models of the Spot Interest Rate," *Review of Financial Studies*, 9:2 (1996).

up the forward curve") plus a random change of the form $v(T)x_t$, where for each t, x_t, is an independent normal random variable with distribution $N(\mu, \sigma(r_t)\sqrt{52})$. (The systematic drift μ of x_t, over time was assumed to be independent of time and the rate level.) The parameters β, γ, and k are estimated as follows. First, using an initial guess for γ, k is estimated by a maximum likelihood fit of the maturity dependence of $v(T)$ to the spot curve changes. Then, using this value of k, another maximum likelihood fit is applied to fit the variance of x_t to the power law model of $\sigma(r_t)$. The procedure is then iterated to improve the estimates of k and γ, but it turns out that the best fit value of k is quite insensitive to the value of γ, and vice versa.

One advantage of looking at the entire term structure is that we avoid modeling just idiosyncratic behavior of the short end, e.g., that it is largely determined by the Federal Reserve. An additional feature of this analysis is proper accounting for the effect of the "arbitrage-free drift" — namely, the systematic change of interest rates due purely to the shape of the forward curve at the start of each period. Prior analyses have typically involved fitting to endogenous short-rate models with constant parameters not calibrated to each period's term structure. The present approach mitigates a fundamental problem of prior research in the context of one-factor models, namely that interest rate dynamics are poorly described by a single factor. By re-initializing the drift parameters at the start of each sample period and studying the volatility of changes to a well-defined term structure factor, the effects of additional factors are excluded from the analysis.

The results for the different time periods are shown in Exhibit 1. (The exhibit doesn't include the best fit values of β, which are not relevant to the empirical issue at hand.) The error estimates reported in the exhibit are derived by a boot-strap Monte Carlo procedure that constructs artificial data sets by random sampling of the original set with replacement and applies the same analysis to them.[22] It is apparent that the different subperiods are well described by very different exponents and mean reversion. The different periods were chosen to include or exclude the monetarist policy "experiment" under Volcker of the late 1970s and early 1980s, and also to sample just the Greenspan era. For the period since 1987, the best fit exponent of 0.19 is significantly different from zero at the 95% confidence level, but not at the 99% level. However, the best fit value is well below the threshold of 0.5 required to guarantee positivity of interest rates, with 99% confidence. There appears to be weak sensitivity of volatility to the rate level, but much less than is implied by a number of models in widespread use — in particular, BDT, BK, and CIR.

The estimates for the mean reversion parameter k can be understood through the connection of mean reversion to the term structure of volatility. Large values of k imply large fluctuations in short rates compared to long rates, since longer rates reflect the expectation that changes in short rates will not persist forever. The early 1980s saw just such a phenomenon, with the yield curve becoming very steeply inverted for a brief period. Since then, the volatility of the short rate (in absolute terms of points per year) has been only slightly higher than that of long-term rates.

---

[22] B.J. Efron and R.J. Tibshirani, *An Introduction to the Bootstrap* (New York: Chapman & Hall, 1993).

Exhibit 1: Parameter Estimates for the Two State Markov Model with Power Law Volatility over Various Sample Periods *

Sample Period	Exponent (γ)	Mean Reversion (k)	Comments
3/1/77 - 3/29/96	1.04 ± 0.07	0.054 ± 0.007	Full data set
3/1/77 - 1/1/87	1.6 ± 0.10	0.10 ± 0.020	Pre-Greenspan
3/1/77 - 1/1/83	1.72 ± 0.15	0.22 ± 0.040	"Monetarist"policy
1/1/83 - 3/29/96	0.45 ± 0.07	0.019 ± 0.005	Post high-rate period
1/1/87 - 3/29/96	0.19 ± 0.09	0.016 ± 0.004	Greenspan

* The uncertainties are one standard deviation estimates based on bootstrap Monte Carlo resampling.

Exhibit 2: 52 Week Volatility of Term Structure Changes Plotted Against the 3-Month Spot Rate at the Start of the Period

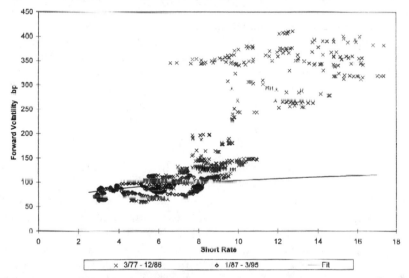

The x's are periods starting 3/77 through 12/86. The diamonds are periods starting 1/87 through 3/95. The data points are based on the best fit k for the period 1/87-3/96, as described in the text. The solid curve shows the best fit to a power law model. The best fit parameters are β=91 bp, γ=0.19. (This is *not* a fit to the points shown here, which are provided solely to give a visual feel for the data.)

Exhibit 2 gives a graphical representation of the data. There is clear evidence that the simple power law model is not a good fit and that the data display regime shifts. The exhibit shows the volatility of the factor in equation (12) using the value of k appropriate to the period January 1987 - March 1996 (the "Greenspan era"). The vertical coordinate of each dot represents the volatility of the factor over a 52-week period; the horizontal coordinate shows the 3-month spot rate (a proxy for the short rate) at the start of the 52-week period. (Note that the maximum likelihood estimation is not based on the data points shown, but on the individual weekly changes.) The dots are broken into two sets: the x's are for start dates prior to January 1987, the diamonds for later dates. Divided in this way, the data suggest fairly strongly that volatility has been nearly independent of interest rates since 1987 — a time during which the short rate has ranged from around 3% to over 9%.

From an empirical perspective, then, no simple choice of model works well. Among the simple models of volatility, the MRG model most closely matches the recent behavior of U.S. Treasury term structure.

There is an issue of financial plausibility here, as well as an empirical one. Some models permit interest rates to become negative, which is undesirable, though how big a problem this is isn't obvious. The class of simple models that provably have positive interest rates without suffering from explosions and match the initial term structure is quite small. The BDT and BK models satisfy these conditions, but don't provide information about future yield curves as needed for the mortgage problem. The Dybvig-adjusted CIR model also satisfies the conditions, but is somewhat hard to work with. There is a lognormal HJM model that avoids negative rates, but it is analytically intractable and suffers from explosions.[23] The lognormal version of the two state Markov model also suffers from explosions, though, as with the lognormal HJM model, these can be eliminated by capping the volatility at some large value. The rational lognormal model has positive rates without explosions, but unreasonable long-term volatility.

It is therefore worth asking whether the empirical question is important. It might turn out to be unimportant in the sense that, properly compared, models that differ only in their assumed dependence of volatility on rates actually give similar answers for option values.

The trick in comparing models is to be sure that the comparisons are truly "apples to apples," by matching term structures of volatility. It is easy to imagine getting different results valuing the same option using the MRG, CIR, and BK models, even though the initial volatilities are set equal — not because of different assumptions about the dependence of volatility on rates, but because the long-term volatilities are different in the three models even when the short-rate volatilities are the same. There are a number of published papers claiming to demonstrate dramatic differences between models, but which actually demonstrate just that the models have been calibrated differently.[24]

The two state Markov framework provides a convenient means to compare different choices for the dependence of volatility on rates while holding the initial term structure of volatility fixed. Choosing different forms for $\sigma(r)$ while setting k to a constant in expression (4) gives exactly this comparison. We can value options using these different assumptions and compare time values. (Intrinsic value — the value of the option when the volatility is zero — is of course the same in all models.) To be precise, we set $\sigma(r, t) = \sigma_0 (r/r_0) \gamma$, where σ_0 is the initial annualized volatility of the short rate in absolute terms (e.g., 100 bp/year) and r_0 is the initial short

---

[23] Heath, Jarrow, and Morton, "Bond Pricing and the Term Structure of Interest Rates."

[24] For a recent example, see M. Uhrig and U. Walter, "A New Numerical Approach to Fitting the Initial Yield Curve," *Journal of Fixed Income* (March 1996).

rate. Choosing the exponent $\gamma=\{0, 0.5, 1\}$ then gives the MRG model, a square root volatility model (not CIR), and a lognormal model (not BK), respectively.

The results can be summarized by saying that a derivatives trader probably cares about the choice of exponent γ, but a fixed-income portfolio manager probably doesn't. The reason is that the differences in time value are small, except when the time value itself is small — for deep in- or out-of-the-money options. A derivatives trader may be required to price a deep out-of-the-money option, and would get very different results across models, having calibrated them using at-the-money options. A portfolio manager, on the other hand, has option positions embedded in bonds, mortgage-backed securities, etc., whose time value is a small fraction of total portfolio value. So differences that show up only for deep in- or out-of-the-money options are of little consequence. Moreover, a deep out-of-the-money option has small option delta, so small differences in valuation have little effect on measures of portfolio interest rate risk. An in-the-money option can be viewed as a position in the underlying asset plus an out-of-the-money option, so the same reasoning applies.

Exhibit 3 shows the results of one such comparison for a 5-year quarterly pay cap, with a flat initial term structure and modestly decreasing term structure of volatility. The time value for all three values of γ peaks at the same value for an at-the-money cap. Caps with higher strike rates have the largest time value in the lognormal model, because the volatility is increasing for rate moves in the direction that make them valuable. Understanding the behavior for lower strike caps requires using put-call parity: an in-the-money cap can be viewed as paying fixed in a rate swap and owning a floor. The swap has no time value, and the floor has only time value (since it is out-of-the money). The floor's time value is greatest for the MRG model, because it gives the largest volatility for rate moves in the direction that make it valuable. In each case, the square root model gives values intermediate between the MRG and lognormal models, for obvious reasons. At the extremes, 250 bp in or out of the money, time values differ by as much as a factor of 2 between the MRG and lognormal models. At these extremes, though, the time value is only a tenth of its value for the at-the-money cap.

If the initial term structure is not flat, the model differences can be larger. For example, if the term structure is positively sloped, then the model prices match up for an in-the-money rather than at-the-money cap. Using the same parameters as for Exhibit 3, but using the actual Treasury term structure as of 5/13/96 instead of a flat 7% curve, the time values differ at the peak by about 20% — about half a point — between the MRG and lognormal models. Interestingly, as shown in Exhibit 4, even though the time values can be rather different, the option deltas are rather close for the three models. (The deltas are even closer in the flat term structure case.) In this example, if a 9.5% cap were embedded in a floating-rate note priced around par, the effective duration attributable to the cap according to the lognormal model would be 0.49 year, while according to the MRG model it would be 0.17 year. The difference shrinks as the rate gets closer to the cap. This $\frac{1}{3}$ year difference isn't trivial, but it's also not large compared to the effect of other modeling assumptions, such as the overall level of volatility or, if mortgages are involved, prepayment expectations.

Exhibit 3: Time Values for Five Year Quarterly Pay Caps for Gaussian, Square Root and Lognormal Two State Markov Models with Identical Initial Term Structure of Volatility and a 7% Flat Initial Yield Curve*

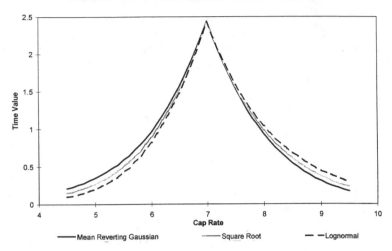

* The model parameters (described in the text) are σ_0=100 bp/yr., k=0.02/yr., equivalent to an initial short-rate volatility of 14.8%, and a 10-year yield volatility of 13.6%.

Exhibit 4: Sensitivity of Cap Value to Change in Rate Level as a Function of Cap Rate*

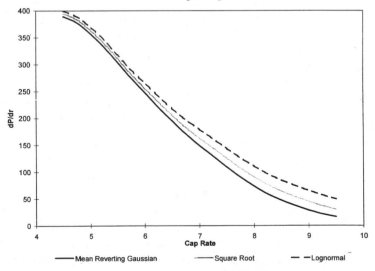

* The cap structure and model parameters are the same as used for Exhibit 3, except that the initial term structure is the (positively sloped) US Treasury curve as of 5/13/96. The short rate volatility is 19.9% and the ten year yield volatility is 14.9%.

Exhibit 5: Valuation of a Continuous Par Call on Zero Coupon and Par Bonds of Various Maturities in the MRG Model

Model parameters are:

σ_0 = 100 bp/year

k = 0.02/year

The value of the call on the zero coupon bond should be zero in every case, assuming non-negative interest rates.

	5% Flat Curve		7% Flat Curve		5/96 US Tsy Yields		10/93 US Tsy Yields	
Term	Zero Cpn	Par Bond	Zero Cpn	Par Bond	Zero Cpn	Par Bond	Zero Cpn	Par Bond
3 Year	<0.01	0.96	<0.01	0.93	<0.01	0.65	<0.01	0.62
5	<0.01	1.93	<0.01	1.83	<0.01	1.43	<0.01	1.27
10	0.06	4.54	<0.01	4.07	<0.01	3.47	0.02	3.06
30	0.60	11.55	0.10	8.85	0.08	7.86	0.09	7.26

These are just two numerical examples, but it is easy to see how different variations would affect these results. An inverted term structure would make the MRG model time value largest at the peak and the lognormal model value the smallest. Holding σ_0 constant, higher initial interest rates would yield smaller valuation differences across models since there would be less variation of volatility around the mean. Larger values of the mean reversion k would also produce smaller differences between models, since the short-rate distribution would be tighter around the mean.

Finally, there is the question raised earlier as to whether one should be concerned about the possibility of negative interest rates in some models. From a practical standpoint, this is an issue only if it leads to a significant contribution to pricing from negative rates. One simple way to test this is to look at pricing of a call struck at par for a zero coupon bond. Exhibit 5 shows such a test for the MRG model. For reasonable parameter choices (here taken to be σ_0=100 bp/year, k = 0.02/year, or 20% volatility of a 5% short rate), the call values are quite modest, especially compared to those of a call on a par bond, which gives a feel for the time value of at-the-money options over the same period. The worst case is a call on the longest maturity zero coupon bond which, with a flat 5% yield curve, is priced at 0.60. This is just 5% of the value of a par call on a 30-year par bond. Using the actual May 1996 yield curve, all the option values — other than on the 30-year zero — are negligible. For the 30-year zero the call is worth just 1% of the value of the call on a 30-year par bond. In October 1993, the U.S. Treasury market had the lowest short rate since 1963, and the lowest 10-year rate since 1967. Using that yield curve as a worst case, the zero coupon bond call values are only very slightly higher than the May 1996 values, and still effectively negligible for practical purposes.

Again, it is easy to see how these results change with different assumptions. An inverted curve makes negative rates likelier, so increases the value of a par call on a zero coupon bond. (On the other hand, inverted curves at low interest rate levels are rare.) Conversely, a positive slope to the curve makes negative rates less likely, decreasing the call value. Holding σ_0 constant, lower interest rates produce larger call values. Increasing k produces smaller call values. The only circumstances that are really problematic for the MRG model are flat or inverted yield curves at very low rate levels, with relatively high volatility.

CONCLUSIONS

For portfolio analysis applications, the mean reverting Gaussian model has much to recommend it. For this model, it is easy to implement valuation algorithms for both path independent securities such as bond options, and path dependent securities such as CMOs. It is one of the simplest models in which it is possible to follow the evolution of the entire yield curve (à la HJM), making it especially useful for valuing assets like mortgage-backed securities whose cash flows depend on longer term rates. The oft raised bogeyman of negative interest rates proves to have little consequence for option pricing, since negative rates occur with very low probability for reasonable values of the model parameters and initial term structure.

Option values are somewhat (though not very) sensitive to the assumed dependence of volatility on the level of rates. The empirical evidence on this relationship is far from clear, with the data (at least in the United States) showing evidence of eras, possibly associated with central bank policy. The numerical evidence shows that, for a sloped term structure, different power law relationships give modestly different at-the-money option time values, and larger relative differences for deep in- or out-of-the-money options. These differences are unlikely to be significant to fixed-income portfolio managers, but are probably a concern for derivatives traders.

Chapter 2

Fixed Income Risk

Ronald N. Kahn, Ph.D.
Director of Research
BARRA, Inc.

INTRODUCTION

Risk analysis has been central to investing since at least the 1950's, when Harry Markowitz showed mathematically exactly how diversification reduced risk.[1] Since then, risk analysis has developed into a very powerful tool relied upon by institutional investors. If expected return is the protagonist in the drama of fixed income portfolio management, then risk is the antagonist.

This chapter will discuss definitions of risk, describe some key characteristics of risk, present approaches to modeling risk, and discuss risk model uses. The important lessons are:

- The standard deviation of return is the best overall definition of risk.
- Risks don't add.
- Duration measures exposure to risk, rather than risk.
- Institutional investors care more about active than total risk.
- Risk models identify the important sources of risk: interest rates, spreads, prepayment factors, volatility, and currencies.
- Risk model uses include current portfolio risk analysis, portfolio construction and rebalancing, and past portfolio performance analysis.

We start with our definition of risk.

DEFINING RISK

All definitions of risk arise fundamentally from the probability distribution of possible returns. This distribution describes the probability that the return will be between 1% and 1.01%, the probability of returns between 1.01% and 1.02%, etc. The return in question can describe a bond or a portfolio, a total return or return relative to a benchmark.

---

[1] H.M. Markowitz, "Portfolio Selection: Efficient Diversification of Investment," *Cowles Foundation Monograph 16* (New Haven CT: Yale University Press, 1959).

The distribution of returns describes probabilities of all possible outcomes. As such, it is complicated and full of detail. It can answer all questions about returns and probabilities. It can be a forecast, or a summary of realized returns.

Unfortunately the distribution of returns is too complicated and detailed in its entirety. Hence all definitions of risk attempt to capture in a single number the essentials of risk more fully described in the complete distribution. Each definition of risk will have at least some shortcomings, due to this simplification. Different definitions may also have shortcomings based on difficulties of accurate forecasting. Let's discuss some possible risk definitions in turn.

The *standard deviation* measures the spread of the distribution about its mean. Investors commonly refer to the standard deviation as the *volatility*. The *variance* is the square of the standard deviation. If returns are normally distributed, then two-thirds of them fall within one standard deviation of the mean. As the standard deviation decreases, the band within which most returns will fall narrows. The standard deviation measures the uncertainty of the returns.

Standard deviation was Harry Markowitz' definition of risk, and it has been the standard in the institutional investment community ever since. It will be our definition of risk. Standard deviation is a very well understood and unambiguous statistic. It is particularly applicable to existing tools for building portfolios. Standard deviations tend to be relatively stable over time (especially compared to mean returns and other moments of the distribution), and econometricians have developed very powerful tools for accurately forecasting standard deviations.

Critics of the standard deviation point out that it measures the possibility of returns both above and below the mean. Most investors would define risk based on small or negative returns (though short sellers have the opposite view). This has generated an alternative risk measure: *semivariance*, or *downside risk*.

Semivariance is defined in analogy to variance, based on deviations from the mean, but using only returns below the mean. If the returns are symmetric, i.e. the return is equally likely to be x percent above or x percent below the mean, then the semivariance is just exactly one-half the variance. Analysts differ in defining *downside risk*. One approach defines downside risk as the square root of the semivariance, in analogy to the relation between standard deviation and variance.

Downside risk clearly answers the critics of standard deviation, by focusing entirely on the undesirable returns. However, there are several problems with downside risk. First, its definition is not as unambiguous as standard deviation or variance, nor are its statistical properties as well known, so it isn't an ideal choice for a universal risk definition. We need a definition which managers, plan sponsors, and beneficiaries can all use.

Second, it is computationally challenging for large portfolio construction problems. In fact, while we can aggregate individual bond standard deviations into a portfolio standard deviation, for other measures of risk we must rely much more on simple historical extrapolation ofportfolio return patterns.

Third, to the extent that investment returns are reasonably symmetric, most definitions of downside risk are simply proportional to standard deviation or variance and so contain no additional information. To the extent that investment returns may not be symmetric, there are problems forecasting downside risk. Return asymmetries are not stable over time, and so are very difficult to forecast. Realized downside risk may not be a good forecast of future downside risk. Moreover, we estimate downside risk with only half of the data, losing statistical accuracy.

Shortfall probability is another risk definition, and perhaps one closely related to intuition for what risk is. The shortfall probability is the probability that the return will lie below some target amount. Shortfall probability has the advantage of closely corresponding to an intuitive definition of risk. However, it faces the same problems as downside risk: ambiguity, poor statistical understanding, difficulty of forecasting, and dependence on individual investor preferences.

Forecasting is a particularly thorny problem, and it's accentuated the lower the shortfall target. At the extreme, probability forecasts for very large shortfalls are influenced by perhaps only 1 or 2 observations.

Value at risk is similar to shortfall probability. Where shortfall probability takes a target return and calculates the probability of returns falling below that, value at risk takes a target probability, e.g. the 1% or 5% lowest returns, and converts that probability to an associated return. Value at risk is closely related to shortfall probability, and shares the same advantages and disadvantages.

Where does the normal distribution fit into this discussion of risk statistics? The normal distribution is a standard assumption in academic investment research and is a standard distribution throughout statistics. It is completely defined by its mean and standard deviation. Much research has shown that investment returns do not exactly follow normal distributions, but instead have wider distributions, i.e. the probability of extreme events is larger for real investments than a normal distribution would imply.

The above five risk definitions all attempt to capture the risk inherent in the "true" return distribution. An alternative approach could assume that returns are normally distributed. Then the mean and standard deviation immediately fix the other statistics: downside risk, semivariance, shortfall probability, and value at risk. Such an approach might robustly forecast quantities of most interest to individual investors, using the most accurate calculations and a few reasonable assumptions. Many currently popular estimates of value at risk use exactly this approach.

Faced with these possibilities, we choose the standard deviation as our definition of risk. It is well understood, unambiguous, and accurately forecastable. And, by assuming normal distributions, we can translate standard deviation into value at risk numbers, for example.

DURATION IS NOT RISK

What about duration, the traditional measure of fixed income risk? There are two problems using duration as risk. First, duration isn't directly connected to the distribution of returns. Duration measures exposure to risk, rather than risk. Second, duration measures only one source of risk: parallel interest rate moves.

For a bond of price P, the duration D measures the return per unit parallel interest rate move Δs:

$$D = -\frac{1}{P} \cdot \frac{\Delta P}{\Delta s} \tag{1}$$

So duration relates bond returns to parallel interest rate moves:

$$r = \frac{\Delta P}{P} = -D \cdot \Delta s \tag{2}$$

Assuming stable duration, bond risk relates to interest rate risk as:

$$STD\{r\} = D \cdot STD\{\Delta s\} \tag{3}$$

If interest rate moves have an annual volatility of 1%, then a 5-year duration bond should exhibit an annual volatility of 5%, based on interest rate risk. Duration measures a bond's exposure to interest rate (parallel shift) volatility.

BASIC RISK MATH

The standard deviation has some interesting and important characteristics. Representing means as μ, standard deviations as σ, and portfolio holdings as h, we know that:

$$\mu\{h_1 \cdot r_1 + h_2 \cdot r_2\} = h_1 \cdot \mu_1 + h_2 \cdot \mu_2 \tag{4}$$

We call this the *portfolio property*. According to equation (4), the portfolio's mean return is the weighted average of the mean returns of its constituents.

The standard deviation does not have the portfolio property. In particular:

$$\sigma^2\{h_1 \cdot r_1 + h_2 \cdot r_2\} = h_1^2 \cdot \sigma_1^2 + h_2^2 \cdot \sigma_2^2 + 2 \cdot h_1 \cdot h_2 \cdot \sigma_1 \cdot \sigma_2 \cdot \rho_{12} \tag{5}$$

where ρ_{12} is the correlation between r_1 and r_2, and $\sigma_{12} = \sigma_1 \cdot \sigma_2 \cdot \rho_{12}$ is the covariance between r_1 and r_2. Then, because correlations must range between -1 and 1:

$$\sigma\{h_1 \cdot r_1 + h_2 \cdot r_2\} \leq h_1 \cdot \sigma_1 + h_2 \cdot \sigma_2 \tag{6}$$

with the equality above holding only if the two returns are perfectly correlated ($\rho_{12}=1$). For risk, the whole is less than the sum of its parts. This is the key to portfolio diversification.

For further insight into this, the risk of an equal weighted portfolio of N bonds, where every bond has risk σ and all bonds have pairwise correlation ρ, is:

$$\sigma_P = \sigma \cdot \sqrt{\frac{1 + \rho \cdot (N-1)}{N}} \tag{7}$$

As the correlation drops to zero this becomes:

$$\sigma_P = \frac{\sigma}{\sqrt{N}} \tag{8}$$

the key to lowering risk is holding many bonds. In the limit that the portfolio contains a very large number of correlated bonds, this becomes:

$$\sigma_P \Rightarrow \sigma \cdot \sqrt{\rho}. \tag{9}$$

This provides a lower bound on risk, even for portfolios containing many bonds.

The Covariance Matrix

In the general case, portfolios contain many bonds of differing volatilities and correlations. Equation (5) then generalizes to:

$$\sigma^2\{h_1 \cdot r_1 + h_2 \cdot r_2 + \dots + h_N \cdot r_N\}$$
$$= h_1^2 \cdot \sigma_1^2 + h_2^2 \cdot \sigma_2^2 + \dots + h_N^2 \cdot \sigma_N^2 + 2 \cdot h_1 \cdot h_2 \cdot \sigma_1 \cdot \sigma_2 \cdot \rho_{12} + \dots \tag{10}$$

For large portfolios, this calculation involves quite a number of terms. We can simplify this notationally by introducing the covariance matrix V which contains all the variances and covariances:

$$V = \begin{bmatrix} \sigma_1^2 & \sigma_{12} & \cdots & \\ \vdots & \sigma_2^2 & & \\ & & \ddots & \\ & & & \sigma_N^2 \end{bmatrix} \tag{11}$$

and then

$$\sigma_P^2 = h_P^T \cdot V \cdot h_P, \tag{12}$$

where h_P is an N-vector containing all the portfolio holdings. Equation (12) has the advantage of notational simplicity, though understanding portfolio risk still involves the calculation in equation (10).

Annualizing Risk

We can use equation (10) to annualize risk. The annual return to a bond is the sum of 12 monthly bond returns:

$$r_A = r_J + r_F + \dots + r_D \tag{13}$$

$$\sigma_A^2 = \sigma_J^2 + \sigma_F^2 + \dots + \sigma_D^2 + \text{covariance terms} \tag{14}$$

Now we will make two generally valid assumptions. First, we will assume stationarity. The return variance is the same each month. Second we will assume that returns are uncorrelated across time, i.e., all the covariance terms in equation (14) are zero. These assumptions mean that:

$$\sigma_A^2 = 12 \cdot \sigma_{monthly}^2 \tag{15}$$

and more generally variance grows with the length of the return horizon. This allows us to measure risk over different horizons, but report it in consistent units.

Active Risk

Investment managers care about relative risk even more than total risk. If an investment manager is being compared to a performance benchmark then the difference in return between his portfolio's return r_P and the benchmark's return r_B is of crucial importance. The difference is called the *active return*, r_A. The *active risk*, ψ_A, is defined as the standard deviation of active return;

$$\psi_P = STD\{r_A\} = STD\{r_P - r_B\} \tag{16}$$

We sometimes call this active risk the "tracking error" of the portfolio, since it describes how well the portfolio can track the benchmark.

HISTORICAL RISK

The key ingredient for calculating portfolio risk is the covariance matrix. A risk model's job is estimating that covariance matrix. The most obvious approach is to use historical variances and covariances. This procedure is neither robust nor reasonable.

Data from T periods is used to estimate the N by N covariance matrix. But the N by N covariance matrix contains $N(N+1)/2$ independent numbers (all the variances and covariances). Each of the T observations includes N numbers (the set of N returns that period), and each variance and covariance requires at least 2 numbers for estimation. Unless $NT \geq 2N(N+1)/2$, or unless $T > N$, there will be active positions that will appear riskless.

So the historical approach requires $T > N$. For a monthly historical covariance matrix of just 500 bonds, this would require over 40 years of data, a severe problem since most bond maturities are less than 40 years. And, even when T is greater than N, this historical procedure still has several problems:

- Historical risk cannot deal with the changing maturity of bonds. Over the course of a year, each bond's risk will change as its maturity shortens.
- Circumventing the $T > N$ restriction requires short time periods, one day or one week, while the forecast horizon of the manager is generally one quarter or one year.

- Sample bias will lead to some gross misestimates of covariance. A 500 asset covariance matrix contains 125,250 independent numbers. If 5% of these are poor estimates, we have 6,262 poor estimates.

The reader will note limited enthusiasm for historical models of risk. We now turn to more structured models of risk.

STRUCTURAL RISK MODELS

In the previous section, we considered historical risk and found it wanting. In this section we look at structural multifactor risk models and trumpet their virtues.[2]

The multiple factor risk model is based on the notion that the return of a bond can be explained by a collection of common factors plus an idiosyncratic element that pertains to that particular bond. We can think of the common factors as forces that affect a group of bonds, for example interest rate or corporate spread movements. Below, we discuss possible types of factors in detail.

By identifying important factors we can reduce the size of the problem. Instead of dealing with 6,000 bonds (and 18,003,000 independent variances and covariances), we deal with approximately 50 factors. The bonds change, the factors do not. The situation is much simpler when we focus on the smaller number of factors and allow the bonds to change their exposures to those factors.

A structural risk model begins by analyzing returns according to a simple linear structure comprised of four components: the bond's exposures to the factors, the excess returns, the attributed factor returns, and the specific returns. The structure is

$$r_n = \sum_k X_{n,k}(t) \cdot f_k(t) + u_n(t) \tag{17}$$

where:

$X_{n,k}(t)$ is the *exposure* of asset n to factor k. This exposure is known at time t. Exposures are frequently called *factor loadings*.

$r_n(t)$ is the *excess return* (return above the risk free return) on bond n during the period from time t to time $t + 1$.

$f_k(t)$ is the *factor return* to factor k during the period from time t to time $t + 1$.

---

[2] For references see Richard C. Grinold and Ronald N. Kahn, *Active Portfolio Management* (Chicago: Probus Publishing, 1995, Chapter 3); Richard C. Grinold and Ronald N. Kahn, "Multiple Factor Models for Portfolio Risk," in John W. Peavy III, (ed), *A Practitioner's Guide to Factor Models* (Charlottesville, VA: AIMR, 1994); Ronald N. Kahn, "Fixed Income Risk Modeling," Chapter 34 in Frank J. Fabozzi, (ed), *The Handbook of Fixed Income Securities*, Fourth Edition (Homewood IL: Business One Irwin, 1995); Ronald N. Kahn, "Fixed Income Risk Modeling in the 1990's," *Journal of Portfolio Management* (Fall, 1995), pp. 94-101; and Andrew Rudd and Henry K. Clasing, Jr. *Modern Portfolio Theory*, (Orinda, CA: Andrew Rudd, 1988), Chapters 2 and 3.

$u_n(t)$ is bond n's *specific return* during the period from time t to time $t + 1$. This is the return that cannot be explained by the factors. It is sometimes called the *idiosyncratic return*, the return not explained by the model. However, the risk model will account for specific risk. Thus our risk predictions will explicitly consider the risk of u_n.

We have been very careful to define the time structure in the model. The exposures are known at time t: the beginning of the period. The asset returns, factor returns, and specific returns span the period from time t to time $t + 1$. In the rest of this chapter, we will suppress the explicit time variables.

We do not require causality in this model structure. The factors may or may not be the basic driving forces for security returns. They are, however, dimensions along which to analyze risk.

We will now assume that the specific returns are not correlated with the factor returns, and are not correlated with each other. With these assumptions and the return structure of equation (17), the risk structure is:

$$V_{n,m} = \sum_{k1,k2} X_{n,k1} \cdot F_{k1,k1} \cdot X_{m,k2} + \Delta_{n,m} \tag{18}$$

where:

$V_{n,m}$ is the covariance of asset n with asset m. If $n = m$, this gives the variance of asset n.

$X_{n,k1}$ is the exposure of asset n to factor $k1$, as defined above.

$F_{k1,k2}$ is the covariance of factor $k1$ with factor $k2$. If $k1 = k2$, this gives the variance of factor $k1$.

$\Delta_{n,m}$ is the specific covariance of asset n with asset m. We assume that all specific risk correlations are zero, so this term is zero unless $n = m$. In that case, this gives the specific variance of asset n.

FIXED INCOME FACTORS

So much for the framework, what are the important factors? In researching this question, we must keep in mind the diversity of fixed income instruments: from Treasury bonds to corporate bonds to mortgages and CMOs; and from fixed coupons to floating-rate notes.

The important factors in the market include interest rates, yield spreads, prepayments, volatilities, and currencies for global bonds.

We have extensively analyzed interest rate risk movements and identified the three most important factors as interest rate shift, twist, and butterfly movements. The most important spread movements include movements in sector spreads and movements in quality spreads. These sources of fixed income risk are well known and fairly well understood.

Prepayment risk concerns the risk of unexpected prepayments. This is a type of model risk and is not well understood. Most models include forecasts of prepayments along interest rate paths. Models then price mortgage-dependent cash flows based on these forecasts. But adjusting mortgage cash flows based on a prepayment model helps to estimate interest rate risk, not prepayment risk. *As defined here, prepayment risk is the risk that the prepayment model is wrong.*

Actually, prepayment risk is somewhat more general than this. A model which correctly predicts prepayments may not match market expectations. And it is market expectations which drive mortgage prices. The prepayment model defines the dimensions of the problem. The volatility along each dimension arises both from forecasting errors and changes in market expectations.

What are these dimensions of the prepayment model? To begin with, the models do not fit all observed prepayments exactly. And so for any particular generic passthrough we expect its prepayments to deviate randomly from the model forecasts. Fortunately these deviations should have mean zero, and so will average out over time and over the different passthroughs in the portfolio.

More critical and systematic sources of prepayment risk involve unexpected changes in model parameters governing baseline (discount mortgage) prepayments, rate dependent prepayments, and burnout. All of these can be significant sources of prepayment risk.

Volatility risk is the risk of unexpected changes in volatility. We use option models to analyze fixed income instruments, and input estimated term structures of volatility. But the option analysis usually extends only to estimating interest rate risk; that is, option-adjusted durations. But what if short- or long-rate volatility is unexpectedly high? How will that affect the portfolio? This is analogous to an option trader's vega risk.

Exposures

The straightforward way to calculate the exposures $X_{n,j}$ in equations (17) and (18), given a model of instrument pricing, is to "shock" the model successively along each dimension of risk and re-value the instruments. For interest rate factors this corresponds to shocking the term structure, re-valuing, and calculating the returns generated by that shock. For unexpected prepayments, this corresponds to shocking the prepayment model, re-valuing the instruments, and calculating the returns generated.

To mitigate problems of instability, we should define our shocks based on realistic expectations of their possible size. For interest rate risk, this approach to estimating exposures is very different from the traditional duration approach. It is not only more meaningful, it is more flexible: it handles negative duration IOs as easily as Treasury bonds.

FACTOR COVARIANCE

Given these exposures, we must also estimate the variances and covariances of the fixed income factors. Here we can use historical analysis, on this significantly reduced set of data. We can also use more sophisticated approaches, including weighting more recent observations more heavily, and scaling the factor covariance matrix **F** up or down based on nonlinear volatility forecasts[3] for overall market volatility.

EXAMPLES

To understand this approach to risk modeling in more detail, we will now apply it to the set of sample instruments shown in Exhibit 1. These include a non-callable Treasury bond, callable and putable corporate bonds, a corporate floating-rate note, a passthrough mortgage, and a PO and IO. The specific analysis date is August 31, 1993, though as you will see, the general pattern of results is typically valid.

To compare magnitudes of risk, we will convert exposures to every risk factor to an equivalent annual movement. (We can impose this definition of the exposures X, as long as we consistently define the covariance matrix **F**.) So, for example, we will interpret the term structure shift exposures as the returns generated by a one-standard-deviation (annual) shift up in interest rates, and the baseline prepayment exposures as the returns generated by a one-standard-deviation (annual) shift up in baseline prepayment rates. For the purposes of this chapter, we will ignore the subtleties of how best to calculate such exposures: based on positive or negative shocks, multiple shocks, and so on.

Let's start with interest rate risk. Exhibit 2 shows monthly shift, twist, and butterfly shapes. For this example we have defined these factors using principal components analysis, but we also could have used more intuitive shapes: a parallel shift, linear twist, and others. Exhibit 3 shows the exposures of the sample instruments to each of these shapes — the X's — scaled to an annual positive movement. So most of the shift exposures are negative because a rise in rates negatively affects returns for most bonds. The IO has a positive exposure because of its negative duration.

Exhibit 1: Term Structure Exposure Examples
Sample Instruments

			Price	Duration
U.S. Treasury	11.875% of November 2003		148.60	6.52
Caterpillar	6.000% of May 2007	(Callable)	93.25	7.45
Dow	8.550% of October 2009	(Putable)	119.34	7.81
Citicorp	8.910% of May 1995	(Floater)	106.84	0.18
GNMA	8.000% issued 1992		104.33	3.49
GNMA	8.000% issued 1992	PO	67.77	18.44
GNMA	8.000% issued 1992	IO	36.56	−24.20

---

[3] For references on nonlinear volatility forecasts, see Tim Bollerslev, Ray Y. Chou, Narayan Jayaraman, and Kenneth F. Kroner, "ARCH Modeling in Finance: A Selective Review of the Theory and Empirical Evidence, with Suggestions for Future Research," *Journal of Econometrics,* Vol. 52 (1992), pp. 5-59; and Robert F. Engle, "Autoregressive Conditional Heteroskedasticity with Estimates of the Variance of U.K. Inflation," *Econometrica*, Vol. 50 (1982), pp. 987-1008.

Exhibit 2: U.S. Shift/Twist/Butterfly Shapes

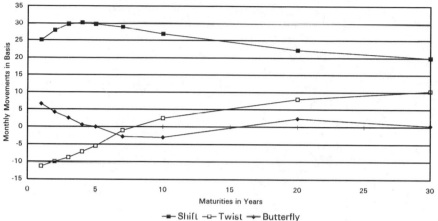

Exhibit 3: Term Structure Exposure Examples

Security	Shift	Twist	Butterfly
Treasury	−7.16%	0.39%	0.61%
Callable Corp.	−8.48%	−0.24%	0.61%
Putable Corp.	−7.86%	0.27%	0.05%
Corp. Floater	−0.24%	0.10%	−0.04%
GNMA	−4.43%	0.28%	−0.31%
PO	−23.15%	3.12%	3.67%
IO	30.28%	−5.02%	−7.69%

For each instrument, the shift is the dominant source of interest rate risk. However we cannot ignore the twist and butterfly risk in many circumstances. Active risk relative to a benchmark, for example, will depend on active exposures. For most institutional portfolios, active durations (and similarly active shift exposures) will be near zero. Also note that the twist and butterfly exposures of the IO are comparable in magnitude to the shift exposure of the long bonds.

Next consider spread risk: the risk that yield spreads could widen or tighten, independent of any moves in interest rates. Exhibit 4 shows yield spread risk exposures for the sample instruments based on a widening spread shock.

Spread risk depends on yield spread volatility and the duration of the instrument. For almost all these examples, spread risk is smaller in magnitude than interest rate shift risk, but comparable or even larger than twist or butterfly risk. Especially for some corporate bonds, it can be the dominant source of active risk (assuming an active shift risk exposure near zero).

Exhibit 4: Yield Spread Risk Exposures

Instrument	Spread Risk Exposure
Treasury Bond	−1.15%
Callable Corp.	−3.21%
Putable Corp.	−3.27%
Corp. Floater	−1.20%
GNMA	−1.45%
PO	−7.67%
IO	10.06%

Exhibit 5: Prepayment Risk Movements

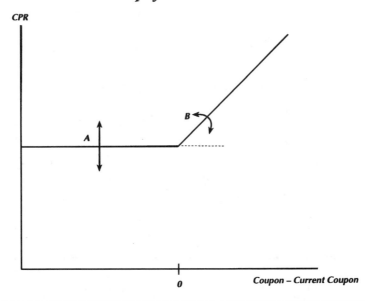

For this example corporate floating-rate note, spread risk dominates interest rate risk. For floaters, the coupon reset mitigates interest rate risk but not default risk. For purposes of interest rate risk, the floater effective maturity is the next reset date. But for spread risk, the relevant cash flows extend all the way out to the true maturity.

Now consider two sources of prepayment risk shown schematically in Exhibit 5, which shows a generic prepayment model with the forecast conditional prepayment rate (CPR) a function of the difference between the mortgage coupon and the current coupon. The movement A denotes baseline prepayment risk and the movement B denotes rate-dependent prepayment risk. Exhibit 6 shows sample instrument exposures to these risk factors. First note that the Treasury bond and the corporate bonds are not exposed to this prepayment risk. If we shock the prepayment model while holding all other parameters fixed, the prices of these bonds will not change. This does not mean that we expect no change in interest rates correlated with a change in prepayments. We account for such effects in the factor covariance matrix, not the factor exposures.

Exhibit 6 also shows that the IO exposure to baseline prepayment risk is comparable to its exposure to interest rate shift risk. If we combine this IO with a Treasury strip to create a zero duration portfolio, we would still be exposed to very significant risks.

In contrast to the IO and PO, the passthrough mortgage has relatively low exposures to prepayment risk. This is because the passthrough is only at a slight premium, so prepayments have only a small impact on price.

To account for volatility risk we can look for shocks to short-rate volatility and/or long-rate volatility. For consistency with our option model, we will parametrize volatility shocks as volatility shifts, where short- and long-rate volatilities move in parallel; and volatility twists, where long-rate volatility moves relative to a fixed short-rate volatility.

Exhibit 7 shows volatility risk exposures for the sample instruments. Since the Treasury bond is noncallable, its volatility risk is zero. Since the floater resets to par at the next reset date no matter what the volatility, its volatility risk is zero. Once again, volatility risk is highest for the IO. Volatility risk in general is smaller in magnitude than other risk sources, but it still may be hard to ignore in some circumstances. For active risk, assuming shift risk exposure near zero, volatility risk is comparable in magnitude to twist and butterfly risk for the callable corporate bonds.

Exhibit 6: Prepayment Exposure Examples

Security	Baseline	Rate Dependent
Treasury	0.00%	0.00%
Callable Corp.	0.00%	0.00%
Putable Corp.	0.00%	0.00%
Corp. Floater	0.00%	0.00%
GNMA	−0.04%	−0.52%
PO	12.14%	4.72%
IO	−22.58%	−10.20%

Exhibit 7: Volatility Exposure Examples

Security	Volatility Shift	Volatility Twist
Treasury	0.00%	0.00%
Callable Corp.	−0.22%	−0.32%
Putable Corp.	0.23%	0.39%
Corp. Floater	0.00%	0.00%
GNMA	−0.20%	−0.25%
PO	0.81%	0.45%
IO	−2.08%	−1.54%

Exhibit 8: Annual Risk Forecasts

Security	Total Annual Risk Forecast
Treasury	7.29%
Callable Corp.	9.10%
Putable Corp.	8.54%
Corp. Floater	1.27%
GNMA	4.71%
PO	26.84%
IO	41.41%

Risk Analysis

We have completed the exercise of calculating each sample instrument's exposures to the risk factors. The exposures of a portfolio of these assets would be just the portfolio-weighted average of the instrument exposures.

To complete the analysis of risk, we must combine these exposures with the covariance matrix **F**, according to equation (18). Only when we combine our risk exposures with the covariance matrix can we see our overall risk.

Equation (18) also includes a contribution from each instrument's specific risk. This risk is idiosyncratic to each instrument and independent of the risk factors.

When we combine these effects, we find the total risk forecasts for the sample instruments listed in Exhibit 8.

The risk rankings aren't surprising — IO's and PO's are riskier than Treasuries, corporates, and straight passthrough mortgages on August 31, 1993 and most other days as well. But the magnitudes of the differences are impressive, and the sources of these differences, as we have observed, are insightful. Significant contributions to IO and PO risk arise from prepayment risks not traditionally analyzed. No combination of Treasuries can hedge out these significant risk factors.

THE USES OF A RISK MODEL

Having now covered in detail the structure of a fixed income risk model, what are its investment applications? Broadly speaking, there are three. They involve the present, the future, and the past. We will describe them in turn, mainly focusing on uses concerning present risk.

The Present: Current Portfolio Risk Analysis

The multiple factor risk model analyzes current portfolio risk. It measures overall risk. More significantly it decomposes that risk in several ways. This decomposition of risk identifies the important sources of risk in the portfolio and links those sources with aspirations for active return.

One way to divide the risk is to look at risk relative to a benchmark and identify the active risk. Another way to divide the risk is between the model risk and the specific risk. The risk model can also perform marginal analysis: what assets are most and least diversifying in the portfolio, at the margin?

Risk analysis is important for both *passive management* and *active management*. Passive managers attempt to match the returns to a particular benchmark. Passive managers run index funds. But, depending on the benchmark, the manager's portfolio may not include all the bonds in the benchmark, possibly due to the prohibitive transactions costs for holding the thousands of assets in a broad benchmark. Current portfolio risk analysis can tell a passive manager the risk of his portfolio relative to his benchmark. This is his active risk, or *tracking error*. It is the volatility of the difference in return between the portfolio and the benchmark. Passive managers want minimum tracking error.

Active managers attempt to outperform their benchmarks. Their goal is not to track the benchmark as closely as possible. Still, risk analysis is important in active management, to focus active strategies. Active managers want to take on risk only along those dimensions they believe they can outperform.

By suitably decomposing current portfolio risk, active managers can better understand the positioning of their portfolios. Risk analysis can tell active managers not only what their active risk is, but why and how to change it. Risk analysis can classify active bets into inherent bets, intentional bets, and incidental bets:

Inherent: An active manager who is trying to outperform a benchmark will have to bear the benchmark risk. This risk is a constant part of the task that is not under the portfolio manager's control.

Intentional: An active portfolio manager has identified bonds that will do well and bonds that will do poorly. The manager should expect that these bonds will appear as important marginal sources of active risk. This is welcome news, it tells the portfolio manager that he has taken active positions that are consistent with his beliefs.

Incidental: These are unintentional side effects of the manager's active position. The manager has inadvertently created an active position on some factor that is a significant contributor to marginal active risk. Incidental bets often arise through incremental portfolio management, where a sequence of decisions, each plausible in isolation, leads to an accumulated incidental risk.

The Future

A risk model helps design future portfolios. Risk is one of the important design parameters in portfolio construction, which trades off expected return and risk.

The Past

A risk model helps to evaluate the past performance of the portfolio. The risk model offers a decomposition of active return and allows for an attribution of risk to each category of return. Thus the risks undertaken by the manager will be clear, as well as the outcomes from taking those active positions. This allows the manager to determine which active bets have been rewarded and which have been penalized.

SUMMARY

Portfolio management centers on the trade-off between expected returns and risk. This chapter has focused on risk. We have quantified risk as the standard deviation of annual returns, though by assuming normal distributions we could report standard deviations as value at risk numbers. Institutional portfolio managers care mainly about active risk. Risk models, and structural risk models in particular, can provide insightful analysis by decomposing risk into total and active risk; and by identifying inherent, intentional, and incidental bets. Accurate risk models include all important sources of risk, especially interest rates, spread movements, prepayment and volatility risk, and currency risk. Risk models can analyze the present risks and bets in a portfolio, forecast future risk as part of the portfolio construction process, and analyze past risks to facilitate performance analysis.

TECHNICAL APPENDIX:
MARGINAL CONTRIBUTIONS TO RISK

The risk model in matrix notation is written as

$$\mathbf{r} = \mathbf{X} \cdot \mathbf{f} + \mathbf{u}, \tag{A-1}$$

where $\mathbf{r}$ is an N vector of excess returns, $\mathbf{X}$ is an N by K matrix of factor exposures, $\mathbf{f}$ is a K vector of factor returns, and $\mathbf{u}$ is an N vector of specific returns.

We assume that the specific returns $\mathbf{u}$ are uncorrelated with the factor returns $\mathbf{f}$, and that the covariance of specific return u_n with specific return u_m is zero, if $m \neq n$. With these assumptions we can express the N by N covariance matrix $\mathbf{V}$ of bond returns as

$$\mathbf{V} = \mathbf{X} \cdot \mathbf{F} \cdot \mathbf{X}^T + \Delta, \tag{A-2}$$

where $\mathbf{F}$ is the K by K covariance matrix of the factor returns and Δ is the N by N diagonal matrix of specific variance.

Marginal Contributions
Although total allocation of risk is difficult, we can examine the marginal effects of a change in the portfolio. This type of sensitivity analysis allows us to see what factors and assets have the largest impact on risk. The marginal impact on risk is measured by the partial derivative of the risk with respect to the asset holding.

We can compute these marginal contributions for total risk and active risk. The N vector of marginal contributions to total risk is:

$$\mathbf{MCTR} = \frac{\partial \sigma_P}{\partial \mathbf{h}_P^T} = \frac{\mathbf{V} \cdot \mathbf{h}_P}{\sigma_P}. \tag{A-3}$$

The $\mathbf{MCTR}(n)$ is the partial derivative of σ_P with respect to $\mathbf{h}_P(n)$. We can think of it as the change in portfolio risk given a 1% increase in the holding of asset n, financed by decreasing the cash account by 1%.

The marginal contribution to active risk is given by

$$\mathbf{MCAR} = \frac{\partial \psi_P}{\partial \mathbf{h}_{PA}^T} = \frac{\mathbf{V} \cdot \mathbf{h}_{PA}}{\psi_P}, \tag{A-4}$$

where $\mathbf{h}_{PA}$ measures the active portfolio holdings.

Using equations (A-3) and (A-4), and the definitions of total and active risk, we can also show that:

$$\mathbf{h}_P^T \cdot \mathbf{MCTR} = \sigma_P \tag{A-5}$$

$$\mathbf{h}_{PA}^T \cdot \mathbf{MCAR} = \psi_P. \tag{A-6}$$

This means that we could, for example, interpret $\mathbf{h}_{PA}(n) \cdot \mathbf{MCAR}(n)$ as asset n's contribution to active risk.

Chapter 3

A Primer on Value at Risk

Michael Minnich
Vice President
Capital Market Risk Advisors, Inc.

INTRODUCTION

The accelerating trend towards measuring and monitoring risk at a firm-wide level has increased the focus on Value at Risk (VAR) and the need for a consistent firm-wide approach. Although VAR is only one of many both quantitative and qualitative factors that should be incorporated into a cohesive risk measurement and risk management approach, it is an extremely important one. Exhibit 1 shows the key components of a risk management framework.

Practitioners, regulators, and academics have embraced VAR, and many view VAR as a vital component of current "best" practices in risk measurement. VAR can be defined as the maximum loss a portfolio is expected to incur over a specified time period, with a specified probability.[1] Exhibit 2 illustrates this point. The shaded area to the left of the graph shows that there is a 5% probability that a sample portfolio of actually traded securities will lose more than $8.2 million ($100 million − $91.8 million) over the next one week period.

One of the most important aspects of VAR is that unlike scenario analysis or stress testing which shows what loss would occur given a certain scenario, VAR actually assigns a probability to a dollar amount of loss occurring. This probability and its corresponding loss amount (5% and $8.2 million in the example above) are not associated with any particular event, but encompass any event that would cause such a loss.[2] It is important to remember that VAR is not the *maximum* loss that will occur, but only a loss level threshold that will be pierced some percentage of the time (5% in the example above). The actual loss that occurs could be much higher than the VAR.

---

[1] In this chapter the term probability is used for purposes of clarity only. "Confidence level" is a more appropriate term that statisticians or mathematicians would prefer.

[2] Any loss figure generated from a VAR calculation can only anticipate losses resulting from events encompassed by the model chosen and that fall within the assumptions made. For example, a VAR that only measures losses due to market risk (such as Riskmetrics) will not capture credit losses. Likewise, most VAR models will not capture losses due to volatility movements.

The author would like to thank his colleagues at Capital Market Risk Advisors, Inc. for their valuable suggestions and help.

Exhibit 1: Key Components of a
Risk Management Framework

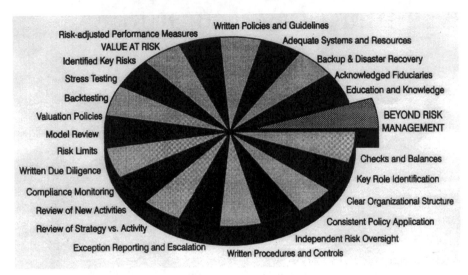

Copyright, Capital Market Risk Advisors, Inc.

Exhibit 2: Illustration of Value at Risk
Probability Distribution of Portfolio Value

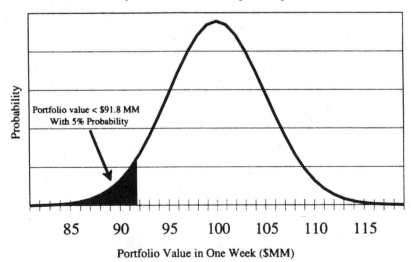

Portfolio Value in One Week ($MM)

Despite all of the support for VAR, it is not a sufficient parameter for risk measurement. VAR is after all only one number from a rich distribution of return information. VAR should be used in conjunction with other risk measures such as scenario testing, stress testing, and other asset/business specific risk measures.

TYPES OF VAR

One of the most difficult aspects of calculating VAR is selecting from among the many types of VAR methodologies and their associated assumptions. Depending on the organization, some of these decisions can be straightforward and clear, but more often than not, certain trade-offs will be made.

There are three main categories of VAR whose primary distinction is the type of calculations performed. These categories are summarized in Exhibit 3. Below we will illustrate how each of these VARs is calculated along with the strengths and weaknesses of each approach. But first we will consider the necessary decisions and assumptions that need to be made regardless of which of the three methodologies is chosen.

VAR CHOICES

The following are decisions that must be decided prior to calculating VAR: (1) time horizon; (2) confidence interval; (3) data series; (4) mapping/selecting relevant risk factors; and, (5) option valuation. Care should be taken when considering each, as the choices made can change not only the actual number,[3] but also the uses and meaning of the VAR number itself

Exhibit 3: Main Categories of VAR

Methodology	Calculations involved
Variance-Covariance	Volatility and correlation matrix
	Matrix algebra to arrive at VAR
Monte Carlo Simulation	Volatility and correlation matrix
	Monte Carlo simulation to generate portfolio return distribution
Historical Simulation	Historical Data set
	Simulate portfolio using historical returns as actual return distribution

[3] Tanya Styblo Beder has clearly demonstrated that the different choices can change the VAR by up to 14 times for some portfolios. See Tanya Styblo Beder, "VAR: Seductive but Dangerous," *Financial Analysts Journal* (September-October 1995), pp. 12-24.

Exhibit 4: Considerations in Selecting a Time Horizon

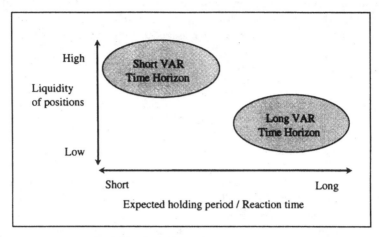

Time Horizon

The choice of time horizon depends upon the objectives of the portfolio and liquidity of its positions. Typically for trading and market making operations, VAR is computed using a one day, one week, or a two week time horizon. However, longer time horizons are often used for proprietary trading firms, institutional investors, and corporations.

Two of the most important considerations for selecting a time horizon are the liquidity of the instruments and the expected holding period. Exhibit 4 illustrates that firms who hold highly liquid securities (such as swaps) for short amounts of time are better suited for a short VAR time horizon, while firms who hold illiquid securities (such as real estate) with a long expected holding period would be wise to choose a longer VAR time horizon.

Confidence Interval

The confidence interval defines the percentage of time that the firm should not lose more than the VAR amount. Commonly used confidence intervals range from 90% to 99%. The actual choice of confidence interval is not as important as understanding the implications of the choice and ensuring that limits are set accordingly. The Bank for International Settlement and the Derivatives Policy Group recommend a confidence level of 99%, while research shows that 95% performs best under backtesting due to "fat tails." The term "fat tails" refers to the fact that large market moves occur more frequently than what would occur if market returns were normally distributed. Despite this fact, many market practitioners and academics assume that returns are normally distributed. This assumption, although usually insignificant, can cause problems in VAR calculations on some asset classes.

Exhibit 5: Normal versus "Fat Tails" Distribution

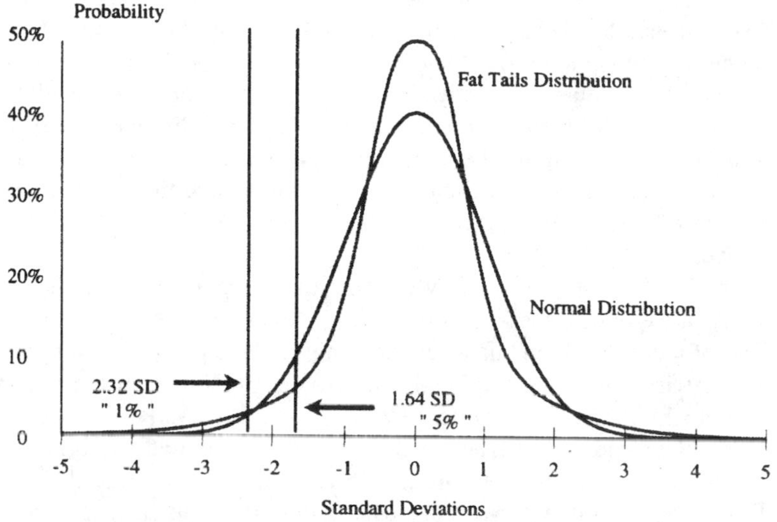

Exhibit 5 illustrates how "fat tails" can cause problems in calculating VAR at higher confidence levels — the VAR should be further to the left for a distribution with "fatter tails" than a normal distribution. As discussed later in this chapter, historical VAR can capture "fat tailed" effects of a return distribution.

Data Series

By most accounts, VAR is fairly data intensive. The choice of historical, implied, or other ways to determine security relationships is important, but typically there is very little choice. Some argue that using implied correlations and volatilities results in a better predictor of risk than historical correlations and volatilities, but very little implied data are available. As a result, historical data sets have become commonplace in VAR calculations, thereby driving the need for additional data decisions to be made.

How much historical data should be used? Longer periods of data have a richer return distribution while shorter periods allow the VAR to react more quickly to changing market events. Three to five years of historical data are typical. In addition, the role of outliers in the data set needs to be considered. Should the Persian Gulf War effects on the oil market be excluded when looking at historical data? Some market participants believe that it should not be excluded because this event reflects real history and adds to the "fat tailed" richness of a data series. Others argue that it should be excluded because the border of its inclusion versus exclusion could imply very different VARs. For instance, consider if a firm were using 10 years of historical data to calculate VAR on an equity portfolio. In October 1997 when the 1987 crash data point falls out of the data set, a risk manager will most likely see a decrease in VAR that has nothing to do with the firm's actual risk, but just the exclusion of one data point due to the passage of time.

One common method that solves both of the above issues is to use exponentially weighted data. Exponential weighting gives more recent data more weight, allowing the VAR to react to changing market conditions quickly. Exhibit 6 illustrates this fact using the Persian Gulf War period as an example. In addition, all of the available historical data are used and hence there is not a discrete trailing point of historical data that would cause the 1987 crash problem mentioned above.[4]

Exhibit 7 shows how equally weighted and exponentially weighted VAR can actually move in different directions due to data issues. Depicted in Exhibit 7 is the VAR of a constantly rebalanced emerging markets portfolio over the course of a 2-year period following the Mexican peso crises. Note that the exponential VAR increases in March 1996, while the equally weighted VAR decreases dramatically during the same period. The increase in the exponentially weighted VAR is caused by the few weeks prior to March 1996 being more volatile than average, while the equally weighted decrease is due solely to the peso crash data point falling out of its one year data set.

Exhibit 6: Exponential versus Unweighted Volatility
S&P 500 Volatility during the Persian Gulf Crisis

[4] Exponential weighting can be approximated in a historical VAR context simply by giving more recent data points more weight in the historical distribution. Depending on how this is implemented, there could be a discrete drop off point in the data series, but the effect will be diminished due to the exponential weighting.

Exhibit 7: $100 Million in an Emerging Markets Portfolio
VAR Stability

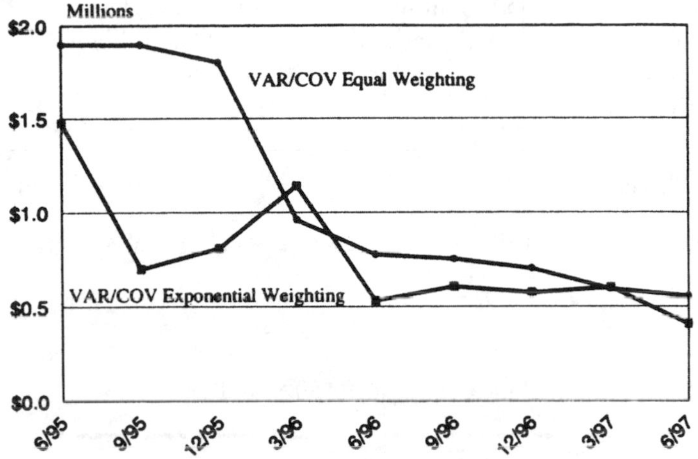

Because slightly different VAR methodologies can yield not only different VARs, but also different relative VAR movements, it is important to either monitor the spread relationships between the VAR calculations on an actual portfolio or at least a sample portfolio. This practice will help avoid placing too much dependence on a single VAR number within an organization.

Mapping/Selecting Relevant Risk Factors

To the extent that historical price series for every position is not available or is too monumental a data problem, assumptions as far as mapping securities into security groups or relating security risk to risk factors need to be made. These assumptions can be considered a balancing act between mapping to such an extent that the ultimate result may not be indicative of the actual portfolio and being so exact that the calculation could take a large team of people several days to compute. The key is to stress test in what areas exactness really matters and then be less exact on the others. This decision is highly dependent on the firm's business and the types of securities it trades.

Option Valuation

The variance-covariance VAR methodologies are not very good at capturing the non-linear behavior of options. So depending on how far in or out of the money an option position is, a VAR number can over or under estimate the real VAR. Depending on the amount of options held, certain second order limits may need to be established or multipliers added to approximate an accurate VAR number. As the next section mentions, Monte Carlo Simulation VAR is considered the best methodology for calculation VAR involving non-linear securities such as options.

Exhibit 8: Portfolio Volatility Example

Position	Treasury Strip	Equity Fund
Units	$100 million	1 million shares
Value	$61.78 million	$60.00 million
Daily Vol	$0.26 million	$0.38 million
Correlation	25%	

$$\text{Vol}_{\text{Portfolio}} = \sqrt{\text{Vol}_{\text{Strip}}^2 + \text{Vol}_{\text{Equity}}^2 + 2 \times \text{Corr} \times \text{Vol}_{\text{Strip}} \times \text{Vol}_{\text{Equity}}}$$

$$\text{Vol}_{\text{Portfolio}} = \sqrt{0.26^2 + 0.38^2 + 2 \times 0.25 \times 0.26 \times 0.38}$$

$$\text{Vol}_{\text{Portfolio}} = \sqrt{0.2614}$$

$$\text{Vol}_{\text{Portfolio}} = \$0.51 \text{ million}$$

$$5\% \text{ VAR} = 1.645 \times \text{Vol}_{\text{Portfolio}} = \$0.84 \text{ million}$$

COMPUTING VAR

Now that we have explored the various VAR choices that need to be tackled, we can show the actual calculations necessary in each of the three major types of VAR. Exhibit 8 illustrates the components of the sample portfolio used in each of the following VAR calculations.

Variance-Covariance VAR

Variance-covariance VAR in its simplest form involves finding the expected volatility in a portfolio of two securities and then multiplying by a factor that is selected based on the desired confidence level. For two securities, the VAR is:

$$VAR = MV \times \text{Factor}$$
$$\times \sqrt{Wt_1^2 \times Vol_1^2 + Wt_2^2 \times Vol_2^2 + 2 \times Corr_{12} \times Wt_1 \times Wt_2 \times Vol_1 \times Vol_2}$$

where

$$Wt_1 + Wt_2 = 1$$

MV   = total market value of portfolio

Factor   = confidence level specific factor derived from cumulative normal distribution

Wt_1 = weight of security 1

Wt_2 = weight of security 2

Vol_1 = volatility of security 1

Vol_2 = volatility of security 2

$Corr_{12}$ = correlation between security 1 and security 2

Exhibit 8 illustrates this calculation for two securities. Note that the factor of 1.645 corresponds to a confidence level of 95%. A factor of 2.326 corresponds to a 99% confidence level. These factors are a function of the normal distribution of security returns that was illustrated in Exhibit 2.

The mathematical relationship can get arbitrarily complex as more and more securities are added. To avoid added complexity, VAR for more than two securities is represented in terms of matrix algebra. The first step in calculating variance-covariance VAR is computing the volatilities and correlations for the selected risk factors. The correlation matrix and volatilities are then combined into a covariance matrix. Next the dollar risk weights for each risk factor are calculated. These weights are arrived at through the mapping process (in the simplest case they are the market value amounts in each asset). Matrix algebra is then used to calculate the portfolio volatility. The portfolio volatility is then scaled by a factor according to the selected confidence level.

The weaknesses of the variance-covariance approach are:

1. It assumes all risk factors are normally distributed. This assumption causes the "fat tails" problem as illustrated in Exhibit 5. Research has shown that this problem is often not significant at the 95% confidence level, but can cause problems at the 99% confidence level.
2. It does not capture non-linear payout functions (e.g., options, callable bonds).
3. It does not capture time decay or time dependency of delta.
4. It assumes a static portfolio.

Monte Carlo Simulation VAR

Monte Carlo simulation VAR follows similar steps. The first step is to calculate the correlation and volatility matrix for the risk factors. Then these correlations and volatilities are used to drive a random number generator to compute changes in the underlying risk factors. Next the resulting values are used to re-price each portfolio position and determine trial gain or loss. This process is repeated for each random number generation and re-priced for each trial. Exhibit 9 illustrates the first 10 trials for the illustration from Exhibit 8. The results are then ordered such that the loss corresponding to the desired confidence level can be determined.

The greatest benefit to Monte Carlo simulation VAR is the ability to use pricing models to revalue non-linear securities for each trial. In this way, the non-linear effects of options that were missed in the variance-covariance VAR can now be captured.

The computation involved in Monte Carlo simulation VAR can be immense for large portfolios, so careful consideration should be paid to the cost versus benefit of calculating a simulation VAR. For instance if a portfolio is composed of linear (non-option) components, there is little added benefit to using

Monte Carlo simulation VAR compared to variance-covariance VAR. Exhibit 10 illustrates how the results from the Monte Carlo simulation VAR approaches the variance-covariance VAR as more and more trials are added.

Monte Carlo simulation, having its roots as a random number generator, is exposed to sampling error. There is the risk of running too few simulations to adequately capture the distribution and this could result in an inferior answer. Fortunately, calculation methods exist to estimate how far off a simulation is so that we can decide whether or not to run more trials.

Exhibit 9: Monte Carlo Simulation Trials
(Values in $ Millions)

Trial	Strip Value	Equity Value	Portfolio	Gain/Loss
1	61.73	59.80	121.53	−0.25
2	62.09	60.01	122.10	0.32
3	61.79	59.64	121.43	−0.35
4	61.61	60.36	121.96	0.18
5	61.79	60.26	122.05	0.27
6	61.79	60.04	121.83	0.05
7	61.65	60.38	122.03	0.25
8	61.65	59.94	121.59	−0.18
9	61.81	60.44	122.25	0.47
10	61.71	59.38	121.09	−0.69

Exhibit 10: Monte Carlo Simulation Results
Portfolio Gain/Loss

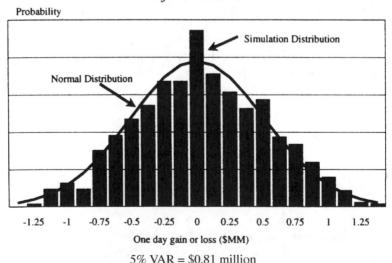

5% VAR = $0.81 million

To analyze the sample error inherent in Monte Carlo simulation, consider the VAR of a portfolio which is between $5 and $6 million with a confidence of 95%. This is simply estimating the range around the estimated VAR in which the real VAR may lie with a certain confidence. This confidence interval can be computed by assuming a binomial distribution with probability equal to the confidence interval (95% in our example) of having a real VAR below the simulated VAR. Using 1,000 trials, we know that the 95% VAR may be viewed as the 50th ranked trial. Using the binomial distribution around the 50th trial, we can compute that with 95% confidence interval around the 50th trial occurs on trials 37 and 64. Therefore in the previous example, the confidence interval for our VAR is $0.75 million – $0.86 million, corresponding to the 64th and 37th ranked trials, respectively.

Historical VAR

Unlike the other two methodologies, historical VAR does not depend on calculated correlations and volatilities. Instead it uses historical data of actual price movements to determine the actual portfolio distribution. In this way the correlations and volatilities are implicitly handled. In fact the most important advantage of historical VAR is that the "fat-tailed" nature of a security's distribution is preserved since there is no abstraction to a correlation and volatility matrix.

Historical VAR is calculated by mapping a portfolio into a historical price distribution. The gains and losses are then added across the portfolio for each day and then ranked in order. The return corresponding to the desired confidence level is then selected as the VAR — meaning that if the desired confidence level were 95% and there were 1,000 data points, we would select the 50th lowest return (50 = (100% – 95%) × 1,000). Exhibit 11 illustrates the historical distribution for the strip and stock example.

One important consideration for computing a historical VAR is the length of the historical period. The historical period should be long enough to form a reliable estimate of the distribution, but short enough to avoid "paradigm shifts."

COMPARISON OF THREE MAJOR VAR TECHNIQUES

Exhibit 12 summarizes the pros and cons of each of the methodologies discussed in this chapter. Recognizing that two different departments with a VAR of $1 million can have very different risk profiles depending on both the nature of their business and the calculation methodology chosen by each is the first step in improving an organization's use of VAR. VAR is a valuable tool, but must be consistently applied to be a meaningful measuring stick.

Exhibit 11: Historical Simulation Results
Portfolio Gain/Loss

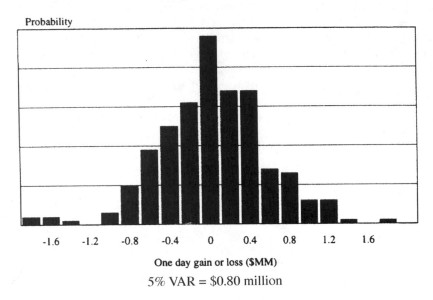

One day gain or loss ($MM)

5% VAR = $0.80 million

Exhibit 12: Summary of Pros and Cons of Each VAR Methodology

Method	Pros	Cons
Variance/ Covariance	Easy to understand. Least computationally intensive. Industry standard.	May misstate non-linear risks. "Fat tails" problem. Computationally intensive.
Monte Carlo Simulation	Accommodates any statistical assumptions about risk factors. Can fully capture non-linear risks.	Sampling error.
Historical Simulation	Naturally addresses the "fat tails" problem. Performs well under back-testing. Can fully capture non-linear risks.	Relies on history. Computationally intensive. Data intensive.

Chapter 4

Portfolio Risk Management

H. Gifford Fong
President
Gifford Fong Associates

Oldrich A. Vasicek
Senior Vice President
Gifford Fong Associates

INTRODUCTION

Fundamental to portfolio risk management is risk measurement. Risk measurement can be thought of as the quantification of the characteristics of risk. Early attempts at risk quantification dealt with investments in relatively simple security types such as Treasury securities and equities. Risk was characterized by volatility of returns and measured by quantities such as variance, standard deviation, or mean absolute deviation.[1]

The development in risk management techniques introduced additional risk measures. In the case of fixed income securities, the concept of duration became a widespread tool for risk management. For equities, the beta coefficient[2] was introduced to provide further capability in managing the risk of equity portfolios. These analytical paths are indicative of the specialization by asset type since the earlier attempts at risk management. In addition, portfolio-oriented measures such as the concept of shortfall risk have been described.[3]

As derivative securities such as options or swap transactions with embedded options were introduced, the structure of marketable assets has become more complex. Derivative securities exhibit an asymmetric price distribution and, hence, cannot be adequately analyzed using the more traditional risk measures suitable for simpler investments. A number of recommendations have emerged to address the perceived need for additional risk analysis insight. The Group of

---

[1] Harry M. Markowitz, *Portfolio Selection* (New Haven, CT: Yale University Press, 1959) and Harry M. Markowtiz, "Portfolio Selection," *Journal of Finance* (March 1952), pp. 77-91.

[2] William F. Sharpe, "Capital Asset Prices: A Theory of Market Equilibrium Under Conditions of Risk," *Journal of Finance*, September 1964, Vol. 19 pp. 425-442.

[3] Martin Leibowitz and Roy D. Henriksson, "Portfolio Optimization With Shortfall Constraints: A Confidence-Limit Approach to Managing Downside Risk," *Financial Analysts Journal* (March-April 1989), pp 34-41.

Thirty[4] reviewed the derivative product industry practice and suggested value at risk as an appropriate risk measure. The Derivative Policy Group (DPG)[5]recommended stress testing under improbable market conditions.

Value at risk provides a useful summarization under prespecified conditions of the amount at risk given the risk characteristics of the portfolio. Stress testing complements the value at risk analysis by providing the results of extreme scenarios of risk factor changes. These two methods view risk from an overall portfolio standpoint rather than at the individual security level.

The focus of attention in this chapter will be the development of the methodologies appropriate for quantifying the risk of complex investments. The discussion concentrates for illustrative purposes on fixed income portfolios, as these contain typically the largest percentage of derivative securities and transactions. The principles of the analysis, however, apply to portfolios of all asset types.

RISK SOURCES

The total risk of a portfolio is represented by the potential decline in the market value of the portfolio. In order to measure this risk, it is necessary to quantify the possible market value changes, under probable as well as extreme circumstances, resulting from the individual risk sources and from their interplay. By identify individual sources of risk, the total and each component risk of the portfolio can be measured. These sources of risk include market risk, option risk, credit risk, foreign exchange risk, and security specific risk, etc.

In the area of fixed income derivatives, market risk arises from changes in the level and shape of the term structure of interest rates. Option risk results from uncertain future interest rate movement. The uncertainty in interest rate movement can be characterized by interest rate volatility. Credit risk stems from changes in the creditworthiness of issuers and can be quantified as the spreads over the default free government rates. Foreign exchange risk for foreign investments is due to exchange rate movements. Security specific risk is the remaining risk not explained by these principal risk factors.

In recapitulation, the principal risk factors for fixed income derivatives can be described as follows:

1. Interest rate level
2. Rates of benchmark maturities
3. Spreads over government rates
4. Volatility of interest rates
5. Exchange rates

---

[4] *Derivatives: Practices and Principles* published by The Group of Thirty, Washington, DC in July 1993.

[5] See Section 1 of *Derivatives: Practices and Principles*. Appendix I: Working Papers.

The investor may be able to hedge or otherwise compensate for some of these risks. For instance, the interest rate risk of the fund can be easily counterbalanced by short positions in interest rate futures contracts. Foreign exchange risk can be eliminated by forward currency hedges. In addition, the specific risk of the fund may be diversified away by the investor's other holdings. For proper risk management, therefore, it is necessary to measure the exposures to the sources of risk in such a way that these can be reduced or eliminated.

RISK EXPOSURES

An essential basis to risk measurement and management is determining the security and portfolio exposures to their risk factors. Suppose we denote the values of the risk factors by F_1, F_2,..., F_n. If P is the value of a security, then the change in the security value resulting from the change in the risk factors can, in the first approximation, be given as

$$\frac{\Delta P}{P} = -\sum_{i-1}^{n} D_i \Delta F_i \tag{1}$$

The quantities D_1,..., D_n in equation (1) are the exposures of the security to each of the risk factors. They measure the percentage change in the value of the security due to a unit change in the value of the factors.

If we postulate a linear relationship between the changes in the value of the factors and the percentage price change represented by equation (1), then the exposures to the factors are defined by the partial derivatives as

$$D_i = -\frac{1}{P}\frac{\partial P}{\partial F_i} \tag{2}$$

For example, if F_i is the interest rate level, the expression (2) is the familiar definition of duration. If F_i is the volatility, the expression (2) gives the exposure to changes in volatility, which is sometimes referred to as "vega." It generalizes in the same form to other risk factors as well. Care needs to be taken that the duration and all other exposures are correctly measured on an options adjusted basis. Therefore, the price sensitivities will have already taken into account any embedded options affecting price changes.

Except as a first-order approximation, however, equation (1) is not a satisfactory representation for the price change of a security for several reasons. First, the price change is not a linear function of the factor change, particularly for derivatives. Secondly, the changes in the factors are not instantaneous, so that a change due to the passage of time needs to be incorporated. Third, there may be a specific component in the value of a security, not explained by the market move. And finally, it is more appropriate to characterize the dollar change, rather than the percentage value change, since derivatives such as swaps and other contracts often start with a low or even zero value.

We will therefore assume that the market value of each security is governed by the equation

$$\Delta P = A - \sum_{i=1}^{n} D_i X_i + \frac{1}{2}\sum_{i=1}^{n} C_i X_i^2 + Y \tag{3}$$

where

$$X_i = \Delta F_i \tag{4}$$

are changes in the value of each risk factor and Y is the risk specific to each security. The quantities D_i, C_i are then the *linear* and *quadratic exposures* of the security value to the factors. They are analogous to the dollar duration and dollar convexity measures of interest rate exposure. In order that the non-linear price response is properly approximated, however, D_i, C_i should be measured for a finite factor change, rather than the infinitesimal one given by equation (2). In fact, there are considerations (related to the theory of Hermite integration) that suggest that the exposures should be determined as

$$D_i = -\frac{P_i' - P_i''}{2\Delta F_i} \tag{5}$$

$$C_i = \frac{P_i' + P_i'' - 2P}{(\Delta F_i)^2} \tag{6}$$

where P_i' and P_i'' are the prices of the security calculated under the assumption that the risk factor F_i changed by the amount of ΔF_i and $-\Delta F_i$ respectively, and ΔF_i is taken specifically to be equal to

$$\Delta F_i = \sigma_i \sqrt{3} \tag{7}$$

where σ_i is the volatility of F_i over the interval Δt. With the definitions (5), (6), (7), the exposures characterize the *global* response curve of the security price rather than the local behavior captured by durations and convexities. Finally, the quantity A in equation (3) is equal to

$$A = \mu - \frac{1}{2}\sum_{i=1}^{n} C_i \sigma_i^2 \tag{8}$$

where μ is the expected return,

$$\mu = E\Delta P \tag{9}$$

With this representation of the price behavior, a risk analysis and measurement is facilitated. Both the linear risk exposures D_i and the quadratic risk exposure C_i combine for the portfolio as simple sums of those for the individual securities. Thus, if D_{ik} is the linear exposure of the k-th security to the i-th risk factor (and similarly for C_{ik}), then

$$D_{ip} = \sum_{k=1}^{m} D_{ik}$$

$$C_{ip} = \sum_{k=1}^{m} C_{ik}$$

would be the risk exposures for the portfolio.

A risk management process may then consist of a conscientious program of keeping all the portfolio risk exposures close to zero,

$$D_{ip} = 0 \qquad i = 1, ..., n$$

$$C_{ip} = 0 \qquad i = 1, ..., n$$

to eliminate an undesirable dependence on market factors. This is equivalent to hedging against all sources of market risk. The specific risks $s_k^2 = Var(Y_k)$ which combine by the formula

$$s_P^2 = \sum_{k=1}^{m} s_k^2$$

can only be reduced by diversification.

The overall variability of the portfolio or security value can be calculated from its risk exposures using the formula

$$\sigma^2 = Var(\Delta P) = \sum_{i=1}^{n}\sum_{j=1}^{n} D_i D_j \sigma_{ij} + \frac{1}{2}\sum_{i=1}^{n}\sum_{j=1}^{n} C_i C_j \sigma_{ij}^2 + s^2 \qquad (10)$$

which is a consequence of the value change equation (3). Here σ_{ij} are the covariances in the changes of the i-th and j-th risk factor,

$$\sigma_{ij} = Cov(X_i, X_j)$$

To the extent possible, the variances and covariances should be obtained from current pricing of derivatives whose values depend on these variances (these are called the *implicit volatilities*). For instance, quotes are available in the swap market for interest rate volatilities, calculated from market prices of swaptions. These volatilities reflect the market's estimate of the prospective, rather than past, interest rate variability. Only when such implicit volatilities are not available for a given risk factor, a historical variability should be used. In this case, care should be taken that the historical period is long enough to cover most market conditions and cycles.

VALUE AT RISK

The *value at risk* (*VAR*) is a single most useful number for the purposes of risk assessment. It is defined as the decline in the portfolio market value that can be expected within a given time interval (such as two weeks) with a probability not exceeding a given number (such as 1% chance). Mathematically, if

$$Prob(\Delta P \leq -VAR) = \alpha \tag{11}$$

then *VAR* is equal to the value at risk at the probability level α.

In order that the *VAR* can be calculated, it is necessary to determine the probability distribution of the portfolio value change. This can be derived from equation (3).

Assume that the factor changes X_i have a jointly normal distribution with mean zero and covariance matrix (σ_{ij}), $i, j = 1,..., n$. Then the first three moments of ΔP are given by equations (9), (10), and (12), where

$$\mu_3 = E(\Delta P - \mu)^3$$

$$= 3\sum_{i=1}^{n}\sum_{j=1}^{n}\sum_{k=1}^{n}D_i D_j C_k \sigma_{ik}\sigma_{jk} + \sum_{i=1}^{n}\sum_{j=1}^{n}\sum_{k=1}^{n}C_i C_j C_k \sigma_{ij}\sigma_{jk}\sigma_{ki} \tag{12}$$

Knowing the three moments, the probability distribution of ΔP can be approximated and the *VAR* calculated. There are theoretical reasons to use the Gamma distribution as a proxy. The resulting formula for the value at risk is then very simple:

$$AR = k(\gamma) \cdot \sigma \tag{13}$$

where σ is the standard deviation of the value of the portfolio or security, obtained as the square root of the variance given in equation (10) above. The quantity γ is the skewness of the distribution,

$$\gamma = \frac{\mu_3}{\sigma^3} \tag{14}$$

calculated using equations (9) and (11). Finally, the ordinate $k(\gamma)$ is obtained from Exhibit 1 (corresponding to the Gamma distribution). (Exhibit 1 only extends to the values $\gamma = \pm2.83$, since this is the highest magnitude attainable for the skewness of the quadratic form in equation (3).)

Exhibit 1: 0.01 Ordinates as a Function of Skewness

γ	$k(\gamma)$
−2.83	3.99
−2.00	3.61
−1.00	3.03
−0.67	2.80
−0.50	2.69
0.00	2.33
0.50	1.96
0.67	1.83
1.00	1.59
2.00	0.99
2.83	0.71

Note that the value 2.33 in Exhibit 1 corresponding to $\gamma = 0$ is the 1% point of the normal distribution. In other words, if the portfolio value change can be represented by the symmetric normal distribution, the VAR at the 1% probability will be VAR − 2.33σ. For most derivative securities and portfolios, however, the probability distribution is highly skewed one way or the other and the normal ordinates do not apply. The numbers in Exhibit 1 represent the proper ordinate values.

It may also be noted that equation (13) does not include the expected return μ. This is because the mean is of lower order of magnitude (namely Δt) than the standard deviation σ (which is of the order $\sqrt{\Delta t}$) and can be neglected.

The VARs can be calculated for individual securities, portfolio sectors, and the total portfolio, as well by the sources of risk. Exhibit 2 illustrates a VAR analysis with a global portfolio. This global portfolio consists of US Treasury securities, a floating-rate loan, a short position in an interest rate cap, and German government bonds hedged with a cross currency swap. The cross currency swap is composed of fixed rate DEM payments in exchange for floating rate USD receipts.

The numbers in Exhibit 2 do not necessarily add up, either down or across. The reason that they do not add up for the sectors and the total portfolio is that the value at risk due to, say, foreign exchange risk may come from rising exchange rate for German government bonds while for the cross currency swap, it comes from declining exchange rates. The reason the numbers do not add up across the sources of risk is that events of a given probability (say, 1%) do not add up: an interest rate change that can happen with 1% likelihood when considered alone is not the same as that which would happen together with, say, an exchange rate movement for a joint 1% probability.

Exhibit 2: Value at Risk (USD)

Security	Market Value	Interest Rate Risk	Derivative Risks	Specific Risks	Foreign Exchange Risks	Total Risk
USA						
TB 01/16/97	973,750	2,980	0	310	0	3,000
T 5.5 11/15/98	989,670	13,860	0	1,580	0	13,950
T 8.5 02/15/20	2,314,560	127,480	0	10,650	0	127,920
T 7.5 11/15/24	1,026,050	62,500	0	6,780	0	62,870
Floating rate loan	5,055,630	9,830	0	1,950	0	10,020
Cap sold	−85,790	46,940	5,540	5,510	0	47,590
USA Total	10,273,860	260,420	5,540	24,980	0	261,670
Germany						
DBR 8.5 08/21/00	80,430	920	0	110	3,220	3,350
DBR 9.0 01/22/01	797,260	10,180	0	1,320	31,900	33.510
DBR 8.0 07/22/02	742,100	12,640	0	1,240	29,690	32.290
DBR 6.0 02/16/06	661,130	16,980	0	1,580	26,450	31.470
Cross currency swap	−150,410	28,330	0	3,450	89,870	94,290
Germany Total	2,130,510	12,610	0	1,460	4,330	13,410
Portfolio Total	12,404,370	267,320	5,540	25,030	4,330	268,580

STRESS TESTING

Although value at risk represents a useful assessment of the potential losses from various sources of risk and their interplay, it should be complemented by a series of stress tests. Value at risk is a proper measure of the instantaneous portfolio riskiness. This is all that would be necessary if all securities in the portfolio were perfectly liquid and if the portfolio risk was managed on a continuous-time basis. But in reality this is not the case. Thus, stress simulations of the portfolio's value response to market condition changes that are more extreme or persistent than those likely to occur in a short time interval are in order for comprehensive risk analyses. In this sense, stress tests are less systematic and somewhat ad hoc compared to the value at risk.

A stress test consists of specifying a scenario of extreme market conditions occurring over a specific time interval, and evaluating the portfolio gains or losses under such scenarios. This is useful for a number of reasons. First, such analysis allows for consideration of path-dependent events, such as cash flows on CMO securities. Second, it does not rely on a specific form of the value response curve, such as the quadratic form in equation (3). Portfolio values including derivatives with embedded options will not change in a linear or quadratic form. Depending on the structure of the portfolio, it may change by a large amount under extreme conditions. Third, it has an appeal to intuition that is lost in the VAR alone by showing the situations under which a loss can occur. And last but not least, it is required or recommended by the various oversight agencies and auditors.

Exhibit 3 is a possible stress test output table for the portfolio described in Exhibit 2. Scenarios 1 and 2 represent U.S. term structure movements, which affect USD denominated securities only. Scenarios 3 and 4 represent U.S. interest rate term structure steepening or flattening, which affects the cross currency swap through the floating-rate USD receipts. Scenarios 5 and 6 are exchange rates changes, which influence DEM denominated securities and the cross currency swap through the fixed-rate DEM payments. Scenarios 7 and 8 represent German interest rate term structure movements, which may affect DEM denominated securities only. Scenario 9 is a combination of a DEM/USD exchange rate change and a German interest rate change, which affects both German government bonds and the cross currency swap.

CONCLUSIONS

Risk measurement of fixed income investments is a complex process due to the asymmetry of their return distribution. By utilizing value at risk and stress testing, an ability to evaluate non-symmetric return outcomes emerges. Each of these techniques has an important role. Value at risk is the expected loss from an adverse market movement with a specified probability over a stated time period. For example, value at risk is defined as the dollar amount that the total loss may exceed within 14 days with a 1% probability. On the other hand, stress testing determines how the portfolio would perform under stress conditions.

Exhibit 3: Stress Tests

Number	Scenario	Gain/Loss (USD)
1	USD interest rate up 100 bps	−451,950
2	USD interest rate down 100 bps	481,560
3	USD interest rate: 2 yr up 50 bps, 10 yr down 50 bps	112,490
4	USD interest rate: 2 yr down 50 bps, 10 yr up 50 bps	−103,640
5	DEM/USD up 10%	−9,840
6	DEM/USD down 10%	12,030
7	DEM interest rate up 30 bps	−137,710
8	DEM interest rate down 30 bps	140,300
9	DEM/USD up 10% & DEM interest rate up 30 bps	−2,290
	etc.	

The market characteristics that affect the value of a security or portfolio are called risk factors. Risk factors that affect fixed income derivatives include interest rate level, benchmark maturity rates, spread over government rates, volatility of rates, and foreign exchange rates. To quantify the risk exposure to those risk factors, a quadratic approximation may be used and then a standard deviation may be calculated. The VAR number may be calculated by a Gamma distribution approximation. While value at risk gives a summary risk number, it does not tell the source or direction of the risk. To see the possible loss under extreme or least favorable market conditions, a series of stress tests must be performed. The value at risk and the result of a comprehensive stress test give a better risk picture than either one of them. In combination, they represent a comprehensive risk measurement necessary for portfolios with complex structures and interrelationships.

Chapter 5

Advanced Risk Measures for Fixed-Income Securities

Teri Geske
Vice President, Product Development
Capital Management Sciences

Gunnar Klinkhammer, Ph.D.
Vice President, Quantitative Research
Capital Management Sciences

INTRODUCTION

Over the past ten years, the evolution of risk and return measures for fixed-income securities has moved from traditional, static measures such as Macaulay's duration, yield-to-maturity, and nominal spread to option-adjusted values such as effective duration, effective convexity, partial or "key rate" durations, and option-adjusted spreads (OAS). All of these concepts focus on the sensitivity of a bond's (or fixed-income derivative's) price to changes in interest rates, as interest rate risk and the relationship between interest rates and the value of a bond's embedded options is the dominant risk factor in this market. However, there are other sources of risk which can have a material impact on the valuation of fixed-income securities. The presence of these additional risk factors highlights the need for risk measures which define and quantify a bond's (or a portfolio's) sensitivity to changes in other variables. This article describes four such measures: prepayment uncertainty, volatility risk (vega), zero-volatility OAS (ZVO), and spread duration. These measures provide an additional dimension to investment analysis, complementing measures such as effective duration, convexity, and OAS. As with effective duration and convexity, these additional risk measures may be calculated both for individual securities and at the portfolio level, allowing portfolio managers to compare individual investment alternatives and overall portfolio strategies.

The four measures are summarized below and are discussed in detail in the following sections.

> *Prepayment uncertainty* — The sensitivity of a mortgage-backed security's price to a change in the level of the prepayment speeds projected by a prepayment model. To calculate this measure, alternative sets of cash

61

flows for the security are produced by shifting each single monthly mortality (i.e., prepayment) rate (SMM) generated by a prepayment model upward and downward by some percentage, e.g. 10%. Based on the security's current OAS, two new prices are computed for the slower and faster prepayments. The average percentage change in these prices compared to today's price is the measure of prepayment uncertainty. The prepayment uncertainty measure recognizes the fact that although a Monte Carlo simulation incorporates interest rate uncertainty, it does not recognize the uncertainty of prepayment forecasts. Prepayment uncertainty may also be calculated for asset-backed securities.

Volatility risk (vega) — The sensitivity of a security's price to a change in the underlying volatility of Treasury rates. To calculate this measure, volatility is increased and decreased along the entire term structure of volatility by specified amounts, and the security's price is recalculated using these higher and lower volatilities, assuming a constant OAS. The average percentage change in price is the measure of volatility risk, or vega. This measure is important for all securities with embedded options, including callable corporates, step-ups, mortgages, CMOs, and ARMs.

Zero volatility spread (ZVO) — The constant spread over the Treasury spot curve which equates the discounted cash flows derived from today's implied forward curve to the current price of the security. As the name suggests, this is the spread an investor would expect to earn if there was no uncertainty about the future path of interest rates. When an OAS is subtracted from the zero volatility spread the result may be interpreted as the time value of the embedded option, since the ZVO assumes that interest rates, and therefore expected future cash flows, will not fluctuate from levels predicted by today's implied forward yield curve.

Spread duration — The sensitivity of a bond's price to a change in its OAS. To calculate this measure, the security's OAS is shifted up and down by some specified amount and the two resulting prices are computed, holding today's term structure of interest rates and volatilities constant. Spread duration equals the resulting average percentage change from the original price (scaled to a 100 bp shift in OAS) and indicates the sensitivity of a bond's price to changes in the risk premium demanded by the market.

PREPAYMENT UNCERTAINTY

Investors have long been aware that the market consensus on expected prepayment rates can change unpredictably. Such changes occur, for example, when new prepayment data indicate that homeowner behavior is no longer adequately described by existing prepayment models. The effect of revised prepayment expectations on the valuation of mortgage-backed securities thus constitutes an additional source of risk. This risk, which we may call prepayment uncertainty risk, is a model risk since it derives from the inherent uncertainty of all prepayment models.

While effective duration and convexity have gained universal acceptance as measures of interest rate risk, no standard set of prepayment uncertainty measures exists yet. Some proposed measures have been called "prepayment durations" or "prepayment sensitivities."[1] Here, we describe three measures that are readily understood and capture the major dimensions of prepayment uncertainty. We call these measures overall prepayment uncertainty, refinancing ("refi") partial prepayment uncertainty, and relocation ("relo") partial payment uncertainty.[2] Our methodology assumes that a (possibly quasi-random) Monte Carlo interest rate path generator is used in conjunction with a prepayment model to compute OASs for mortgage-backed securities.

Overall prepayment uncertainty measures the price effect of a proportional increase or decrease of all projected prepayment rates that underlie the valuation of a given security. To this end, all single month mortality rates (SMMs) that are predicted along the various Monte Carlo paths used for the security's valuation are scaled up by 10% from what the prepayment model would normally predict. The security's price is then recomputed using the OAS derived from the original market price (and the original prepayment model). The price is also recomputed for SMMs that are scaled down by 10% from their originally predicted levels, holding the OAS constant. The price for faster prepayments is then subtracted from the one for slower prepayments, and the overall prepayment uncertainty measure equals one-half the difference, expressed as a percentage of the original price. Thus, an overall prepayment uncertainty of 0.2 indicates that a security's market price will increase (decrease) by 0.2% if all projected prepayment rates are revised downward (upward) by 10%.

In many situations, investors might be less concerned with the possibility of an overall revision of expected prepayments than of expected refinancings. Therefore, the *refinancing partial prepayment uncertainty* is based on a 10% up and down scaling of the refinancing portion of each predicted SMM. The calculation is otherwise analogous to the overall prepayment uncertainty. To complete the picture, one can also compute a *relocation partial prepayment uncertainty* measure which quantifies the exposure to revisions of the projected baseline prepayment rate (the "demographic prepayment rate").

[1] Andy Sparks and Frank Feikeh Sung, "Prepayment Convexity and Duration," *Journal of Fixed Income* (March 1995), pp. 7-11; and, Gregg N. Patruno, "Mortgage Prepayments: A New Model for a New Era," *Journal of Fixed Income* (December 1994), pp. 42-56.
[2] These measures have been implemented by Capital Management Sciences (CMS) in the BondEdge® fixed-income portfolio analytics system.

Exhibit 1: Prepayment Uncertainty Measures for FNMA 30-Year Passthroughs (June 1995)

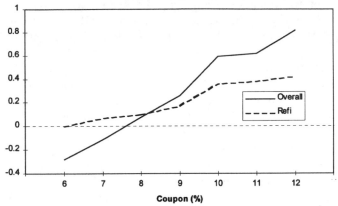

Source: Capital Management Sciences

Exhibit 1 shows overall and partial refinancing prepayment uncertainties for FNMA 30-year passthroughs as of June 1995. For discount coupons, the overall prepayment uncertainty measure is negative because a slow-down of prepayments decreases the security's value. Furthermore, the overall prepayment uncertainty for discounts is approximately equal to the relocation uncertainty, since the effect of a revised refinancing expectation on discount mortgages is small. By contrast, premium coupons gain value under an overall slow-down of prepayments and thus have a positive overall prepayment uncertainty. They also have an appreciable refinancing uncertainty. Note that the refinancing uncertainty is positive (or zero) for all coupons since refinancings are projected only for those times and interest rate paths where the coupon bears a premium. For leveraged mortgage securities, such as volatile CMO tranches or mortgage strips, the prepayment uncertainty measures can attain much greater magnitude, both positive and negative, than for passthroughs.

The prepayment uncertainty measures presented here can assist with trading decisions on a single security basis, as differences in prepayment uncertainty may explain why two securities with seemingly very similar characteristics trade at different OASs. On a portfolio basis, these prepayment uncertainty measures allow the user to construct portfolios with controlled exposures to the basic drivers of prepayment uncertainty.

VOLATILITY RISK (VEGA)

Implicit in the valuation of fixed-income securities with embedded options is an estimate of the volatility of interest rates. Obviously, changing one's volatility estimates will affect the value of such securities. The value of an option increases as volatility increases because higher volatility makes it more likely that the option will be in the money on its exercise date (European option) or some time during its exercise period (American option). The investor who holds a security with an embedded option exercisable by the issuer (e.g., a callable corporate bond) therefore faces a drop in value as volatility increases. The opposite is true when the investor is long an embedded option (e.g., in a putable corporate bond). The volatilities implied by the market prices of fixed-income securities with embedded options change over time. These changes are tied to the changing volatility outlook of the markets for interest rate derivatives (caps, floors, swaptions, etc.). If implied volatilities in the markets for callable corporate bonds, mortgage-backed securities and similar assets exhibited large deviations from the volatilities implied by the prices of these derivatives, arbitrage opportunities would arise.

Absent the ability to predict changes in implied volatilities, investors need one or more risk measures to quantify the exposure of their holdings to volatility changes. To value fixed-income securities with embedded options, one needs a dynamic model of the term structure of interest rates. Since different term structure models treat interest rate volatility differently, there is no unique way to measure volatility risk. In particular, models with a term structure of volatility allow the computation of more than one measure of volatility risk, because long-rate volatilities may be changed differently from short-rate volatilities. For simplicity, we present a fundamental measure of volatility risk, which we shall call vega.[3] This risk measure quantifies the sensitivity of a security's price to an overall upward or downward shift of the term structure of volatility. In other words, vega measures the change in a security's value when the volatilities of interest rates of all maturities rise or fall in tandem. In this respect, vega resembles effective duration, which measures exposure to a parallel shift of the term structure of interest rates.

Of course, how one implements the notion of all volatilities rising or falling in tandem may still depend on one's dynamic term structure model. For example, the term structure of volatility in the BondEdge® system is completely characterized by the specification of any two of the following parameters: volatility of the short rate, volatility of the long rate (i.e., the 30-year par bond yield), and mean reversion, which governs the steepness of the term structure of volatility. Building on this term structure model, one can implement a straightforward definition for vega: the percentage change of a security's value under a change in long volatility of one percentage point, with the mean reversion rate and the security's OAS held constant. For example, if the initial long volatility is 11%, vega will involve recalculating a security's price for 10% and 12% long volatility, respectively, holding the security's original OAS constant. The price for 12% long volatility is then subtracted from the one for 10% long volatility, and vega equals one half the difference, expressed as a percentage of the security's original price.[4]

---

[3] *Vega* is a common name for the volatility sensitivity of options, particularly when the option value is assumed to depend on only one volatility parameter (such as in the basic Black-Scholes option formula).

[4] Since mean reversion is held constant, the volatilities of shorter interest rates also move up and down in this calculation, although typically by more than one percentage point.

Exhibit 2: Vega for 30-Year FNMA Passthroughs (September 1995)

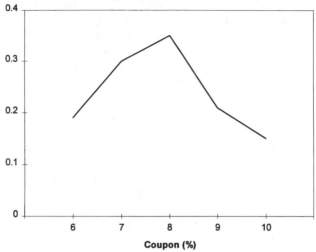

Source: Capital Management Sciences

Mortgage-backed securities provide a good illustration of how a security's characteristics determine its sensitivity to volatility changes. As we discuss in the section on zero volatility spreads, the prepayment options held by homeowners can be thought of as a portfolio of calls and puts. Depending on interest rates, homeowners will prepay faster (thus exercising calls) or slower (thus exercising puts) than expected for a specified base case. Increasing volatility increases the value of the prepayment options and thus reduces the value of a mortgage passthrough. Given our definition, vega should be positive (greater than zero) for passthroughs. Exhibit 2 shows vega for representative 30-year FNMA issues, as computed in September 1995. For example, the 8% issue's vega of 0.35 means that the price of this passthrough would fall by 0.35% if long volatility were to increase by one percentage point. Conversely, the price would increase by 0.35% if long volatility were to fall by one percentage point.

It is not surprising that the near-current coupon issues exhibit the largest vegas. For current coupon mortgages, the prepayment options allow for both accelerated prepayments under falling interest rates and slowed prepayments under rising interest rates. By contrast, for a discount mortgage, homeowners' put options are in the money and gain little additional value under rising interest rates. Similarly, for a premium mortgage, the calls are in the money and gain little additional value under falling interest rates. In other words, the value of the prepayment options in a current-coupon mortgage is most sensitive to changes in volatility because both the puts and the calls are at the money. We see, also, that the volatility sensitivity of the 10% premium collateral is low due to burnout and shorter maturity.

Vega can be negative for some mortgage-backed securities. For example, as of September 1995, a PO backed by 6.50% FNMA collateral maturing in 2024 had a vega of −0.53. This discount collateral hardly has any extension risk, but falling interest rates could cause principal to be returned faster. Thus, volatility creates value for the holder of this PO strip. This last conclusion may seem to conflict with the fact that the prepayment option is still with the homeowners and not with the holder of the PO. The contradiction is solved by considering the third party involved: the holder of the corresponding IO. In our example, the IO backed by the same collateral had a strongly positive vega of 1.65. If one weights the vegas of the IO and the PO by their market values one obtains a combined vega of 0.24 for the IO/PO pair. As we expect, this equals the vega computed for the underlying collateral.

In summary, vega helps to manage the exposure of assets with embedded options to fluctuations of the implied volatility levels in the fixed-income markets.

ZERO VOLATILITY SPREAD

Zero volatility spread (ZVO) is the spread an investor would expect to earn on a bond if there was no uncertainty about the future path of interest rates. It is the spread (in basis points) over the Treasury spot curve which equates the present value of expected future cash flows to the current price of the security, where the "expected" cash flows are determined by today's term structure of interest rates. ZVO is similar to OAS as it is a spread over the entire Treasury curve, unlike nominal spread which is computed relative to a single point on the yield curve. The difference between OAS and ZVO is that OAS incorporates the possibility that interest rates will vary into the future, thereby reflecting the impact of any embedded options under different interest rate environments. The ZVO calculation uses a single set of expected cash flows based on today's term structure to determine whether any embedded options will be exercised. As described below, the difference between ZVO and OAS provides interesting information about the nature of the embedded options in the security.

Intrinsic Value versus Time Value of Options

As discussed earlier, we know that the value of a fixed-income security with embedded options depends on the amount of volatility that interest rates are expected to experience in the future. The greater the volatility, the more valuable the embedded options, and vice versa. When considering the impact of volatility on option value, it is useful to think of options as having both intrinsic value and time value. The intrinsic value is the amount the option holder would realize if the option were exercised today, and in many cases the intrinsic value is zero. A simple example of this is a currently callable corporate bond priced below its call price, e.g., priced at 98 and callable at 102. Although this option's intrinsic value is zero its overall value is greater than zero as long as we assume interest rates can deviate from current levels.

This value which exceeds the intrinsic value is called the *time value of the option*. The longer the time to the option's expiration and the more volatility we assume interest rates will experience in the future, the greater its time value (all other things being equal) because there is more opportunity for the option to end up in-the-money prior to its expiration date. In the example of a corporate bond priced at 98 and currently callable at 102, the option's time value could be considerable (perhaps $2, $3, $4, etc.) depending upon the bond's coupon rate, maturity date, and our expectations for interest rate volatility into the future. If we assume that interest rates will have zero volatility in the future, the time value of this option would also be zero, because there would be zero probability that the call would ever end up in-the-money.

The impact of volatility on an option's time value also applies to the prepayment option embedded in mortgage-backed securities, and to interest rate caps in floating rate CMOs and adjustable-rate mortgages (ARMs). At CMS, we define the intrinsic value of the prepayment option by the level of prepayments which are expected given today's term structure of interest rates. The time value of the prepayment option is derived from the fact that, assuming there is some interest rate volatility going forward the level of prepayments can deviate from current expectations. For those who prefer to think in terms of puts and calls, the prepayment option in a mortgage may be thought of as a combination of a call option and a put option, since homeowners have the right to accelerate prepayments (to call their high coupon mortgages away from investors) when rates fall, and can reduce prepayments below original expectations when rates rise (forcing the investor to hold the mortgage for a longer period when its value has declined) — a put option. As with the example of the callable corporate bond, the time value of the prepayment option depends upon the level of volatility we assume interest rates will experience over the life of the mortgage. If we assume no volatility of interest rates in the future, the time value of the prepayment option drops to zero.

ZVO and OAS

Since the ZVO calculation is equivalent to an OAS calculation with volatility "turned off," the difference between ZVO and OAS expresses the time value of embedded options in basis points. The greater the level of volatility assumed in valuing a security, the greater the difference between the ZVO and OAS. If we turn off volatility, OAS would be equal to ZVO. Therefore, comparing ZVO and OAS tells the investor the cost of future volatility, in basis points. As noted above, for mortgage-backed securities, the difference between ZVO and OAS represents the time value of the prepayment option. For ARMs and CMO floaters, the difference also reflects the time value of periodic and lifetime caps.

CMOs are also affected by the value of the homeowner's prepayment option, with the added complexity of the deal structure. VADM tranches and PACs with short average lives are not particularly sensitive to changes in the time value of the prepayment option because their cash flows are stable. We would therefore expect there to be little difference between the ZVO and the OAS for these instruments, since interest rate volatility in the future will have little impact on the pattern of cash flows received by the investor. We see a greater difference between ZVO and OAS for support tranches which absorb most of the prepayment risk, indicating the cost of future interest rate volatility for these securities.

The difference between the ZVO and OAS for an ARM or CMO floater may be greatly affected by changes in the time value of the lifetime and periodic caps. Even if the bond's coupon is below the cap rate, the cap (which the investor has shorted) has time value because there is a positive probability that the coupon formula will exceed the cap rate during the remaining life of the security. The time value of a cap is also impacted by the slope of the yield curve. For CMO floaters with long average lives, and for ARMs, a positively sloped yield curve implies that a short-term index, such as 1-month LIBOR or the 1-year CMT, will rise into the future. If the curve steepens, the likelihood that a coupon based on one of these rates will ultimately encounter its lifetime cap increases, thereby increasing the time value of the embedded option. The difference between ZVO and OAS measures that value.[5]

Computing ZVO and comparing it to OAS allows the investor to quantify the impact of uncertainty about the future of interest rates. It can be used to compare investment alternatives across different types of fixed-income securities, and to track over time how the time value of embedded options changes.

SPREAD DURATION

Spread duration measures the sensitivity of a bond's price to a change in its OAS. To calculate spread duration we hold the Treasury spot curve fixed at its current level, increase and decrease the security's OAS by some amount and compute two new prices. Spread duration equals the average percentage change from the original price and indicates the sensitivity of the bond's price to changes in the risk premium demanded by the market.

Recall that OAS is the average spread which, when added to the possible future Treasury spot curves, equates the discounted present value of the security's option-adjusted cash flows to its market price. (See Exhibit 3.)

OAS may be interpreted as a summary measure of the possible future returns offered by a security based on the expected cash flows across different interest rate paths. OAS allows investors to compare risk/reward characteristics across different types of fixed-income securities with embedded options, such as callable corporate bonds, mortgage passthroughs, and CMOs. Often, investors are just as concerned with the magnitude and direction of changes in spreads as with changes in interest rates, and spread duration allows the portfolio manager to measure the impact of changes in OAS across a variety of fixed-income investment alternatives.

---

[5] For ARMs and floating-rate CMOs the difference between ZVO and OAS also reflects the time value of the prepayment option, but this is typically less important than for fixed rate mortgage-backed securities.

Exhibit 3: Treasury Curve and OAS

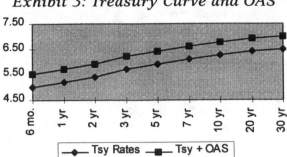

An interesting contrast between corporate bonds and mortgage-backed securities may be observed when analyzing spread duration. With mortgage-backed securities, a change in OAS does not alter the cash flows which the investor expects to receive, as a homeowner's prepayment option is unaffected by changes in OAS demanded by investors.[6] Similarly, a change in OAS for an adjustable-rate mortgage has no impact on the evolution of its coupon rate and therefore would not impact the likelihood of encountering the ARM's reset or lifetime caps. Therefore, spread duration for mortgage-backed securities reflects the fact that a change in OAS affects the present value of expected future cash flows, but the cash flows themselves are unaffected by the change in the OAS.

However, a change in the OAS of a callable (or putable) corporate bond does affect the cash flows an investor receives, since the corporate issuer who owns the call option will decide whether or not to call the bond (or the investor decides to put the bond) on the basis of its price in the secondary market. If a bond's OAS narrows sufficiently a bond's price could rise above its call price, causing the issuer to call the issue (likewise, a sufficient widening of OAS would cause an investor to put a bond to the issuer). Thus a small change in the OAS of an "at-the-money" callable bond could mean the difference between receiving cash flows based on the maturity date or the call schedule.

Consistent with these observations, we see that the spread duration for a mortgage passthrough often resembles its Macaulay's duration, with good reason. Macaulay's duration calculates the change in a bond's price given a change in yield, assuming no change in cash flows. Similarly, spread duration is calculated by discounting the mortgage passthrough's projected cash flows using a new OAS, which is analogous to changing its yield. Spread duration for a mortgage passthrough will not be exactly equal to Macaulay's duration, as spread duration is derived from projected mortgage prepayments along a variety of possible interest rate paths (using a Monte Carlo simulation), whereas Macaulay's duration

---

[6] One could argue that changes in the secondary market ultimately affect the interest rate charged on new mortgages, thereby impacting the homeowner's refinancing incentive, but any potential impact is assumed to be negligible for purposes of this discussion.

uses the single set of cash flows generated by a lifetime PSA speed. For CMOs, the difference between the single set of so-called "PSA cash flows" used to calculate Macaulay's duration and the multiple sets of cash flows resulting from the various interest rate paths can cause spread duration to be markedly different than Macaulay's duration.

In contrast, the spread duration for a corporate bond is actually equal to its effective duration.[7] Recall that a corporate issuer will decide whether or not to call a bond based on its price in the secondary market. Since changing a corporate bond's OAS by x basis points has the same impact on price as shifting the underlying yield curve by an equal amount, the calculation for spread duration and effective duration produce the same result. Therefore, either one can be used to estimate the impact of a change in OAS on a corporate bond's price. For example, the impact of a 20 basis point shift in OAS on the price of a bond with an effective duration of 4.37 is estimated by $[0.20 \times 4.37] = 0.874\%$.[8]

Why go to the trouble of calculating spread duration for corporate bonds when it is equal to effective duration? The benefit becomes clear when we consider a portfolio which contains both mortgage-backed securities and corporate bonds. The spread duration of the portfolio measures the portfolio's sensitivity to a change in OASs across all security types, giving the portfolio manager important information about a portfolio's risk profile which no other duration measure provides.

CONCLUSION

The risk measures discussed in this chapter recognize that investment analysis and portfolio management must go beyond interest rate risk measurement and address other sources of risk which impact all fixed-income securities. They can assist with trading decisions on a single security basis, helping to explain why two securities with seemingly similar characteristics have different OASs and offer different risk/return profiles. At the portfolio level, these risk measures allow the portfolio manager to manage exposure to these sources of risk, trading off one type of exposure for another, depending upon one's expectations and risk tolerances.

---

[7] Assuming effective duration is calculated using the same basis point shift used to calculate spread duration.

[8] This assumes effective duration and spread duration are calculated using a 100 basis point shift in the term structure.

Chapter 6

Dissecting Yield Curve Risk

Wesley Phoa, Ph.D.
Vice President of Research
Capital Management Sciences

INTRODUCTION

For many years, modified duration was regarded as the sole interest rate risk measure of importance to bond investors. Its appeal was that it was simple to calculate, yet had explanatory power. Its use is still widespread.

However, yield curve risk is complex. The growth of indexing, and the proliferation of complex products with embedded options, have both revealed inadequacies in the concept of modified duration. Portfolio managers have been forced to devise a variety of more detailed measures in an attempt to represent yield curve risk more completely.

These new duration measures include effective or option-adjusted duration, non-parallel durations, such as slope or curvature durations; and partial durations, such as key rate durations. It is not immediately obvious where these measures come from, why they are meaningful or how they should be used. Furthermore, the concept of modified duration itself has unexpected subtleties.

This chapter reviews each of these duration measures, the intuition behind it, how its use is justified by the empirical data, and the role it plays in managing a bond portfolio.

EFFECTIVE DURATION

Modified duration is computed using a fixed set of bond cash flows. If a bond contains embedded options, so its cash flows vary under different scenarios, modified duration does not measure interest rate risk correctly.

For example, consider a callable bond. One could work out the modified duration in at least two possible ways: based on the cash flows to maturity, or the cash flows to the call date. Neither is correct, since each calculation ignores the fact that the other scenario may occur. The correct duration instead lies somewhere in between the two figures.

Exhibit 1: Change in Effective Duration for a Callable Bond
Issue: Cincinnati Gas & Electric 8.125%, 8/1/2003
Call information: Call price: $102.31 from 8/1/95
Price: $102.09

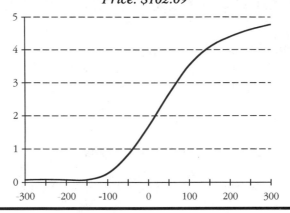

The obvious solution is to compute the modified duration under all possible scenarios and then weight by their probabilities. This correctly captures the uncertain timing of the bond's cash flows.[1]

Note that effective duration can vary significantly as yields change — intuitively, a change in yields changes the probabilities of the different scenarios. This is partly captured by the bond's convexity; but for large parallel shifts in yields, even convexity does not fully describe the price effect.

Exhibit 1 shows how the effective duration of a typical callable bond varies under parallel shifts in the yield curve. Note that if convexity fully described all these changes, the graph would be a straight line. The bond is a Cincinnati Gas & Electric 8.125% 8/1/2003, callable at $102.31 from 8/1/95 and currently valued at $102.09.

Another way that effective duration differs from modified duration is that it can depend on option-adjusted spread. Intuitively, the OAS is incorporated into every interest rate path, and partly determines whether an option will be exercised along a given path. The following example uses the Cincinnati Gas & Electric callable bond:

Price	OAS	Effective duration
$102.09	33 bp	1.68
$101.50	60 bp	2.17

[1] Strictly speaking, risk-neutral rather than "real world" probabilities must be used in the calculation. For readers familiar with option pricing, the explanation is as follows: the effective duration of a contingent security is the derivative of the security price P with respect to an overall yield level y; to see why this is equivalent to the above definition, first note that P is the expected value:

E[NPV of cash flows discounted at riskless rate]

where the integral is taken over all interest rate paths under the risk-neutral probability measure, and cash flows are computed for each interest rate path — then differentiate under the integral sign.

Finally, both the passage of time and changes in volatility affect the probability distribution of interest rate paths, and hence the effective duration of a callable bond.

All the above remarks apply equally to mortgage-backed securities. In fact, the behavior of a CMO effective duration can be much more complex than the above examples, and also dependent on the prepayment model.

To sum up: if a portfolio contains bonds with embedded options, a single effective duration (and convexity) does not fully describe its parallel risk; effective durations must be computed under a range of yield and OAS scenarios.

WHAT DOES DURATION MISS?

Effective duration describes how the bond price responds to a change in bond yields. It is a conceptually simple measure of interest rate risk. However, in using effective duration as a *portfolio* risk measure, three assumptions must be made:

1. The price-yield relationship is linear.
2. Yield changes are perfectly correlated.
3. Bond yield volatilities are all identical.

If these all held, then, for example, portfolio risk would not be affected by executing a duration-matched switch out of a 2-year Treasury into a 30-year Treasury.

All three assumptions are false:[2]

1. The above switch increases portfolio convexity, and thus changes its risk profile. But if a bond has no embedded options, its convexity is relatively small.

2. Changes in the 2-year and 30-year Treasury yields have a (10-year) historical correlation of only 0.73; it is possible that the 2-year bond will rally while the 30-year bond remains unchanged, in which case the investor will underperform.

3. The (10-year) historical annual volatility of the 2-year and 10-year Treasury yields is 107 bp and 94 bp. If the 2-year bond rallies by 22 bp but the 30-year bond rallies by only 18 bp, the investor will underperform.

In the light of 2 and 3, how is it possible to justify the use of effective duration as the primary portfolio risk measure? In order to answer this question, it is necessary to look more closely at the dynamics of the term structure. It turns out that effective duration is indeed of primary importance.

---

[2] For a further discussion, see R. Jarrow, *Modeling Fixed Income Securities and Interest Rate Options* (NY: McGraw-Hill, 1996), pp. 113-117.

Exhibit 2: Principal Component Analysis Applied to Treasury Yields: 1986-1996

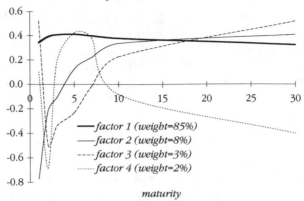

maturity

A common tool for identifying and analyzing different kinds of term structure shifts is *principal component analysis*.[3]

The dynamics of a physical (or financial) system — described in terms of coupled quantities — can be broken down into "normal modes" which by definition act independently of each other: mathematically, these are the eigenvectors of the system. Given a theoretical description of the system, the eigenvectors can be derived mathematically. However, if we do not yet have a formal model of the system, but only empirical data on its behavior, statistical methods must be used to estimate the eigenvectors. This is termed principal component analysis.

In this case, the procedure is as follows: one computes the covariance matrix of weekly changes in constant maturity Treasury yields; then the eigenvectors of this matrix may be regarded as underlying, uncorrelated "factors" affecting the term structure, while the eigenvalues indicate their relative importance. A small eigenvalue suggests that the corresponding factor is not meaningful.

Exhibit 2 shows the results of a principal component analysis applied to daily 1-, 2-, 3-, 5-, 7-, 10- and 30-year Treasury yields, from the period 1986–1996. Since the eigenvectors can be interpreted as yield curve shifts, it is helpful to graph each of them as a function of maturity.

Exhibit 2 indicates that:

- The most important factor, which explains 85% of observed yield curve shifts, is a parallel shift in the yield curve.

---

[3] An early reference is by R. Litterman and J. Scheinkman ("Common Factors Affecting Bond Returns," *Journal of Fixed Income* (June 1991)). More recent examples of the results of this kind of analysis appear in E. Canabarro ("Where Do One-Factor Interest Rate Models Fail?" *Journal of Fixed Income* (September 1995)), and R. Rebonato and I. Cooper ("The Limitations of Simple Two-Factor Interest Rate Models," (*Journal of Financial Engineering* (March 1996)). Principal component analysis provides an empirical underpinning for Arbitrage Pricing Theory, the successor to CAPM; for an example of how its results are consistent with economic theory, see the appendix to this chapter.

- The second most important factor is a change in yield curve slope, where the short end of the curve suffers a shock whose impact decays with maturity, so that 10–30 year yields are hardly affected.

- The remaining factors are hard to interpret, but appear to be relatively unimportant; we will revisit them later in this chapter. The smallest factors are not even shown, as they appear to be pure noise.

For a bond with no embedded options, modified duration measures portfolio exposure to the dominant factor, parallel shifts in the yield curve; it ignores all the other factors. That is, modified duration accurately captures the most important source of yield curve risk, and ignores all the other kinds of yield curve risk. A duration-matched switch is neutral with respect to parallel risk, but can drastically affect portfolio risk in other ways.

Note that the results of a principal component will in general depend on both the bond yields included and the historical period used; this is discussed in the next section. This is related to the fact that principal component analysis does not capture all important aspects of yield curve risk, such as individual rate correlations; we return to this point later in this chapter.

NON-PARALLEL DURATION

The analysis presented in the previous section identified slope risk as a significant factor determining bond returns. Although it was far less important than parallel risk, for investors closely tracking an index duration its relative importance is much greater.

A portfolio manager can monitor portfolio slope risk by computing a non-parallel duration. This shows the impact on a security's value of a change in the slope of the yield curve.

For example, suppose an investor redistributes portfolio holdings across the yield curve without changing portfolio duration. Exposure to a yield curve steepening or flattening may be radically different, and non-parallel duration is required to detect this.

It will be helpful to give the precise definition. Recall that effective duration measures the impact on bond value of a 100 bp change in yields across the whole curve. By contrast, non-parallel duration measures the impact on bond value of a more complex "slope shift;" very short-dated yields move by 100 bp, but longer maturity yields move by less than this — 10-year yields move by only 13 bp and 30-year yields do not move at all.

Exhibit 3 shows the precise slope shift used by a proprietary model (CMS BondEdge's Structured Products module) and compares it to the "slope factor" derived earlier in this chapter.

Exhibit 3: Slope Shift Assumed by Proprietary Model and Slope Factor

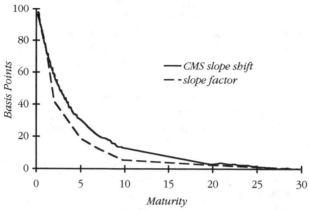

The slope factor appears to show more rapid attenuation than the proprietary slope shift, probably due to the fact that different datasets were used in the estimation process; but the discrepancies are fairly small. In general, there is good agreement between the two.[4]

The shape of the proprietary slope shift is thus reasonable. What about the 100 bp scale? The choice of a 100 bp shift in short-end yields was arbitrary, but turns out to be convenient: it corresponds to a change of 60 bp in the 2-year/30-year spread. (From the perspective of a bond portfolio, maturities under 2 years are of secondary interest.)

This means that if a portfolio has a non-parallel duration of 1.10 and the 2-year/10-year spread falls by 30 bp, one expects portfolio value to decline by $1.10 \times 30/60 = 0.55\%$.

Now the 2-year/30-year spread has a historical volatility of around 60 bp per annum, compared to around 100 bp for the 30-year Treasury yield. So from the point of view of volatility, the scale of the proprietary slope shift is consistent with the scale of the parallel shift used to compute effective duration.

This means that, broadly speaking, it makes sense to compare parallel and slope risk by comparing the effective and non-parallel durations in absolute terms: if a portfolio has an effective duration of 4.00 and a non-parallel duration of 1.00, then slope risk is indeed "about 25% as important" as parallel risk for that portfolio. If the slope shift involved a 100 bp change in the 2-year/10-year spread, it would have been less convenient to make this comparison.

---

[4] Both the BondEdge slope shift and the slope factor in the previous section were derived purely empirically. It is also possible to take a more theoretical approach to defining a "slope shift." See, for example, R. Willner, "A New Tool for Portfolio Manager: Level, Slope, and Curvature Durations," *Journal of Fixed Income* (June 1996). The appendix to this chapter explains how this can be done in an economically motivated context.

Exhibit 4: Parallel and Non-Parallel Durations for Noncallable Treasury Bonds

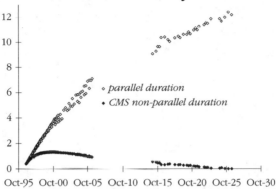

As a concrete illustration of non-parallel duration, Exhibit 4 shows both parallel and non-parallel durations for non-callable Treasury bonds. Note that non-parallel duration tends to be much smaller than modified duration, which is consistent with the observation in the previous section that in absolute terms, parallel risk is much more important than slope risk.

Non-parallel duration is highest for bonds with maturities of 3–5 years. For shorter bonds, any change in yields has little effect; whereas for longer bonds, the proprietary slope shift gives only a small change in yields.

Two obvious — related — questions are:

- A single "typical slope shift" was identified using 1986–1996 data. What if the shape of the "typical" slope shift is different from one year to the next? Then we might be using the wrong shape now. This would not have been picked up by the analysis that was carried out, which somehow averages over the whole period.

- Is it possible to identify a "curvature" factor that affects mid-range bond yields? If so, how important is it compared to the parallel and slope factors? Recall that the initial principal component analysis in the previous section did *not* unambiguously reveal the existence of a curvature factor.

To answer these questions, it is helpful to look at the historical data in a way which strips out both parallel and slope shifts, but which does not depend on principal component analysis. We will use an analysis which looks at *ratios* of yield spreads: it takes the 2-year/10-year spread on any given day as the definition of "slope," and divide all other spreads to the 10-year bonds by this "slope." This might be termed relative spread analysis.

The reason for using 2-year and 10-year yields rather than, say, 3-month and 30-year yields is that we suspect that both the very short and the very long ends of the yield curve are "special" in some sense. The analysis will confirm this suspicion.

Exhibit 5: Historical Spread Between 2-Year and 10-Year Treasury Yields: January 1981 to September 1996

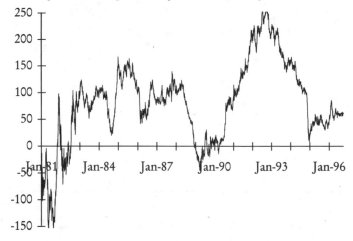

Exhibit 6: Spread to 10-Year, Relative to 2-Year/10-Year Spread

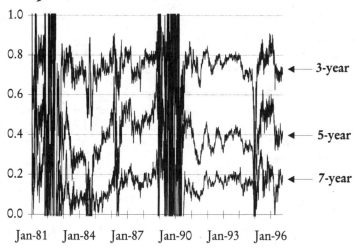

Note that this method cannot give stable results when the yield curve is flat or nearly flat. Exhibit 5 shows the historical spread between the 2-year and 10-year Treasury yields from January 1981 to September 1996. Clearly, before 1983, between December 1988 and June 1990, and in December 1994 and January 1995, the results will probably be meaningless.

Exhibits 6 and 7 show the results of this simple analysis, when applied to 1981–1996 Treasury data. For convenience, signs of the 30-year relative spreads have been inverted. The analysis indicates that:

Exhibit 7: Spread to 10-Year, Relative to 2-Year/10-Year Spread

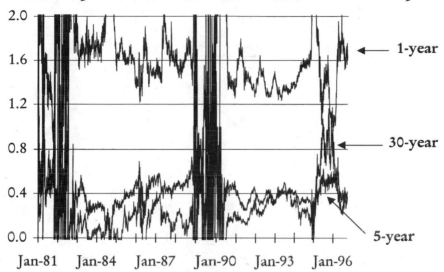

- The mid-range (3-, 5- and 7-year) relative spreads are closely correlated. Note that when these mid-range relative spreads are smaller, there must be more curvature in the yield curve.

- The mid-range relative spreads are not obviously correlated with the economic cycle, but instead appear to mean revert to "normal" values over periods significantly shorter than the cycle; these values characterize the slope factor of presented in the previous section.

- The 30-year relative spread tends to move in line with the mid-range relative spreads, but it does not appear to have a "normal" value, and instead seems to exhibit medium-term trends.

- The 1-year relative spread tends to move in the opposite direction to the mid-range relative spreads – as expected – but it is also subject to wide random fluctuations that seem to be completely unrelated.

Broad conclusions are as follows:

1. The 2- to 10-year part of the yield curve, including the mid-range bonds, forms a relatively homogeneous market.

2. There is a "curvature" factor explaining changes in mid-range relative spreads.

3. Market segmentation affects 1- and 30-year bond yields; that is, the 1- to 30-year part of the yield curve is, to some extent, a heterogeneous market.

Exhibit 8: Principal Component Analysis Without 1-Year and 30-Year Yields

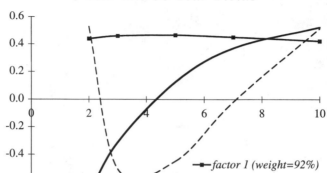

Maturity

Taken together, 1 and 3 suggest that if we eliminate 1- and 30-year bond yields from the dataset and carry out a principal component analysis again, we should be able to identify the curvature factor mentioned in 2.

Exhibit 8, which shows the results, illustrates that this is indeed the case. The findings are:

- The two most important factors are again parallel and slope shifts. The slope shift has a lower weight here because it had the greatest impact on 1-year yields, which were eliminated from the new dataset.

- The third most important factor emerges clearly as a change in the curvature of the mid part of the curve; however, this is only about half as important as the slope factor — even before taking into account the fact that the true significance of slope shifts is understated in this dataset.

- The other factors appear to be noise.

However, this is not the only possible point of view. It might be argued that the short end of the yield curve, corresponding to the region in which Eurodollar futures were actively traded, also constitutes a "market." An analysis which focused on the short end of the curve — for example, which included 3-, 6-, 9-, and 18-month yields but excluded maturities longer than 3 years — would not reveal the above "curvature" factor, but might instead reveal a "humping" factor at the short end.

The point is that since principal component analysis is highly dataset-dependent, its use is based on a subjective judgment. An investor might be interested in analyzing a curvature factor; a cap/floor trader might be more interested in analyzing a humping factor.

YIELD CORRELATIONS

It is tempting to believe that principal component analysis — if it is carried out carefully enough, and perhaps in several stages — can provide a complete description of term structure dynamics and thus yield curve risk, comprehensively broken down into factors.

This is not the case. There are a number of related reasons why this idea does not work. First, as we have seen, there are always a number of factors which are simply meaningless "noise," representing yield changes which the analysis fails to explain. Second, the analysis only gives statistically significant results if it is applied to a relatively long time series; but this means that short-term phenomena are obscured.

What this means in practice is that yields at adjacent maturities are, historically, appreciably less correlated than a factor model would predict. The reason is that yield spreads often show significant short-term fluctuations. This was observed — for forward rates rather than bond yields — by Rebonato and Cooper, in their evaluation of two-factor term structure models.[5] They use a comparative correlation analysis of forward rates, which can equally well be applied to Treasury yields.

Exhibit 9 shows the empirical correlations of various Treasury yields, based on 1986–1996 daily yield data. Exhibit 10 shows what the correlations would be if only parallel and slope changes had occurred. The actual correlations between adjacent rates, shown in italics, are significantly lower than those predicted by a factor model with parallel and slope factors only. Rebonato and Cooper provide a theoretical explanation for this phenomenon.

Concretely, this implies that, for example, the 2-year/3-year spread is more volatile than the factor model predicts. This extra volatility means that a portfoilo manager who is only monitoring parallel risk and slope risk will experience some inexplicable fluctuations in returns. These might arise, for example, from fluctuations in relative spreads as in the previous section.

Exhibit 9. Empirical Correlations of Various Treasury Daily Yields: 1986-1996

	1	2	3	5	7	10	30
1	1.00	0.78	0.78	0.71	0.68	0.64	0.58
2		1.00	0.92	0.88	0.85	0.82	0.73
3			1.00	0.92	0.91	0.87	0.78
5				1.00	0.93	0.91	0.83
7					1.00	0.94	0.87
10						1.00	0.93
30							1.00

[5] Rebonato and Cooper, "The Limitations of Simple Two-Factor Models."

Exhibit 10: Empirical Correlations of Various Treasury Daily Yields if Only Parallel and Slope Changes had Occurred: 1986-1996

	1	2	3	5	7	10	30
1	1.00	0.95	0.92	0.80	0.73	0.62	0.54
2		1.00	0.99	0.94	0.90	0.83	0.77
3			1.00	0.97	0.94	0.88	0.83
5				1.00	0.99	0.97	0.94
7					1.00	0.99	0.97
10						1.00	0.99
30							1.00

These fluctuations will generally be quite small. It is also possible that they exhibit a degree of mean reversion, and are therefore less significant determinants of medium-term portfolio returns. However, mean reversion in relative spreads, where it occurs at all, generally occurs over timeframes longer than the typical interval between portfolio performance measurement.

Adding a curvature factor will improve the fit to empirical correlations, but — by definition — it is not possible to recover the precise correlations without adding all the factors back in, including the meaningless "noise" factors which are too unstable to be useful.

To sum up, factor durations such as effective duration, non-parallel or slope duration, and curvature duration will not fully capture yield curve risk. To achieve this, it is necessary to monitor the portfolio's sensitivity to each individual rate that enters the construction of the yield curve.

This method — which was first developed for managing dealers' OTC derivative positions and has now been widely adopted on derivative trading desks — is becoming increasingly widespread in bond portfolio management. This method computes *key rate durations* for each on-the-run Treasury yield — these are the "key rates" on the Treasury curve. For example, the 5-year key rate duration of a bond measures the change in bond value if the 5-year zero coupon Treasury yield changes but all other zero coupon Treasury yields (and the bond's OAS) remain the same.

By definition, the sum of all the key rate durations is equal to the effective duration of the bond. Thus the key rate durations may be regarded as decomposing a parallel shift in the yield curve into its component parts.[6]

As a bond's yield changes, or as it grows shorter, its modified or effective duration is rebalanced amongst its key rate durations. One way of understanding this is to observe that the key rate duration calculation attempts to replicate a bond by a portfolio of zero coupon Treasuries; the key rate durations are then simply the durations of these Treasury bonds, multiplied by their weights in the replicating portfolio.

---

[6] More abstract "point" duration measures have been proposed, which decompose a parallel shift in different ways. While these are valid ways of looking at risk, key rate durations have the advantage of being more concrete and intuitive.

Thus, unlike parallel and slope duration, key rate durations are not independent. It is necessary to develop some experience with key rate durations and how they can interact as the yield curve moves around.

Finally, it must be mentioned that the issues raised in this section may simply be irrelevant to some investors, depending on the nature of the portfolio and the investment strategy. For example, an investment manager might focus mainly on effective duration and non-parallel duration; imposing constraints on key rate durations might compromise the manager's ability to search for relative value opportunities along the yield curve, without delivering appreciable benefits in terms of risk control. On the other hand, an asset-liability manager might need to monitor key rate durations much more closely.[7]

A critical point is that, while effective duration and non-parallel duration are in some sense linked to economic risk factors (as discussed in the appendix), key rate durations are not. The yield curve shifts used to calculate key rate durations do not correspond to independent, meaningful sources of risk, and do not arise from changes in market fundamentals. Rather, they are related to more transitory market phenomena.

CONCLUSION

At first sight, duration appears to be a simple concept; but yield curve risk is actually very complex. It is dangerous to rely on preconceptions, whether based on "market intuition" or term structure theory, without carefully examining the empirical data.

It is also wasteful to monitor a large number of risk measures without a proper understanding of what they mean, how they work, and when they are — or are not — important. The use of inappropriate risk measures can actually subtract value by limiting flexibility.

This chapter has presented a number of different ways of looking at the empirical data, and shown how they naturally lead to a variety of different duration measures. Each duration measure was related to a specific kind of yield curve risk. Some connections to market experience, to economics, and to term structure theory were also described, particularly in the appendix.

Although only U.S. data were discussed here, similar results are obtained for other mature bond markets. However, the precise details — such as the optimal way to measure slope risk — vary between different markets.

---

[7] The role of empirical analyses — like those presented here — in designing regulatory frameworks is a controversial question.

APPENDIX: MACROECONOMIC EXPLANATION OF THE TWO MOST IMPORTANT FACTORS DRIVING CHANGES IN BOND YIELDS

Both market experience and principal component analysis confirm that overall changes in the level and slope of the yield curve are the dominant factors in the Treasury market. This appendix sketches an explanation, essentially due to Frankel, of why this is the case.[8]

Frankel uses a macroeconomic argument to derive a theoretical shape which the yield curve must have under a certain set of macroeconomic assumptions. Because the actual economy is not fully characterized by these theoretical assumptions, the yield curve rarely assumes this form in practice.

However, in the course of the analysis, potential factors affecting bond yields are identified; and, most importantly, it is possible to characterize the yield curve shifts arising from these factors. Moreover, these theoretical shifts may be identified with the two dominant factors which emerge, independently, from a principal component analysis.

To sketch the argument, first define:

y_t = log of current (time t) output
y_{long} = log of normal or potential output

n_t = current nominal short rate
i_{long} = long-run inflation rate
r_{long} = long-run real interest rate

m_t = log of the current money supply
p_t = log of the current price level

Consider a model consisting of the following assumed relationships, where Greek letters denote fixed adjustment rates or elasticities:

1 (IS) $\quad y_t - y_{long} = -\zeta\,(n_t - i_{long} - r_{long})$

2 (LM) $\quad m_t - p_t = \phi\,y_t - \lambda\,n_t$

3 (supply) $\quad dp_t/d_t = \rho(y_t - y_{long}) + i_{long}$

Intuitively, the first assumption relates the output gap to the current real rate via investment demand; the second relates real money demand to income and the current nominal short rate; and the third asserts that price changes are determined by excess demand and expected inflation.

---

[8] J.A. Frankel, *Financial Markets and Monetary Policy* (Cambridge, MA: MIT Press, 1995).

Using the fact that dm_t/dt and dp_t/dt both tend to i_{long}, it can be shown that:

$$dn_t/dt = -\delta\,(n_t - i_{long} - r_{long})$$

where $\delta = \rho\zeta\,(\phi\zeta+\lambda)^{-1}$. This integrates to:

$$n_t = (i_{long} + r_{long}) + (n_0 - i_{long} - r_{long})\,e^{-\delta t}$$

In other words, the current nominal short rate approaches an "equilibrium" nominal short rate at an exponentially decaying rate.

This analysis is claimed to be applicable to a wide variety of macroeconomic models that include a money-demand and a price-adjustment equation. It also generalizes to a model with stochastic disturbances to the level and trend of the money supply.

Even if the actual economy does not satisfy the above assumptions, if investors implicitly believe that they are valid, then the argument shows that *expected* future short rates have this form. In this case i_{long} and r_{long} should be understood as the market expected long-run inflation and real interest rates.

Specifying a yield curve is equivalent to specifying a forward rate curve; and it can be shown that a forward rate must be equal to the expected future short rate plus a risk premium related to volatility.

The above analysis therefore describes a theoretical term structure of forward rates and bond yields, which is assumed to depend on investors' inflation and growth expectations.

The yield curve rarely conforms to this theoretical shape. Investor expectations cannot be perfectly described by an economic model; furthermore, there are arguably periods when bond yields are not solely determined by investor expectations. However, the analysis turns out to be a useful way to understand the dynamics of the term structure. In terms of the above model, a change in the path of future nominal rates can result from:

1. a change in the current nominal rate;
2. a change in long-run inflation; or
3. a change in the long-run real interest rate.

Here 2 and 3 should be understood to mean a change in investor expectations.

If the initial nominal rate n_0 changes by an amount Δ, then future nominal rates nt will change by the amount $\Delta e^{-\delta t}$; in particular, the impact on long-term bond yields is negligible. So 1 corresponds to a yield curve slope shift.

If investors adjust their long-run inflation expectations, so i_{long} changes by an amount Δ, then all future nominal rates nt will change by the same amount Δ; all bond yields will be equally affected. That is, 2 corresponds to a yield curve parallel shift. The same argument shows that 3 also corresponds to a yield curve parallel shift.

Summing up, the analysis suggests that parallel shifts and "exponentially decaying" slope shifts should be the major factors driving the dynamics of the term structure. This is consistent with the empirical evidence.

If only nominal bonds are traded, parallel shifts arising from 2 and 3 cannot be distinguished in the bond market. However, if both nominal and inflation-linked bonds are traded, then these two kinds of term structure shifts can be distinguished.

The above analysis actually suggests a two-factor time homogeneous affine yield model in the sense of Brown and Schaefer,[9] or Duffie and Kan.[10] The derived parameter δ can be regarded as speed at which the short-term rate approaches an expected long-term equilibrium level, and in fact can be identified with the mean reversion parameter κ_s of Brown and Schaefer; unlike the underlying elasticities, it is in principal an observable constant. There are several possible ways to measure it; however, it is somewhat difficult to derive stable estimates.[11]

Note that the model apparently sheds no light on the possible source of a curvature factor. Curvature shifts do not have an obvious interpretation in the above framework.

It might be argued that they occur when investors revise their structural assumptions about the economy, and hence their estimates of the elasticities in the model; but the proposed mechanism is obscure.

The explanation also seems to conflict with market experience, which tentatively suggests that curvature shifts are not driven by fundamentals, but are related to transient supply/demand factors, temporary market segmentation and investor psychology.

In other words, bond yields are not fully explained by economic fundamentals — hardly a surprising observation.

---

[9] R. Brown and S. Schaefer, "Interest Rate Volatility and the Shape of the Term Structure," in S.D. Howison, F.P. Kelly, and P. Wilmott (eds.), *Mathematical Models in Finance* (London: Chapman & Hall, 1995).

[10] D. Duffie and R. Kahn, "Multi-Factor Term Structure Models," in *Mathematical Models in Finance*.

[11] Frankel attempted to estimate δ directly, and obtained an estimate of 0.46 based on 1958–1978 Treasury data. Treasury data from 1986 to 1996 were used to compute an estimate of 0.38 for the U.S. economy, consistent with the estimate of 0.42 obtained by Brown and Schaefer from 1987–1993 swap yields. (Their estimate based on 1930–1979 Treasury data was 0.78, but as a number of structural changes in the U.S. economy occurred during this time period, this estimate is probably not meaningful.) By way of comparison, our estimates for a number of international government bond markets ranged from 0.28 to 0.62, suggesting that the shape of a "typical" yield curve slope shift may indeed vary from country to country.

Chapter 7

Measuring and Managing Interest-Rate Risk

Scott F. Richard, DBA
Partner
Miller Anderson & Sherrerd, LLP

Benjamin J. Gord
Vice President
Miller Anderson & Sherrerd, LLP

INTRODUCTION

How do we predict what will happen to the value of a client's fixed-income portfolio when interest rates change? This is one of the most important questions we have to answer in managing fixed income assets. In this chapter we report on our research aimed at answering this question and explain how we use the results of this research in portfolio management.

If a client's portfolio contained only one bond, then the answer would be given, to a good approximation, by the bond's (modified) duration. The duration of the bond measures its percentage price change for a small change in the bond's yield. Suppose a portfolio contained only a 10-year-maturity Treasury note with a 6.5% coupon selling at par. Standard calculations indicate a duration of 7.3 years for this bond. Hence, if the 10-year note's yield rises 10 basis points, the bond's value, and the portfolio's value, will fall by approximately 73 basis points; conversely, if the 10-year note's yield declines 10 basis points, the value of the bond and the portfolio will rise by about 73 basis points.

In reality, portfolios are never so simple that they contain only one bond. The highly diversified portfolios that we manage typically contain more than 100 securities with a wide variety of maturities. Is duration a good measure of the relative interest-rate sensitivity of different portfolios? Consider another portfolio composed of 44.6% in cash, with a duration of zero years, and 55.4% in a 30-year Treasury bond with a 6.5% coupon, selling at par with a duration of 13.1 years. Standard calculations show that the portfolio has a duration of 7.3 years, which is the weighted average of zero years and 13.1 years. Usually portfolio managers who use duration as a measure of interest-rate risk think of this barbell as having about the same interest-rate risk as the 10-year bullet we just discussed. But what does this duration figure mean? Presumably, it means that if yields rise by 10 basis points, the portfolio will decline in value by about 73 basis points. We must be more precise, however, about exactly what we mean by "if yields rise by 10 basis points" in order for 73 basis points to be the realized loss. In fact, both the 30-year and 10-year yields must change in the same direction and in the same amount for the price change of the bullet to equal the price change of the barbell. If both yields do not typically change in the same direction or by the same amount, then the change in the portfolio's value will be different, and duration will mismeasure the interest-rate risk of the portfolio.

Now let's extrapolate our reasoning to a portfolio containing many bonds with all maturities between cash and 30 years (or longer). Separating these bonds into their coupon and principal payments, we see that such portfolios commonly have cash flows at all points on the yield curve. Will the average duration[1] of all the bonds be an accurate measure of the portfolio's interest-rate risk? Extending our reasoning from the two bond portfolios, *we see that duration is an accurate measure of interest-rate risk for a portfolio only if all yields typically change in the same direction and by the same amount (i.e., if a typical yield-curve change is a parallel shift).*

We have now deduced that duration is an adequate measure of interest-rate risk only if parallel shifts typify changes in the yield curve. Luckily, this is an empirical issue that we test by examining yield-curve data.[2] If it is true, then we are done; if not, we must create a new measure of interest-rate risk that is consistent with the way yield curves actually reshape.

HOW DO YIELD CURVES CHANGE?

To answer this question, we examined yield data for zero-coupon Treasury bonds. We used zero-coupon bonds for two reasons. First, zero-coupon bonds are the building blocks for all coupon bonds, which can be separated into portfolios of zero-coupon bonds. Second, zero-coupon bonds give us a much richer set of bond durations to examine. The maturity of a zero-coupon bond is nearly equal to its duration, so that the duration range for zero-coupon bonds is one to 30 years. In contrast, coupon bonds have a duration range of about one to 13 years, the duration of a 30-year Treasury security.

---

[1] Actual Portfolios contain callable bonds such as mortgages and corporates. For callable bonds, when we refer to "duration," we mean the option-adjusted duration.

[2] There are solid theoretical foundations for thinking that parallel shifts are not likely. For example, if interest rates mean-revert, even very weakly, then long yields must be less volatile than short yields, which rules out a parallel shift. There is an increasing volume of empirical evidence from term-structure modeling and option pricing showing that interest rates mean-revert very slowly.

Exhibit 1: Zero-Coupon Yields

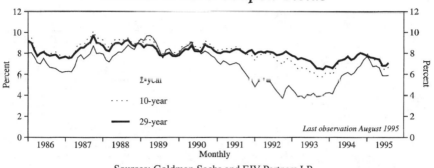

Sources: Goldman Sachs and EJV Partners LP.

Exhibit 1 shows monthly yield data for the 2-year, 10-year, and 29-year zero-coupon Treasury bond since 1986.[3] It appears that yields tend to change in the same direction across the yield curve, but not by the same amount. Just by looking at the data, it is difficult to identify a typical yield-curve shift, but it appears that short-term interest rates are more volatile than long-term interest rates (i.e., short-term yields have tended both to fall more and to rise more than long-term yields). In other words, the yield curve has tended to steepen during a rally and to flatten during a sell off.

Although Exhibit 1 is sufficient to confirm this general observation, we need to use statistical techniques to estimate typical yield-curve movements more precisely. In making this analysis, we examined beginning-of-month yields from October 1986 through August 1995 on zero-coupon bonds of constant maturities one through 29 years. Although these data represented 29 different yield series, the results — not surprisingly — did not suggest that there are 29 independent sources of change in the yield curve. Indeed, using principal-components analysis (discussed in the Appendix) we found that two types of systematic yield-curve reshapings explained almost 97% of the variation in interest rates. Remaining changes in yields at different maturities appear random.

We call the first type of systematic change a "yield-curve shift." This shift describes the movement in the yield curve that typically accompanies a general upward or downward movement of interest rates. Exhibits 2a and 2b show shifts for the yield curve of August 1, 1995. The yield-curve shift shown in Exhibit 2a corresponds to a bond-market decline and causes all yields to rise, but not by equal amounts; typically, short yields rise twice as much as very long yields. Exhibit 2b shows the yield curve shift for the corresponding bond-market rally scenario; again all yields fall, but not by equal amounts. Yield-curve shifts account for about 90% of the systematic variation in monthly yields over our sample. Each month the yield-curve shift will be slightly different because it depends on the level of yields and the shape of the yield curve.

---

[3] Our data for zero-coupon Treasury bonds begin in 1986 because that is when a 29-year-maturity noncallable zero-coupon bond was first available. We have replicated our study using coupon-bond data from 1952 through 1995 and have found nearly identical results.

Exhibit 2: Yield-Curve Shift
(a): Yield Curve Shift Up

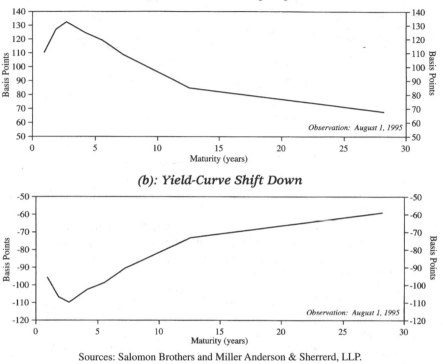

Observation: August 1, 1995

(b): Yield-Curve Shift Down

Observation: August 1, 1995

Sources: Salomon Brothers and Miller Anderson & Sherrerd, LLP.

Yield-curve shifts are not the whole story, though. There is a second systematic change, called a "yield-curve twist," as shown in Exhibits 3a and 3b for the yield curve of August 1, 1995. The yield-curve twist shown in Exhibit 3a causes yields under five years to rise and those over five years to fall. The opposite twist, shown in Exhibit 3b, causes short yields to fall and long yields to rise. Yield-curve twists account for approximately another 7% of the systematic variation in monthly yields. Yield-curve shifts and yield-curve twists are independent reshapings of the yield curve: knowledge of the direction and magnitude of a yield-curve shift is not helpful in predicting either the direction or magnitude of any simultaneous yield-curve twist.

Although yield-curve twists explain a smaller amount of systematic variation than yield-curve shifts, they are nevertheless quite important. The actual change in the yield curve during 1994 and the changes predicted by a yield-curve shift are shown in Exhibit 4. The predicted yield-curve shift shown in Exhibit 4 is calculated by observing the actual change in the yield of the 5-year zero-coupon bond and then using the statistical model to predict the change in the rest of the yield curve.[4] That is why the actual and the predicted changes exactly agree for a 5-year bond. The yield-curve shift captures most of what happened in 1994.

---

[4] Exhibit 4 shows the concentration of monthly changes for 1994.

Exhibit 3: Yield-Curve Twist
(a): Flattening Yield Curve

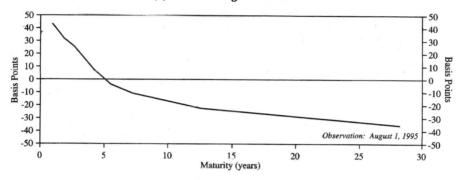

(b): Steepening Yield-Curve Twist

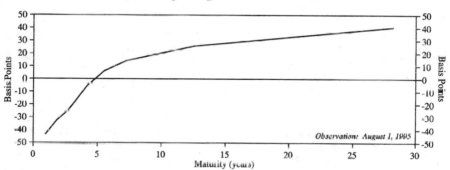

Sources: Salomon Brothers and Miller Anderson & Sherrerd, LLP.

Exhibit 4: Yield-Curve Shift in 1994

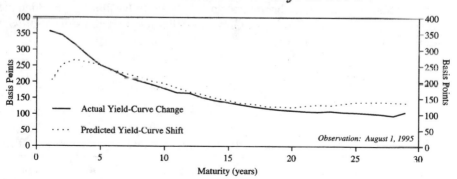

Sources: EJV Partners LP and Miller Anderson & Sherrerd, LLP.

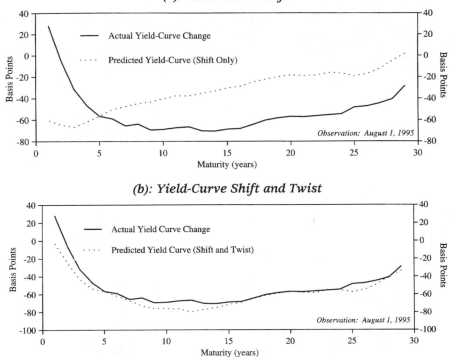

Exhibit 5: Yield Curve Changes in 1995
(a): Yield-Curve Shift

(b): Yield-Curve Shift and Twist

Sources: EJV Partners LP and Miller Anderson & Sherrerd, LLP.

For 1995, however, the yield-curve twist is vital in explaining changes in yields. Exhibit 5a shows the changes in actual yields from year-end 1994 to August 1, 1995, and the effect of a yield-curve shift. We can see that something besides a yield-curve shift has been important in 1995. In Exhibit 5b we added the appropriate yield-curve twist for 1995 to show that together the shift and twist capture the dynamics for the year.[5]

MANAGING INTEREST-RATE RISK

Recall that duration is a good measure of interest-rate risk only if a parallel shift is the predominant form of yield-curve change. Examining Exhibits 2a and 2b, we see that we can rule out a parallel shift as the usual yield-curve change. Rather,

---

[5] To calculate the effect of a yield-curve twist, we first observe the actual change in the yield of 5-year zero-coupon bonds and use the statistical model to predict a yield-curve shift. Next, we observe the part of the change in the yield of a 20-year zero-coupon bond that is not explained by the yield-curve shift and use the statistical model to predict the yield-curve twist. This is why the actual and the predicted changes exactly agree for both a 5-year bond and a 20-year bond.

we see that short yields usually move more than long yields; duration is therefore not an accurate measure of interest-rate risk for a diversified portfolio.

We have replaced duration with *interest-rate sensitivity* (IRS) as our standard measure of portfolio interest-rate risk. Duration measures a portfolio's percentage price change in response to a parallel shift in the yield curve. IRS measures a portfolio's percentage price change in response to a yield-curve shift. The unit of both measures is years. Exhibit 6 shows the relationship between duration and IRS as of August 1, 1995. IRS is measured relative to the yield change in a benchmark zero-coupon bond. We typically choose the 5-year zero-coupon bond as the benchmark because its interest-rate risk is closest to the inter-est-rate risk in the broad market indices, such as the Lehman Brothers Aggregate Index and the Salomon Brothers Broad Index. In constructing Exhibit 6, we used the 5-year zero-coupon bond as our benchmark security, so its duration and IRS are equal. The IRS of a lower-duration bond (e.g., the 2-year zero-coupon bond) is usually slightly higher than its duration, while a large-duration bond (e.g., the 25-year zero coupon bond) has an IRS substantially lower than its duration.

The importance of using IRS instead of duration can be demonstrated by running an experiment that compares the performance of two portfolios, one man-aged with duration and one with IRS. Suppose a portfolio manager thought, in Sep-tember 1992, that long yields were too high and likely to decline and that the yield curve was too steep and likely to flatten.[6] Hence, the manager thought that the rewards for bearing interest-rate risk and yield-curve risk were unusually high. To profit from the view that the bond market would rally, the manager wanted a portfo-lio with longer duration than the index's, and to profit from the view that the yield curve would flatten, he wanted a barbell portfolio. The manager recommended a portfolio composed of cash and long-maturity zero-coupon Treasury bonds with 50% more interest-rate risk than that of the broad market index. The question he had to answer was how many long zero-coupon bonds to buy. The table below shows the calculations for constructing the portfolio using duration and IRS.

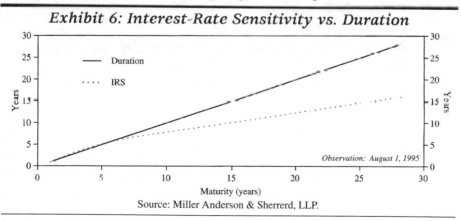

Exhibit 6: Interest-Rate Sensitivity vs. Duration

Observation: August 1, 1995

Maturity (years)

Source: Miller Anderson & Sherrerd, LLP.

---

[6] This is an unusual situation. Typically a downward yield-curve shift produces a steepening yield curve (i.e., yield curves typically steepen in a rally.)

	Duration Management	IRS Management
Index	4.5 years	4.6 years
Target	6.75 years	6.9 years
30-Year Zero-Coupon Treasury Bond	29.0 years	17.8 years
Fraction of Portfolio in Zero Coupons	23.3%	38.8%
Fraction of Portfolio in Cash	76.7%	61.2%

The subsequent bond-market rally would have resulted in some disappointment for an investor using duration, but not for someone using IRS. From September 30, 1992, to September 30, 1993, the yield curve rallied strongly and flattened as shown in Exhibit 7. Over this 12-month period, cash (1-month CDs) returned 3.3%, and 30-year zero-coupon Treasury bonds returned 56.0%. The portfolio constructed using duration returned 15.6%, which is only 30 basis points better than the 15.3% return on the equal-duration bullet portfolio composed of the 7-year zero-coupon Treasury bond. There was very little extra return from the equal-duration barbell portfolio over that of the bullet portfolio, despite a substantial flattening of the yield curve. In contrast, the portfolio constructed with use of IRS has a return of 23.7%, which is 840 basis points above that of the equivalent-IRS 7-year zero-coupon Treasury bond.

Since 1993, we have used IRS rather than duration as our primary measure of interest-rate risk. Over this period, the risk of our core portfolios relative to a broad market index differs significantly when calculated using the two risk measures. In Exhibit 8, we show the duration of our core fixed-income portfolios in comparison with that of the Salomon Brothers Broad Index.

If duration is used as a measure of interest-rate risk, it appears that we were longer than the index until March 1995, significantly so throughout most of 1993. However, in 1993, our portfolios were barbelled, using long-maturity zero-coupon Treasury bonds as part of the barbell, and the distinction between IRS and duration was vital, as can be seen in Exhibit 9. This exhibit compares the IRS of our core fixed-income portfolios with the IRS of the Salomon Brothers Broad Index.

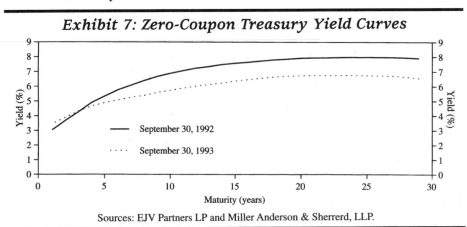

Exhibit 7: Zero-Coupon Treasury Yield Curves

——— September 30, 1992

· · · · September 30, 1993

Sources: EJV Partners LP and Miller Anderson & Sherrerd, LLP.

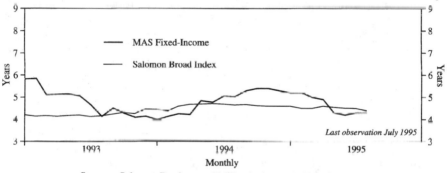

Exhibit 8: MAS Core Fixed-Income Duration

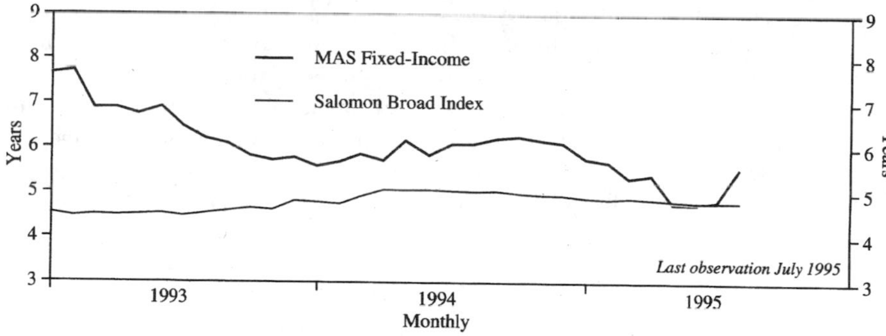

Sources: Salomon Brothers and Miller Anderson & Sherrerd, LLP.

Exhibit 9: MAS Core Fixed-Income Interest-Rate Sensitivity

Sources: Salomon Brothers and Miller Anderson & Sherrerd, LLP.

In our core portfolios, interest-rate risk as measured by IRS has varied much less than interest-rate risk as measured by duration. In fact, for 1993, 1994, and 1995, we have been alternately longer or shorter than the index rather than uniformly longer. The distinction between the two measures is important   not only as an internal tool for better managing assets, but also as a means of communicating our decisions to our clients. Solely on the basis of the duration of our core fixed-income portfolios, one would probably conclude that we have been bullish since the middle of 1993; on the basis of IRS, one can see that we have been alternately slightly bullish and slightly bearish.

Although IRS is a useful tool for portfolio management, its successful use requires a mixture of technical skill and judgment. Technically, using IRS requires a daily updating of our proprietary empirical model because IRS measures are sensitive to both the level of yields and the shape of the yield curve. Furthermore, the internal analytical models we use to evaluate callable securities, such as mortgages, are consistent with IRS in that the typical changes in the yield curve are very similar to empirical yield-curve shifts and yield-curve twists. This internal consistency is very important in managing a highly diversified portfolio of mortgage, corporate, and Treasury securities.

IRS is not a substitute for the critical judgments of our interest-rate team, which seeks to add value by deciding how much interest-rate risk and yield-curve risk we should bear. Our interest-rate team still must form a judgment about the likely direction of a yield-curve change. The team's view is then implemented with our IRS model rather than duration to ensure that our portfolios have the proper amount of interest-rate and yield-curve risk relative to their benchmark indices.

APPENDIX

In this appendix, we give a brief description of the statistical analysis through which we found the systematic yield-curve changes. The first step in our analysis is to adjust the data so that percent yield changes are of similar volatility over time.[7] This adjustment is required so that the data from periods of predictably high volatility do not swamp the statistical analysis. In Exhibit A-1, we have plotted the volatility of percent yield changes for 2-year, 10-year and 29-year zero-coupon bonds. We see that yield volatility generally declines with maturity. In other words, the volatility of zero-coupon yields typically falls as maturity lengthens.

We can also see from Exhibit A-1 that there is reason to believe that yield volatility is not constant over time. A comparison of Exhibit 1 and Exhibit A-1 suggests that yield volatility is related to yield levels. For example, for short-maturity zero-coupon bonds volatility tends to be high when rates are low and vice versa. Conversely, at long maturities we find the opposite effect: Volatility tends to be high when rates are high. The adjustment we make uses the beginning-of-month yield to help explain subsequent volatility. This adjustment is most important for shorter-maturity yields, especially those under five years. For example, Exhibit A-2 shows the effect of this adjustment on 2-year zero-coupon yield volatility. Having adjusted the data for changing volatility over time, we are now ready to perform our statistical analysis.

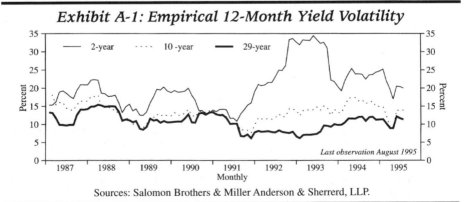

Exhibit A-1: Empirical 12-Month Yield Volatility

Sources: Salomon Brothers & Miller Anderson & Sherrerd, LLP.

[7] Technically, we use the changes in the natural logarithms of the yields.

Exhibit A-2: Two-Year Yield Volatility

Sources: Salomon Brothers & Miller Anderson & Sherrerd, L.P.

The question we want to answer is how the yield curve is ordinarily reshaped. We answer this question by using a statistical technique called principal-components analysis. Principal-components analysis allows us to identify and to simplify the joint movement (or covariation) of many data series. Our complete data series are the beginning-of-month yields from October 1986 through August 1995 on zero-coupon bonds of constant maturities one through 29 years. We performed principal-components analysis on the correlation matrix of the volatility-adjusted series of monthly yield-curve changes. As we reported in the text, we found two statistically significant principal components, which taken together explain 97% of the correlation in our monthly yield series. We also analyzed the covariance matrix of the volatility-adjusted series of monthly yield-curve changes, with very similar results.[8]

---

[8] The original study of systematic risks in the yield curve is Robert Litterman and José Scheinkman, "Common Factors Affecting Bond Returns," *Journal of Fixed Income* (June 1991). Our findings differ in two ways. First, they report that there are three systematic risks affecting yield-curve changes, while we found only two that are statistically significant. More important, their yield-curve shift is nearly a parallel shift. There are two reasons our results differ from theirs. First, we adjusted our data for the change in yield volatility associated with changes in yield levels. Second, we used more data from a longer time period. When we restrict our study to their time period (1984-1989) and do not adjust for yield levels, we closely replicate their results. As we mention in footnote 2, we have replicated our study using coupon-bond data from 1952 through 1995 with results nearly identical to our original ones. We conclude that the parallel yield shift found in data from 1984 through 1989 was an anomaly.

Chapter 8

Value Measures for Managing Interest-Rate Risk

Michele A. Kreisler
Vice President
Miller Anderson & Sherrerd, LLP

Richard B. Worley
Partner
Miller Anderson & Sherrerd, LLP

INTRODUCTION

At the beginning of 1995, the economy was strong, real interest rates were high, and the front end of the yield curve was steep. Economists and investors expected interest rates to rise and stay at higher levels. Instead, the economy slowed and yields fell 200 basis points over the course of the year. A year later, the economy appeared weak, real rates were significantly lower, and the front end of the yield curve was inverted. The market expected interest rates to continue to decline. Again, the market forecast was incorrect; several months passed and bond yields were 100 basis points higher, not lower. There is nothing unusual about these two episodes. The bond market has trouble "getting it right" when it tries to forecast interest rates.

Given the difficulty of forecasting interest rates, the obvious question is whether it is possible to add value by managing the level of interest-rate risk in bond portfolios. We think that it is possible to do so; however, to succeed, one must pay more attention to measures of bond value than to forecasts. Ironically, a value approach to managing interest-rate risk works *because, even though* it is difficult to forecast changes in interest rates, investors do forecast, their forecasts affect prices, and the mispriced securities provide investment opportunities for value-oriented investors.

We rely on two principal measures of value to inform our interest-rate-risk management process: the steepness of the yield curve and the level of the real interest rate. The real interest rate reflects the restrictiveness of monetary policy and thus broadly indicates the longer-term trend of inflation and nominal interest rates. The steepness of the yield curve reveals the expectations about future interest rates that are priced into bonds. In short, bonds are a better value when the yield curve is steep (when it contains forecasts of rising interest rates) and when they offer a high real interest rate than when the curve is flat and the real interest rate is low. Success in managing interest-rate risk requires paying at least as much attention to these measures of value as to rate forecasts. In this chapter, we describe our approach.

THE STEEPNESS OF THE YIELD CURVE

The steepness of the yield curve measures the extra yield that an investor receives for extending maturity. For example, Exhibit 1 shows the basis-point spread between the yield of a 3-month Treasury bill and that of a 2-year Treasury note. The yield advantage fluctuates significantly; in the fall of 1982, an investor was offered more than 350 basis points to extend from 3-month Treasury bills to 2-year Treasury notes, but in the beginning of 1981, the yield curve was inverted, and an investor forfeited 200 basis points of yield for the same extension of maturity.

The steeper the yield curve, the larger the initial yield advantage of the longer-maturity security, the greater the gain from riding down the curve, and the more interest rates have to rise in order to wipe out that initial yield advantage. For example, for an investor to earn as high a return from holding a 3-month bill as from holding a 2-year note that initially yields 100 basis points more, the yield on the 2-year note must rise by approximately 27 basis points over the subsequent three months. If instead the yield advantage of the 2-year note had been 200 basis points, the required yield increase would be more than twice that amount.

Exhibit 1: The Steepness of the Yield Curve: Basis-Point Spread Between 2-Year Notes and 3-Month Bills

Figure: Basis-point spread between the 2-year Treasury note yield and the 3-month bill yield.
Sources: Salomon Brothers and Miller Anderson & Sherrerd, LLP.

The yield advantage that investors require to extend maturity depends on their forecasts of interest rates and their evaluation of the riskiness of the longer security. Whether a steeper-than-average yield curve indicates that bonds represent attractive values depends on whether the additional yield received for extending maturity adequately compensates investors for the increased risk or the increased likelihood of interest-rate increases. If the extra yield advantage is not correlated with an increase in the risk of price depreciation, then it is an attractive value, i.e., it offers a higher yield for the same amount of risk.

Conceptually, we can divide the steepness of the yield curve into the yield pickup that reflects a risk premium and the increment that reflects market forecasts of future interest rates. Long-maturity securities are more volatile than short-maturity securities, and therefore investors require a higher yield on longer securities to compensate them for the additional risk. The yield curve normally slopes upward, reflecting this risk premium. The size of the risk premium is influenced by investors' tastes, their appetite for risk, and their perception of the riskiness of the longer security. Investors will demand a larger risk premium to extend maturity whenever they view the future as more risky.

Interest-rate forecasts also influence the steepness of the yield curve. When investors expect interest rates to rise, they demand a larger-than-usual yield advantage to protect against expected price depreciation (see Exhibit 2). The more they expect interest rates to rise, the larger the yield advantage they require. On the other side, the more borrowers expect interest rates to rise, the larger the yield premium they are willing to pay to lock in fixed-rate financing. Similarly, forecasts of declining rates are the primary cause of flat or inverted curves.

Exhibit 2: Steep Curves Reflect Forecasts of Rising Rates

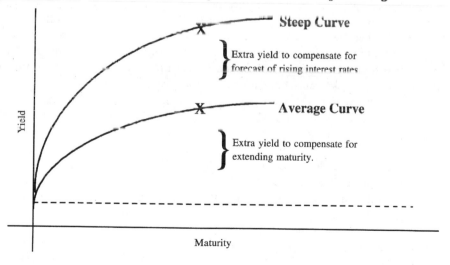

Of course, not everyone has a forecast of interest rates. Some do. Others don't. But most borrowers and lenders think of the possible or probable future movement of interest rates as they develop a notion about which part of the yield curve is most attractive for their purposes. Their choices contain implicit, if not explicit, forecasts.

A steep curve reflects participants' forecasts of rising rates and/or their perception of greater-than-normal risk of rising rates, but for our purposes the distinction makes little difference. What is important is whether the market generally gets it right. If a steep curve correctly signals greater risk of rising rates, then it does not signal extra value in long maturities — only the likelihood of price loss that wipes out the extra yield advantage. On the other hand, if the market does not forecast well but forecasts anyway or if it offers greater risk premia in the absence of higher risk, then an investor who responds to steepness as a value signal by investing counter to either market forecasts or large risk premia will add value over time.

One way to test whether steepness is a good measure of value is to test the market's ability to forecast. We used the steepness of the yield curve to estimate the market's forecast and then compared this estimate with subsequently realized spot rates. If the forecasts had been accurate on average, then changes in the steepness of the yield curve would have accurately reflected changes in the risk of extending.

From the current yield spread we calculated a forward rate. The forward rate is the interest rate that must exist in the future for an investor to earn the same return from rolling a short-term investment as from investing in a longer-term security. It is a break-even rate and is influenced by market forecasts. The forward 3-month rate, for example, is the rate on a 3-month bill three months hence that would be necessary to equate the return on tandem 3-month bills with the return of a 6-month bill over six months. The higher the forecast for future 3-month bill yields, the higher the forward rate.

If there is a risk premium, rolling short-term bills will generally offer a smaller return than a longer-term bill, and forward rates will tend to overestimate subsequent spot rates even when the market forecasts well. In the bill market, the forward rate does tend to overestimate subsequent spot rates. This bias is too strong and too persistent over too long a period to be nothing more than the result of faulty forecasts. We attribute the bias to the risk premium.

In estimating the market's interest-rate forecast, we accounted for the average risk premium by subtracting the average forecast error from the forward rate. A yield curve that is steeper than average indicates a market forecast of rising interest rates; a yield curve that is flatter than average indicates a forecast of declining interest rates.

For a portion of the period we studied, we have an independent measure of market forecasts. The *Goldsmith and Nagan Bond and Money Market Letter* has conducted a survey of market participants since 1970. The surveys are sent quarterly to a group of market economists and practitioners. The survey's findings corresponded closely to our estimates of market forecasts, lending support to our conjecture that most of the change in the steepness of the curve results from changing market forecasts (see Exhibit 3).

We compared the forecasted change in interest rates with the actual interest-rate change. No one would expect a perfect fit. But if the market forecasts accurately on average, we should find a positive correlation between its forecast and the actual change. The higher the correlation, the greater the market's forecasting ability.

We found no such correlation. A scatter of the actual interest-rate changes against the forecasted changes suggests that no relationship exists between the forecasted and the actual changes in interest rates (see Exhibit 4). It appears that increases in interest rates are as likely to follow from curves that forecast declining interest rates as from curves that forecast rising interest rates.

This finding is important. Recall that our estimates of market forecasts are derived from market prices — from the steepness of the yield curve. If a steeper-than-average yield curve is not normally, or on average, associated with subsequent increases in interest rates, then it is a signal of value in longer maturities. The investor is earning a higher-than-average yield premium without bearing more risk. We have performed the same test for 6-month and 1-year interest rates. The results are similar.

We have also examined whether a steep curve predicts the short-term movement in *long-term* interest rates. It does not. Steep curves are more often followed by decreases in long-term interest rates.

Exhibit 3: Forward Rates (Adjusted for Risk Premium) Reflect Market Forecasts

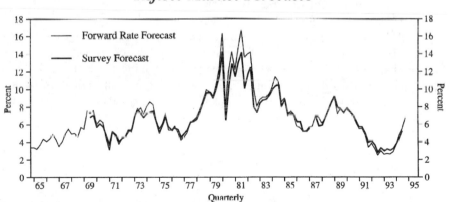

Note: Forecasts for the 3-month bill yield. The forward-rate forecast is the 3-month forward rate adjusted for the average risk premium. The survey forecast is from the *Goldsmith-Nagan Bond and Money Market Letter*.

Sources: Salomon Brothers, *Goldsmith and Nagan Bond and Money Market Letter*, and Miller Anderson & Sherrerd, LLP.

Exhibit 4: The Market Does Not Forecast Well

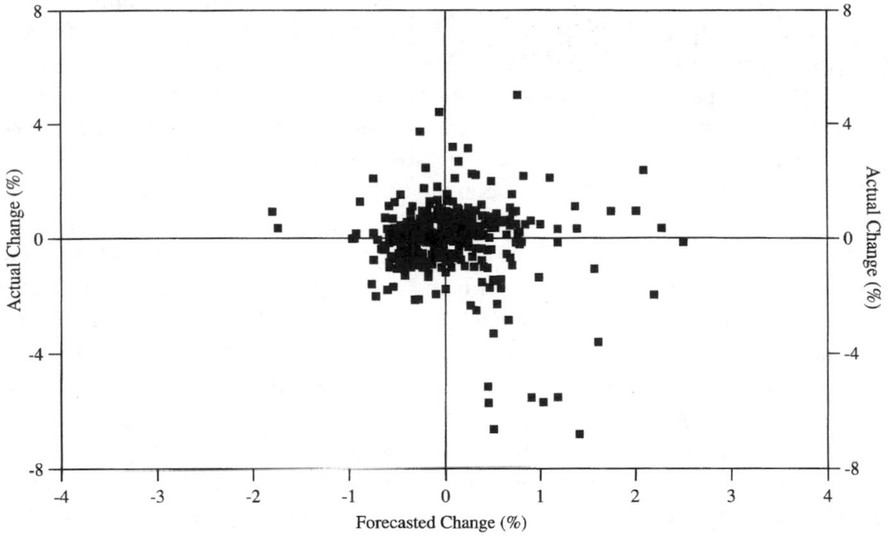

Note: Forecasted changes in the 3-month bill rate versus the actual change. If the market were proficient at forecasting interest rates, the points would be scattered around a 45° line from bottom left to upper right. Data are from 1965 through 1995.

Sources: Salomon Brothers and Miller Anderson & Sherrerd, LLP.

The implications of these findings for the bond investor are significant. When the market forecast for interest rates is wrong, the market "corrects." When interest rates do not rise as much as initially expected, longer-maturity securities outperform shorter maturities (see Exhibit 5). The larger the forecast error, the greater the outperformance of the longer security.

In summary, if a steep curve indicates correctly (on average) the risk or likelihood of higher interest rates, then it is not an indication of bond value. If, on the other hand, there is little or no relationship between the slope of the curve and subsequent interest-rate movements, then a steep curve is an indication of bond value, and a flat or inverted curve indicates its absence. The data support the latter conclusion.

THE REAL INTEREST RATE

Our other measure of value is the real interest rate. Interest rates are determined not only by the actions of the Federal Reserve Board but also by the willingness of individuals to save and the desire of the corporate sector and the government to borrow. If businesses want to borrow more dollars at the current interest rate than households wish to save, then interest rates will rise.

The willingness to save and the desire to borrow depend more on the *real interest rate* than on the nominal interest rate. For example, because an increase in expected inflation increases the income that a real-estate developer expects to earn, the developer will be willing to pay a higher nominal interest rate. Similarly, households' decisions to save should depend on the real interest rate since the object of saving is to increase future purchasing power. By affecting people's behavior, the real interest rate affects the growth of the economy and the path of inflation.

There is no reason that the real interest rate should be constant (see Exhibit 6). It should vary with monetary policy, budget deficits, and investment opportunities among other things. However, we view the long-run return on capital in the economy as reasonably stable, and we interpret real rates that exceed the long-run return on capital as "high." When the real interest rate is higher than the average return on capital, there are fewer investment opportunities that appear profitable; when the real interest rate is lower, borrowers will choose to make more purchases today (for example, of houses, cars, and other durables) rather than saving at the low real interest rate. High real interest rates also indicate more restrictive or at least less expansive monetary policy, which lowers the threat of inflation. High real interest rates thus help the bond investor in several ways: they provide a high real yield, they discourage speculation, and they are usually followed by stable or declining inflation — which increases the chances that price appreciation will supplement the high real yield.

Exhibit 5: Long Notes Outperform When the Forecast Is Too High They Underperform When the Forecast Is Too Low

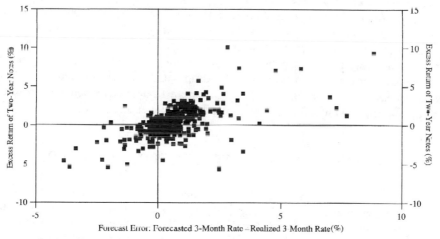

Note: The "Forecast Error" is the difference between the 3 month forward rate adjusted for the average risk premium and the realized 3-month rate three months hence. This is plotted against the excess return of the 2-year Treasury note over the return of the bill over the 3-month forecast period. Data are from 1965 through 1995.

Sources: Salomon Brothers and Miller Anderson & Sherrerd, LLP.

Exhibit 6: The Real Interest Rate

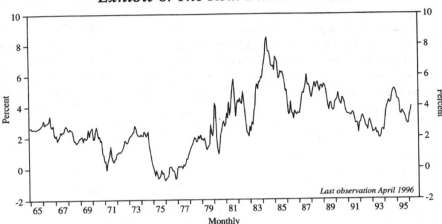

Note: The real interest rate calculated from the 10-year Treasury yield and the 3-year historical inflation rate.
Sources: Salomon Brothers, Department of Commerce, and Miller Anderson & Sherrerd, LLP.

The "real" real interest rate is unobservable. It is the nominal interest rate adjusted for the market's expectation of inflation over a bond's life. We cannot directly measure the market's expectations of inflation. Instead, in our research we adjust nominal interest rates by past inflation — we use a 3-year average giving extra weight to the latest year. We believe that this approach provides a reasonable estimate to the extent that people form expectations of the future largely by extrapolating recent events.

We know that if we could predict inflation perfectly, we would have an even better measure of the real interest rate and of the value of bonds. In our management of assets, we think prospectively about the real interest rate; i.e., we adjust the nominal rate not only for past inflation but also for our forecast of inflation. If our forecasts are better than forecasts created by extrapolating historical inflation, we have a better measure of value. However, the real interest rate, even when calculated only on the basis of past inflation, has proven useful as a measure of bond value.

COMBINING THE TWO CONCEPTS OF VALUE

We examine the importance of the two concepts of value by comparing returns from different real-interest-rate and yield-curve starting points and by simulating interest-rate-risk management strategies. In order to measure the benefit from holding longer-maturity securities directly, we examine "excess" returns — the amount that the longer-maturity note's return exceeds that of the 3-month bill.

For the real interest rate, we compare the excess returns of a series of longer notes from periods of high and low real interest rates. We do not torture the data to find the boundary that would give the best result. Instead, we use the assumption that a real long-term interest rate that is higher than the long-term growth rate of the economy is a high real interest rate. The results show that over the past 30 years, longer notes have outperformed the bill by a larger amount starting from high real interest rates than starting from low real interest rates (see Exhibit 7). We find that the level of the real interest rate also indicates bond value in foreign bond markets (see Exhibit 8). In addition, the real interest rate has been useful in selecting among countries: the countries with the highest real rates have had, on average, the highest real bond returns (see Exhibit 9).

Exhibit 7: High Real Interest Rates Lead to Outperformance by Longer Securities
Average Monthly Excess Returns 1965 - 1995

	2-Year	5-Year	10-Year
High Real Rates	0.21%	0.33%	0.46%
Low Real Rates	0.04	−0.11	−0.30

Figure: Average monthly returns of the Treasury note in excess of a 1-month Treasury bill from high- and low-real-rate starting points. The real rate was calculated by discounting the nominal yield by the average inflation over the prior three years (with the most recent year overweighted). High real rates were above 2.5%.

Sources: Department of Commerce, Salomon Brothers, and Miller Anderson & Sherrerd, LLP.

Exhibit 8: High Real Interest Rates Indicate Bond Value Around the World

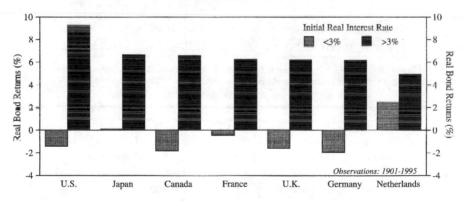

Note: Nominal long-term bond returns adjusted for the increase in the GNP deflator (3-year holding period). Returns in local currencies. Initial real interest rates based on inflation over the previous three years. Excluded data: World Wars I and II for Continental Europe and Japan and hyperinflationary periods (1920s) for France and Germany.

Sources: Sidney Homer and Richard Sylla, *A History of Interest Rates*, Third Edition (New Brunswick, NJ: Rutgers University Press, 1991); Morgan Stanley; The WEFA Group; and Miller Anderson & Sherrerd, LLP.

Exhibit 9: Countries with Higher Real Interest Rates Have Higher Returns

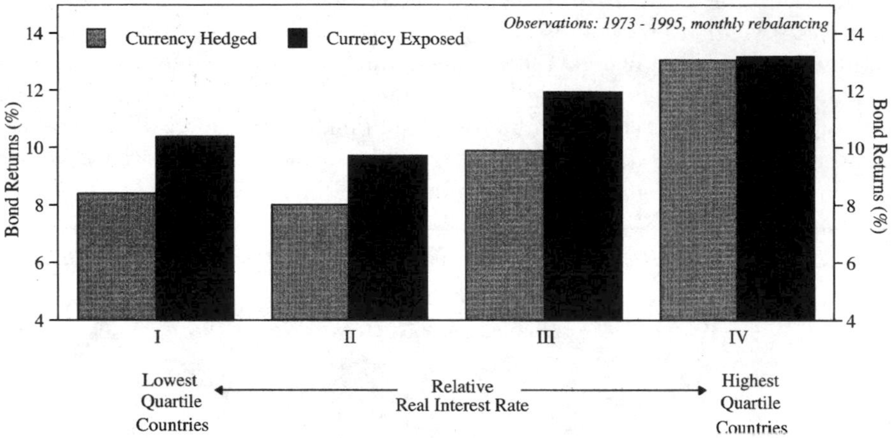

Note: Annualized monthly return on 10-year bonds of the G7 countries and the Netherlands, measured in U.S. dollars and sorted by real interest rate (e.g., quartile I shows the return from investing each month in the two bond markets with the lowest real interest rates). Real interest rates based on the average annual increase in the GNP deflator over the previous three years.

Sources: First Boston, Morgan Stanley, OECD, The WEFA Group, and Miller Anderson & Sherrerd, LLP.

Exhibit 10: Steep Yield Curves Lead to Outperformance by Longer Securities

Average Monthly Excess Returns 1965 - 1995

	2-Year	5-Year	10-Year
Steep Curves	0.31%	0.36%	0.50%
Normal Curves	0.11	0.15	0.07
Flat or Inverted Curves	−0.09	−0.15	−0.23

Note: Average monthly returns of the Treasury note in excess of a 1-month Treasury bill from steep, normal, and flat (or inverted) yield-curve starting points.

Sources: Salomon Brothers and Miller Anderson & Sherrerd, LLP.

We conduct a similar analysis for the steepness of the yield curve. We calculate the average steepness between a series of points on the curve — for example, between 3-month bills and 2-year notes — and sort monthly observations for the last 30 years into three categories: steep, normal, and flat (including inverted). In the sorting process, we use only information that would have been available at the time of each observation; i.e., a steep curve is a curve that was steep relative to curves that had preceded it rather than steep relative to unknown future curves. We compare the returns from each category (see Exhibit 10). For every maturity, the return of the note relative to the bill is greater from steep curves than from normal curves and greater from normal curves than from flat or inverted curves. The difference in average return starting from steep curves versus that starting from flat curves is statistically significant.

We can also measure how much value can be added by active management based on these concepts. To do so, we simulate two active investment strategies, one that uses the steepness of the yield curve as a signal and one that uses the real interest rate. We add or subtract interest-rate risk on the basis of our yield-curve and real-interest-rate signals respectively — for example, from a benchmark we add interest-rate risk when real rates are high (yield curve is steep), and reduce interest-rate risk when real rates are low (yield curve is flat). A simulated investment strategy that uses either signal had higher returns than passive benchmarks.

Next, we combine the two concepts of value. The real interest rate improves our ability to discriminate between notes and bills for any yield-curve shape and vice versa. Exhibit 11 shows the average monthly excess returns for 2-year, 5-year, and 10-year notes from each combination of real-interest-rate and yield-curve starting points.

Given the analysis thus far, it should not be surprising that a simulated trading strategy that uses both concepts of value outperforms a passive benchmark. The benchmark we consider is a 50-50 weighting of a 2 year note and a 10-year note. This portfolio has a duration similar to that of the Lehman Aggregate or Salomon Broad Index. Our simulated strategy allocates assets between the two notes. When the signals are the most bullish, we hold all 10-year notes, and when the signals are the most bearish we hold all 2-year notes. We vary the proportion in each note for varying degrees of bullishness and bearishness. The results are impressive in terms of both average return and risk (see Exhibit 12). The strategy outperforms the index by an average of almost 100 basis points per year.

CONCLUSIONS

In practice, we also use our judgment and our forecasts of the economy and Federal Reserve policy in managing the interest-rate risk and the country allocation of our bond portfolios. However, we start the process with a strong predisposition to follow our value signals. We modify our value signals rather than overrule them.

It is often very difficult to retain confidence in a forecast that is different from the current trend of economic reports. No approach always gives the correct signal. The market occasionally "gets it right," as it did earlier in 1994. Our value measures help us to understand what is priced into the market and to evaluate the risk-reward trade-off of extending or shortening the interest-rate sensitivity of portfolios. Over a long horizon, using a disciplined value approach to adjust the interest-rate sensitivity of a portfolio can add significant value.

Exhibit 11: Steep Yield Curves and High Real Rates Signal the Most Value Average Monthly Excess Returns of Treasury Notes 1965 - 1995

	Steep Yield Curves	Normal Yield Curves	Flat Yield Curves
Two-Year Notes			
High Real Rates	0.36%	0.29%	−0.03%
Low Real Rates	0.28	−0.06	−0.16
Five-Year Notes			
High Real Rates	0.54	0.30	0.22
Low Real Rates	0.23	−0.02	−0.57
Ten-Year Notes			
High Real Rates	0.73	0.41	0.25
Low Real Rates	0.23	−0.33	−0.69

Figures: Average monthly returns of the 2-year, 5-year and 10-year Treasury note in excess of a 1-month Treasury bill from combinations of real-rate and yield-curve starting points. The real rate was calculated by discounting the nominal yield by the average inflation over the prior three years (with the most recent year overweighted).

Sources: Salomon Brothers, Department of Commerce, and Miller Anderson & Sherrerd, LLP.

Exhibit 12: A Simulated Investment Strategy Based on Our Concepts of Value
Summary Statistics 1965 - 1995

	Strategy	50/50
Average Return	8.59%	7.64%
Standard Deviation	5.77	5.60
Sharpe Ratio	0.35	0.20
Value of $1 invested in 1965	$12.85	$9.79

Sources: Center for Research in Security Prices, Department of Commerce, Miller Anderson & Sherrerd, LLP, and Salomon Brothers.

Chapter 9

Improved Measurement of Duration Contributions of Foreign Bonds in Domestic Portfolios

Ram Willner, Ph.D.
International Market Strategist and Risk Control Manager
PIMCO

INTRODUCTION

Managers of domestic bond portfolios are facing increasing opportunities for investments in non-benchmark foreign securities. This brings into question the tool of *domestic* duration as the primary instrument of portfolio management. It was Macaulay who first pointed out that matching the duration of one portfolio to another would, for small yield changes, ensure that the relative values of the portfolios would not change much. His idea has been applied as a general tool for managing any portfolio against a benchmark portfolio. However, implicit in that application is that both portfolios be exposed to the same source of interest rate risk. This is not true in the case of foreign versus domestic bonds. Moreover, as portfolio management becomes increasingly sophisticated, we recognize that Macaulay's concept of duration is only sufficient at an aggregate level. We can gain precision by considering duration or sensitivity of portfolios to changes in rates along the whole yield curve rather than just to the aggregate portfolio yield. Consequently, today's domestically benchmarked bond portfolio manager who is tempted to include attractive non-benchmark foreign bonds must face the somewhat inscrutable sensitivity of those bonds to the entire domestic yield curve.

In other research, Lee Thomas and I discuss the calculation of a portfolio's duration when bonds of a foreign nation are included in a domestic portfolio.[1] To the domestic portfolio manager, duration measures the sensitivity of the portfolio to domestic interest rate changes. For a conventional government bond,

---

[1] L.R. Thomas and R. Willner, "Measuring the Duration of an Internationally Diversified Portfolio," *Journal of Portfolio Management* (Fall 1997).

its duration can be calculated directly by assuming a yield change for the relevant local yield. The change in yield for a bond issued by another government may or may not have any effect on the original government bond and vice versa. In fact, without a theory that links the two economies, there is no reason to presuppose any coincident effect at all. Lee Thomas and I show that there generally is an empirical linkage and a relationship between yield changes in one country and another. However, these changes certainly are not one-to-one as is often assumed, and if so assumed can cause significant miscalculation of the portfolio's duration with respect to domestic interest rates. Consequently the exposures and risk experienced by the portfolio manager can be significantly different than what was anticipated. We propose a methodology for calculating the contribution to the domestic duration of the portfolio by the foreign bonds, as well as providing some guidelines and estimations for the degree of error in that methodology. Our recommendation is that the inclusion of foreign bonds in a domestically benchmarked portfolio be in reverse proportion to the anticipated degree of error.

Now let's turn to the other issue of the need for more precision in duration estimates altogether. In previously published research, I describe how conventional duration alone cannot explain the complete sensitivity of a portfolio to changes in the entire yield curve.[2] A functional representation of the yield curve based on three parameters — level, slope, and curvature — is employed. The conventional duration can be extended to duration with respect to each of the three parameters. This extension allows for a much more comprehensive description of the relationship between yield curve changes and changes in portfolio value. Conventional duration essentially relates only to changes in yield curve level. Other researchers have confirmed the significance of these first three moments or principal components of the yield curve in the determination of changes in portfolio value due to yield curve changes.[3]

In this chapter, we marry the concept of adjusting the duration contribution of a foreign bond to a domestic portfolio to the notion that a level, slope, and curvature representation of the yield curve is a more accurate way to measure the exposure of a portfolio to yield curve changes. We investigate the use of level, slope, and curvature duration contributions of foreign bonds within a domestic portfolio. The approach is a fairly straightforward extension of the basis analysis performed in my previous research.[4] The next section presents a review of that analysis and of the level, slope, and curvature duration model I developed in order to familiarize the reader with the two components of the married system pre-

---

[2] R. Willner, "A New Tool for Portfolio Managers: Level, Slope, and Curvature Durations," *Journal of Fixed Income* (June 1996), pp.48-59.

[3] See F.J. Jones, "Yield Curve Strategies," *Journal of Fixed Income* (September 1991), pp. 43-51; W.T. Golub and L.M. Tilman, "Measuring Yield Curve Risk Using Principal Components Analysis, Value at Risk, and Key Rate Durations," *Journal of Portfolio Management* (Summer 1997), pp. 72-84; and, R. Litterman and J. Scheinkman, "Common Factors Affecting Bond Returns," *Journal of Fixed Income* (June 1991), pp. 54-61.

[4] Thomas and Willner, "Measuring the Duration of an Internationally Diversified Portfolio."

sented in this chapter. The third section presents the methodology for combining the two. The fourth section presents the results of calculating the foreign adjusted level, slope, and curvature durations for 15 countries. The concluding section reviews the results of the analysis and provides some guidelines and cautions for the practical application of the methodology.

THE FOREIGN DURATION BASIS APPROACH

The problem of including foreign bonds in a domestic portfolio is essentially a basis problem with respect to duration due to the imperfect correspondence of domestic and foreign interest rate changes. Knowing the duration of the foreign bond and knowing the change in domestic interest rates is not sufficient to know the new value of the bond. We will focus the analysis on investigating this relationship. Assuming that duration alone explains capital appreciation or depreciation of a bond, that change in value can be written:

$$\text{Change in value} = \text{Duration} \times \text{Change in yield} \tag{1}$$

The "Change in yield" refers to a change in yield due to a change in *domestic* interest rates. If the bond in question is a foreign bond, then the change in value can be written:

$$\text{Change in value} = \text{Duration} \times \text{Change in foreign yield}$$

But if we are interested in the change in foreign bond value given a change in *domestic* yield, we must explicitly recognize an interrelationship between domestic yield changes and foreign yield changes. This results in the relationship.

$$\text{Change in value} = \text{Duration} \times (\text{Change in foreign yield given a change in}$$
$$\text{domestic yield} + \text{Other unrelated changes in foreign yield}) \tag{2}$$

Note that we must include other unrelated (to domestic interest rate changes) but coincident effects on the foreign yield since these will also affect the value of the foreign bond — and since the portfolio manager will be subject to them. Such unrelated effects need not be unexplainable "noise" but can be due to persistent factors which are measurable but are not related to domestic interest rates. Since such factors can introduce variability into the portfolio, the portfolio manager must consider their impact. We shall discuss these factors later in this chapter.

The Thomas-Willner methodology considers the "Change in foreign yield given a change in domestic yield" in equation (2) as a basis problem in which one tries to calculate the optimal hedge ratio minimizing the variance between changes in foreign yields and domestic yields. This hedge ratio adjusts the duration of a foreign bond for its related but imperfect sensitivity to domestic interest rates. The adjustment is given by a beta coefficient which can be calculated through a regression of foreign yield changes on domestic yield changes. We also use the regression to get a sense of the impact of the other factors which might cause coincident but unrelated changes in bond value. We review this approach below.

We formulated the foreign to domestic bond relationship [applying equation (1)] as the following regression relationship:

$$d\Delta y_{foreign} = \alpha + \beta d\Delta y_{domestic}$$

where

$$d = \text{duration}$$
$$y = \text{yield}$$

Or since the durations are essentially the same for both foreign and domestic bonds, they are dropped from the equation giving:

$$\Delta y_{foreign} = \alpha + \beta \Delta y_{domestic} \tag{3}$$

The β is termed a "country beta." Duration attributed to a foreign bond in the domestic portfolio is calculated as $\beta \times d$. This means that the measured relationship between changes in domestic and foreign interest rates are incorporated into the assessment of a foreign bond's sensitivity to domestic interest rates.

Further, β can be decomposed into:

$$\beta = \text{correlation} (\Delta y_{foreign}, \Delta y_{domestic}) \times \sigma_{foreign}/\sigma_{domestic}$$

In general, the higher is the correlation component of beta, the greater the amount of the foreign bond which can be included in the domestic portfolio with the expectation that the beta adjusted duration will accurately represent the duration contribution of the foreign bond. However as stated previously, the alpha in the regression also plays a role in the accuracy of the estimated beta adjusted duration contribution. The alpha term represents the average contribution of all factors unrelated to domestic interest rates, but still affecting the change in foreign bond value. The smaller is this value relative to the standard variation (deviation), the better will be the accuracy of the beta adjusted duration estimate.[5] Exhibit 1 gives such betas measured over the period July 1992 to July 1997.

---

[5] R^2 measures a similar phenomenon: the degree of variation explained by the regression. The distinction here is that the measure of interest is not the degree of variation but its economic significance. For instance, if only 50% of the variation was explained, but overall that variation was quite small, that may be preferable to explaining 90% of a very large variation

Exhibit 1: Country Betas

Country	β	(t stats)	R^2
Australia	1.04	(8.68)	0.49
Austria	0.23	(3.61)	0.13
Belgium	0.29	(3.00)	0.09
Canada	0.89	(8.67)	0.49
Denmark	0.48	(3.68)	0.14
France	0.51	(4.95)	0.23
Germany	0.42	(5.32)	0.26
Holland	0.45	(5.51)	0.27
Ireland	0.55	(4.65)	0.21
Italy	0.43	(2.53)	0.06
Japan	0.30	(2.75)	0.08
Spain	0.47	(2.82)	0.08
Sweden	0.49	(2.95)	0.09
Switzerland	0.25	(2.59)	0.07
UK	0.51	(4.30)	0.18

The Level, Slope & Curvature Model

The level, slope, and curvature (LS&C) duration model I developed represents the change in bond value as dependent on the sum of changes of each one of the yield curve parameters times the sensitivity of the bond to changes in the particular parameter.[6] The Nelson and Siegel mathematical function for representing the yield curve is employed.[7] Their function, dependent on three parameters which represent the level, slope, and curvature of virtually any yield curve, can be used to estimate every discount rate along the yield curve. Since the value of a bond is given as a sum of discounted cash flows, knowing the three parameters for the function, means knowing the discount rate estimates at every maturity along the yield curve, and thus the bond's value. A change in any parameter induces a change in discount rates and therefore a change in the bond's value. The sensitivity of the bond's value to a change in any parameter is its duration with respect to that parameter. In theory, the three parameters comprehensively describe the yield curve so that the complete sensitivity of the bond to the yield curve can be known by knowing the function and the changes in the parameters. In practice the description is generally not completely comprehensive but very close, so that the amount of noise introduced is small.

The LS&C model's extension to the simple formulation of change in a bond's value given by equation (1) is:

---

[6] Willner, "A New Tool for Portfolio Managers: Level, Slope, and Curvature Durations."
[7] C. Nelson and A. Siegel, "Parsimonious Modeling of Yield Curves," *Journal of Business* (1987).

Exhibit 2: An Example of LS&C Bond Change Valuation*

	Level	Slope	Curvature	Total
A. Duration	7.0	1.6	1.0	—
B. Start month value	5.5	2.5	0.5	—
C. End month value	5.3	2.0	0.5	—
D. Parameter Change (Line C − Line B)	−0.2	0.5	0.0	—
E. Value Change (Line A × − Line D)	1.4	−0.8	0.0	0.6

* Based on equation (4).

$$\text{Change in value} = d_L\,\Delta L + d_S\,\Delta S + d_C\,\Delta C \tag{4}$$

where d_X refers to the bond's duration with respect to parameter X and ΔX refers to the change in parameter X. If we assume that our portfolio starts at an initial value of 100, then "Change in value" gives the percent return of the portfolio.

Consider the following application of equation (4). Suppose that a French bond has level, slope, and curvature durations of 7.0, 1.6, and 1.0, respectively. Now suppose that the French yield curve was fit at the beginning of the month with best fit values for the level, slope, and curvature parameters of 5.5, 2.5, and 0.5, respectively, and at the end of the month the best fit parameters were 5.3, 2.0, and 0.5, respectively. Then the corresponding changes in level, slope, and curvature are −0.2, 0.5, and 0.0, respectively. This means that the level of the yield curve went down, the slope of the yield curve diminished (i.e., the short end of the yield curve came up somewhat) and the curvature remained unchanged. Given the assumed durations, the net effect was a gain in value of 0.6% (= 1.4 − 0.8 + 0.0). Exhibit 2 presents this example.

COMBINING THE LEVEL, SLOPE, AND CURVATURE MODEL AND THE FOREIGN DURATION BASIS APPROACH

Equation (4) gives us the starting point to extend the Thomas-Willner methodology to the LS&C model representation of the yield curve and its characterization of three durations. The problem is essentially the same: find the hedge ratio for each of the three durations (jointly) which provide the historically minimizing variance between the return of the foreign bond and the hedged (adjusted) exposure to the level, slope, and curvature durations of the domestic bond. This is a problem which is solved by conventional multiple regression[8] — an extension of the simple regression case previously presented. There is one caveat. Notice that in equation (4),

---

[8] A sketch of the proof that this is a multiple regression problem is to formulate the problem as: Minimize Variance $(R - H_L\,d_L\,\Delta L - H_S\,d_S\,\Delta S - H_C\,d_C\,\Delta C)$ where each term is a time series vector, yielding $\{H^*_L, H^*_S, H^*_C\}$. The problem is solved using matrix algebra and differential calculus, and thereby also considers the cross correlations between the durations. The solution is $\{H^*_L, H^*_S, H^*_C\} = \{\beta_L', \beta_S', \beta_C''\}$.

unlike in the conventional duration case, the duration itself does not drop out. We estimate the beta coefficients, three in this case, by performing the following time series regression which includes the duration factor, monthly over five years:

$$R_{\text{foreign}} = \alpha + \beta_L' d_L \Delta L + \beta_S' d_S \Delta S + \beta_C' d_C \Delta C \tag{5}$$

where R_{foreign} is the return of the foreign bond. Once we have estimated $\{\beta_L', \beta_S', \beta_C'\}$ we might notice that over the time period estimated, the duration values $\{d_L, d_S, d_C\}$ are virtually constant. We will consider them as constant at their average value over the time period we studied. We can then define the three values $\{\beta_L, \beta_S, \beta_C\}$ as $\beta_L', \beta_S', \beta_C'$ divided by the average values of d_L, d_S, d_C, respectively. The resulting values $\{\beta_L, \beta_S, \beta_C\}$ can then be compared to the beta parameter described and calculated by Lee Thomas and me. We shall term the values $\{\beta_L, \beta_S, \beta_C\}$ "country level, slope, and curvature betas."

Exhibit 3 presents the results of regressions for the period July 1992 to July 1997 for 15 countries versus the United States (as well as including the conventional duration country betas (Exhibit 1) for comparison). The exhibit presents (1) the beta coefficients for level, slope, and curvature durations (equation (5)), (2) the adjusted R^2 for the regression, and (3) the beta associated with a regression of conventional duration (equation (3)) and its R^2. To use the exhibit in practice we would *multiply the foreign measured duration(s) by the corresponding beta coefficient* in the exhibit.

For example, suppose a Canadian bond has foreign (i.e., local) level, slope, and curvature durations of 7.34, 2.13, and 1.87, respectively. If that bond was to be included in a U.S. domestic portfolio we would assign it — multiplying by the corresponding beta — domestic (U.S.) level, slope, and curvature durations of 6.98, 2.07, and 1.76, respectively. According to the Exhibit 3, if the bond had a *conventional* foreign duration of 7.20, we would assign it a domestic duration of 6.41. Consider the performance of these approximate duration measures over July 1997. During this month there was a rally in the Canadian bond market. The yield on this bond dropped by 55 basis points which corresponded to a gain in value of about $4.00 per $100 bond (ignoring any currency effects). The yield on a U.S. bond of equivalent duration dropped by 50 basis points, suggesting an increase in value for the Canadian bond of $3.20 (= 0.5 × 0.89 × 7.2). Using the LS&C model, for the month of July 1997, we would have measured a change in level, slope, and curvature of −0.43, 0.29, and −0.61, respectively. Multiplying those changes in U.S. yield curve parameters by the *adjusted* level, slope, and curvature durations and summing — that is, equation (5) — we get an anticipated change of $3.50 (= 0.43 × 6.98 - 0.29 × 2.07 + 0.61 × 1.76), which is closer to the actual value of $4.00. Exhibit 4 summarizes this situation.

We see in Exhibit 3 that for most countries the adjusted R^2 for the LS&C durations regression is greater than that for conventional duration. We also notice that for most countries the beta coefficient for level duration is closer to one than the corresponding beta coefficient for conventional duration. Note that a beta of 1.0 means that the durational effect of a foreign bond is equivalent to that of a domestic bond.

Exhibit 3: Duration Betas (July 1992 - July 1997)

Country	β_L (t-stat)	β_S	β_C	R^2	β	R^2
Australia	1.08	1.14	1.20	0.47	1.04	0.49
	(5.97)	(3.00)	(5.77)		(8.68)	
Austria	0.35	0.54	0.07	0.16	0.23	0.13
	(3.87)	(2.90)	(0.71)		(3.61)	
Belgium	0.48	0.82	0.04	0.13	0.29	0.09
	(3.58)	(2.91)	(0.24)		(3.00)	
Canada	0.95	0.97	0.94	0.47	0.89	0.49
	(6.30)	(3.07)	(5.44)		(8.67)	
Denmark	0.74	1.04	0.18	0.16	0.48	0.14
	(3.99)	(2.65)	(0.83)		(3.68)	
France	0.73	0.99	0.24	0.26	0.51	0.23
	(5.13)	(3.32)	(1.48)		(4.95)	
Germany	0.64	1.04	0.11	0.35	0.42	0.26
	(6.17)	(4.81)	(0.93)		(5.32)	
Holland	0.62	0.93	0.19	0.32	0.45	0.27
	(5.74)	(4.09)	(1.56)		(5.51)	
Ireland	0.72	0.84	0.40	0.20	0.55	0.21
	(4.18)	(2.33)	(2.02)		(4.65)	
Italy	0.83	0.74	0.16	0.07	0.43	0.06
	(2.92)	(1.24)	(0.48)		(2.53)	
Japan	0.22	0.03	0.36	0.07	0.30	0.08
	(1.66)	(0.12)	(2.38)		(2.75)	
Spain	0.79	0.70	0.26	0.08	0.47	0.08
	(2.99)	(1.26)	(0.86)		(2.82)	
Sweden	0.91	0.81	0.12	0.12	0.49	0.09
	(3.64)	(1.54)	(0.43)		(2.95)	
Switzerland	0.31	0.14	0.17	0.06	0.25	0.07
	(2.51)	(0.54)	(1.19)		(2.59)	
UK	0.77	1.00	0.24	0.20	0.51	0.18
	(4.49)	(2.77)	(1.23)		(4.30)	

Exhibit 4: Predicted Performance from Linking U.S. to Canadian Yield Curve Changes by Beta Adjusting Duration

	Actual	Expected from Adjusted Conventional Duration	Expected from Adjusted LS&C Durations
Canada	$0.40	—	—
U.S.	—	$0.32	$0.35

UNDERSTANDING THE SIGNIFICANCE OF THE
LS&C DURATION BETA: EXAMINING SPECIFIC COUNTRIES

By examining the results presented in Exhibit 3, we can get a sense of the extra information provided by the disaggregation of duration into the components described by the LS&C model. We will examine the results presented with respect to explanatory power and statistical validity so that we can be more confident of our conclusions regarding the relationship between interest rates in different countries.

R^2 and t-Statistics for the LS&C and the Conventional Duration Models

Exhibit 3 indicates that in most cases the R^2 statistic, which indicates the degree of variation in foreign versus domestic interest rates explained by the model factor(s), is greater for the LS&C representation of duration(s) than for conventional duration. This is even after having adjusted for the two extra factors in the LS&C representation. In those cases, when the conventional duration approach provides a higher R^2, the numbers are very close and could be explained by the somewhat arbitrary approaches used to adjust R^2 for having two additional factors.[9] It is also interesting to note that this condition occurs only when the t-statistic for the conventional duration beta is greater than the t-statistic for the level duration beta. In general however, the LS&C model beta regressions are more explanatory. This should give the portfolio manager more confidence in applying this model and its associated betas.

Examining the t-statistics carefully, we observe a reassuring phenomena. In every case where the t-statistic is insignificant, the corresponding beta coefficient is close to zero. An example is the coefficient for the slope of Switzerland which has a t-statistic of 0.54, which is not at all significant, and a beta of 0.14. This indicates that there is no truly reliable (low t-statistic), nor measurable relationship (beta close to zero) between changes in the slope of the U.S. yield curve and the Swiss yield curve. In that case, the portfolio manager should be aware that there may be lots of unrelated fluctuation in Swiss bonds due to changes in the Swiss yield curve slope that will affect the value of Swiss bonds in the portfolio but will not be associated (correlated) to U.S. slope variations. However, Swiss changes in yield curve *level* can be more confidently attributed (t-statistic = 2.51) to be about one third of the contemporaneous change (β = 0.31) in U.S. level changes. Changes in curvature (t-statistic = 1.19), like those for slope, are less reliable than for those of level. This might suggest to the portfolio manager trying to manage risk and seeking confidence in domestic duration to hold *long maturity* Swiss bonds. Such bonds have the least exposure to slope and curvature variations.

---

[9] In all cases the actual (unadjusted) R^2 was higher for the LS&C case versus the conventional duration case.

Examining the Relationship Between the Beta for Level Changes and Yield Changes

The conventional duration model relies on changes in the overall yield of the bond to arrive at a country beta (equation (3)), and the overall yield must incorporate the net effect on yield of changes in the whole yield curve. If that is indeed the case, and if there is correlation between the factors of slope and curvature, then there is spurious noise introduced into the estimate of the country beta. In general, the correspondence between foreign and domestic level changes in the yield curve will be closer than that estimated by a (conventional duration) country beta — implying that the country beta should be closer to 1.0. The LS&C model would be expected to better segregate the effect of level changes in the yield curve when estimating the country level beta. We would expect the country level beta, which after all corresponds quite closely to the country beta,[10] to be closer to 1.0. In our sample this is true for all countries except Australia and Japan. We will examine the typical case using Canada as the example, and then Australia and Japan as two exceptional cases.

The Canadian country level beta is 0.95 and the country beta is 0.89. Both are highly statistically significant. In this case, the country level beta is closer to 1.0 as predicted. In fact for Canada, the country slope and curvature betas are also close to 1.0; they are 0.97 and 0.94, respectively. This indicates that Canada can be used as a fairly close substitute for the United States along all three dimensions of yield curve movements. Further, Canadian bonds can be included to a greater degree than, say, Dutch bonds (see Exhibit 3), while maintaining a higher degree of confidence that portfolio performance will be close to that of a purely domestic portfolio. Exhibit 5 presents the correlations between level, slope, and curvature in Canada over the 5-year period we consider. We notice that all correlations are fairly low, but not negligible. This explains why the country beta, albeit farther from 1.0 than the country level beta, is still quite close to 1.0. This also reaffirms that the LS&C model better sorts out the noise inherent in the slope and curvature correlations; that noise is only summarized in the conventional duration approach.

Exhibit 5: Canada: Correlations of Changes in Level, Slope, and Curvature Parameters

Correlation	Level	Slope	Curvature
Level	1.00		
Slope	−0.03	1.00	
Curvature	−0.12	−0.16	1.00

---

[10] For a discussion of this issue, see Willner, "A New Tool for Portfolio Managers: Level, Slope, and Curvature Duration."

Exhibit 6: Australia: Correlations of Changes in Level, Slope, and Curvature Parameters

Correlation	Level	Slope	Curvature
Level	1.00		
Slope	–0.45	1.00	
Curvature	–0.27	0.24	1.00

Exhibit 7: Japan: Correlations of Changes in Level, Slope, and Curvature Parameters

Correlation	Level	Slope	Curvature
Level	1.00		
Slope	–0.50	1.00	
Curvature	–0.52	0.22	1.00

The Australia country level beta is 1.08 and the country beta is 1.04. In this case the country beta is closer to 1.0. This result may appear to be puzzling at first since we would expect in general (for the reasons stated earlier) that that relationship would be reversed. However, Exhibit 6 may give us some insight into what is causing this condition. The exhibit shows us that there is significant negative correlation between level changes and slope and curvature changes (for instance, compare Exhibit 6 to Exhibit 5). The negative correlations may be creating a mitigating effect. Recall that the country beta is proportional to the covariance of changes in Australian versus U.S. yields. The offsetting effects of intra-Australian yield curve large negative correlations can depress the size of the overall covariance with the United States. Therefore, the volatility adjustment inherent in the country beta may be biased lower. We also note that the t-statistics for the level, slope, and curvature beta are all highly significant. This makes us comfortable that the non-level changes are significant so that their movement and its associated correlations are not spurious but a persistent part of the yield curve dynamics of Australian interest rates. These effects are therefore likely to be represented in the country beta.

The Japanese country level beta is 0.22 and the country beta is 0.30. In this case the country beta is closer to 1.0. However, the correlations in Exhibit 7 reveal an even more onerous situation. The correlations of level changes to slope and curvature changes are particularly high (in absolute value), suggesting that the single point estimation inherent in the conventional duration, yield-oriented model, can be misleading. Moreover, only the country curvature beta (representing the weakest yield curve change effect) is statistically significant. The conclusion drawn from these statistics is that Japan can be considered as fairly independent from the United States. Perhaps the best conclusion to be drawn is that no (or not much of a) relationship exists between U.S. and Japanese yield curves. The portfolio manager that hazards including Japanese government bonds (JGBs) in the portfolio is adding close to pure tracking error. Of course, lack of correlation with U.S. securities affords valuable diversification. However, this is not the issue we are addressing. Our research indicates that if a JGB is included in a domestic portfolio, its contribution to the domestic duration of the portfolio cannot be calculated reliably.

This analysis for Canada, Australia, and Japan indicates how every country should be analyzed and evaluated on its own merit. Clearly, LS&C durations are more elucidating than country betas alone since they present the marginal contribution of sensitivity of each type of yield curve movement rather than an aggregate which necessarily obfuscates the individual contributions. Exhibit 3 is easily revised for successive five year or other periods. The portfolio manager can then adjust the duration using the betas presented in Exhibit 3 and be more confident of a reasonable representation of the domestic duration contribution engendered by the inclusion of foreign bonds. The *degree* of confidence is the topic of the next section which concludes this chapter.

CONCLUSION

Previous analysis indicates the potential for basis risk engendered by including foreign bonds in a domestically benchmarked portfolio. Considering this issue as a hedge problem provides a way to quantify the indirect durational response of the foreign bonds to domestic interest rates and a methodology to adjust for it. The question we have addressed so far is: given the inclusion of a foreign bond in a domestic portfolio, how can its domestic duration be reasonably calculated? The conclusion is that the use of a hedge approach with derived country betas is good, while the use of a hedged approach with level, slope, and curvature betas is better. What we have not yet addressed is how good is it. How much of the differential reaction to domestic interest changes have we explained? And consequently, how much of the foreign bond can be included in a domestic portfolio?

The conclusive answer would require a comprehensive model of interest rate changes across and within the nations of the world. Then we could describe the performance of foreign bonds in total since all the effects on their interest rates would be modeled. Our hedge approach only picks up that movement of interest rates co-varying with domestic interest rates. If domestic interest rate change was the only factor necessary to explain interest rate changes in all countries (i.e., all other non-correlated foreign interest rate movement was simply noise), then our model could be comprehensive. In that case a well diversified holding of foreign bonds would substantially reduce risk and the durational behavior of bonds would very much be captured by this hedge approach. The danger comes about when the unexplained component of variation has covariance between two countries represented in our domestic portfolio, but not with the domestic country itself. An example might be two European countries vying to be members of the European Monetary Union (EMU) and having this affect their interest rates, while being represented in a U.S. domestic portfolio — whereas the U.S. interest rates are generally independent of EMU considerations.

Nontheless, a portfolio manager is interested in whether or not to include foreign bonds and how much of them to include. Elsewhere this issue is discussed at some length and the reader is referred to that more extensive discussion.[11] We shall only review some of the points here.

Recall that a beta can be dissected into a correlation term times a relative volatility term. A beta of 1.0, which generally indicates close correspondence between foreign and domestic interest rates, can be misleading. It may be close to 1.0 if the foreign and domestic interest rate performance is similar. But it may also be close to 1.0 if relatively high foreign volatility offsets low correlation of performance. For instance, when the correlation is 0.5 and relative volatility of interest rates is 2.0, $0.5 \times 2.0 = 1.0$. Therefore it is not sufficient to know the beta when trying to identify close substitute bonds. What is desirable is that foreign interest rates be highly correlated with local interest rates. Unfortunately, there is no single comprehensive correlation number when we extend country betas to the county level, slope, and curvature beta framework. However, for the purpose of determining the general correlation between interest rates as a guide to the inclusion of foreign bonds in a domestic portfolio, the conventional duration country beta is probably sufficient. The higher is the correlation, the more of the foreign bond which can be safely included. Exhibit 8 presents correlations for the 15 countries. The actual amount of the foreign bond to include is a topic of managerial discretion which we will not address here. Obviously, the more of the foreign bond, the more domestic benchmark tracking error introduced. The expected return is the reward for taking on such risk and the allowable tradeoff is a decision for the portfolio manager.

Exhibit 8: Correlations to U.S. Interest Rate Changes

Country	Correlation	Country	Correlation
Australia	0.70	Ireland	0.47
Austria	0.38	Italy	0.28
Belgium	0.32	Japan	0.30
Canada	0.70	Spain	0.31
Denmark	0.39	Sweden	0.32
France	0.49	Switzerland	0.28
Germany	0.52	UK	0.44
Holland	0.53		

[11] Thomas and Willner, "Measuring the Duration of an Internationally Diversified Portfolio."

Exhibit 9: UNFIRM Statistics Measured Against U.S. Interest Rate Changes

Country	%	Country	%
Canada	18	Holland	29
Ireland	19	Italy	29
UK	19	France	29
Australia	20	Switzerland	32
Germany	24	Spain	35
Sweden	24	Belgium	39
Denmark	24	Japan	41
Austria	28		

In the Thomas-Willner study, a statistic called "Unrelated foreign interest rate movement" or UNFIRM was also introduced. This statistic is measured as $2|\alpha|/\sigma$ where α is from the regression given in equation (5) and σ is the standard deviation of the return term (left hand side) of equation (5). We explain that this statistic is a proxy for the economic value of potential factors not included in the regression. The statistic attempts to measure the economic significance of these factors by comparing their average contribution to the typical value change. The UNFIRM statistics for the same 15 countries are presented in Exhibit 9.

Exhibit 9 is presented in ascending UNFIRM order, which reflects the closest substitutes for the United States first. It is interesting to note that the ordering occurs by block! First is the Anglo-block, with Canada the closest substitute, next is the European block, and finally there is Japan. This appeals to our intuition about the natural substitutes for the United States, at least, block by block. For instance, we would expect that more of Canada than Switzerland can be included in a U.S. portfolio for the same degree of tracking error of U.S. interest rates.

Our discussion has presented tools and approaches for careful inclusion of foreign bonds in domestic portfolios. We note the need for caution and a case-by-case approach for the bonds of each country. The domestic portfolio manager wishing to include foreign bonds may find it wise to apply the country level, slope, and curvature beta adjustments to their corresponding durations (or at least the country beta adjustment to conventional duration). Further, the manager should examine the betas' associated statistics, the corresponding country correlations and the UNFIRM statistics, to gauge the accuracy of such adjustments. This approach will assist in maintaining the usefulness of domestic duration as a guide for managing such portfolios. In the absence of a comprehensive transnational interest rate model, such an approach may be the best alternative.

Chapter 10

The Basics of Cash-Market Hedging

Shrikant Ramamurthy
Senior Vice President
Prudential Securities Incorporated

INTRODUCTION

Fixed-income instruments, like securities in other asset classes, exhibit price volatility on a daily basis. For many participants in these markets, these price fluctuations are not always desirable. For investors who want to reduce price volatility, hedging offers a way to minimize or eliminate price risk. Hedging strategies are of interest to many market participants including, among others, dealers and traders whose goal is to provide liquidity to investors without incurring large losses, portfolio managers who need to protect positions from potential loss, and corporate treasurers who want to lock in rates prior to issuing fixed-income debt.

This chapter provides an introduction to hedging fixed-income securities using the "dollar-value-of-a-basis-point" (DVBP) approach and develops a framework for analyzing and managing risk through the use of hedging strategies in the cash market. While many types of financial instruments can serve as hedge vehicles, this chapter will focus on Treasury securities as hedge instruments. Treasuries are by far the most commonly employed hedge instruments for reasons that are readily apparent; they have no credit risk, the Treasury market is very liquid, and most importantly, Treasuries have an appropriate sensitivity to interest-rate movements.

We begin by discussing the sources of price risk and the goals of any particular hedging strategy. We then discuss the mechanics of developing and implementing optimal hedging strategies for risk management. As we will show, DVBP-based hedging strategies are flexible and can incorporate the nuances of different markets. However, as we shall also illustrate, ultimately any hedging strategy has its limits in providing absolute price protection. Numerous examples of constructing and evaluating hedges for bullet bonds, option embedded bonds, and mortgage-backed securities are included.

I would like to thank Boris Loshak and Michael Valente for many useful suggestions and comments. I am also indebted to Richard Chin of Goldman, Sachs & Co., with whom an earlier version of this research was coauthored.

THE MECHANICS OF HEDGING

The design and implementation of a successful hedge strategy involves:

- identifying the causes of a security's price fluctuations
- determining the amount of price volatility that is acceptable
- finding the appropriate hedge instrument
- determining the appropriate position in the hedge instrument
- analyzing the cost of the hedge strategy

Identifying the Sources of Price Risk

Different securities have different sources of price risk; no single hedge strategy or hedging vehicle is optimal in all situations. For example, a short-term corporate bond's price changes as short-term interest rates change, or as perceptions of the issuer's credit quality changes. In contrast, an MBS's price changes primarily due to changes in long-term interest rates, the shape of the curve and/or the prepayment outlook. Thus, a hedge strategy suitable for a corporate bond may not be as suitable for a mortgage-backed security.

Price movements in the fixed-income markets are largely, but not solely, determined by interest-rate movements. Other factors, such as liquidity, supply, changes in credit risk, event risk, expectations of future economic growth and inflation, etc., all can affect the pricing of a particular fixed-income issue or portfolio. However, since the price movements of most fixed-income securities are dominated by interest-rate movements, hedging interest-rate risk is generally the first goal of any hedging strategy. Hedging other risks, like credit risk, may not be possible and, if possible, may not be the objective of a hedging strategy.

Balancing Risk and Return

We said that a hedging strategy is used to reduce the effect of price uncertainty of a security. A "perfect" hedge eliminates all price risk for the hedged portfolio and, in effect, "locks in" the future price of the hedged portfolio under any scenario. In contrast, a less-than-perfect hedge eliminates some, but not all, price uncertainty and, consequently, the hedged portfolio will display some price volatility, but the volatility will be less than that of an unhedged portfolio.

By controlling a portfolio's price fluctuations through hedging, an investor may be insulated from a decline in portfolio value but may, at the same time, be prevented from realizing any appreciation in value. The fundamental tenet of finance, "the lower the risk, the lower the return," is certainly applicable to hedging. Exhibit 1 compares the returns for hypothetical hedged and unhedged portfolios over a range of interest-rate scenarios. In effect, a hedge changes a security's risk/return profile, thus creating a synthetic security with a lower risk/return profile than if the security was not hedged. Various synthetic securities with differing risk/return profiles can be created by changing the degree to which a position is hedged. For example, hedging only half the position in a particular bond creates a different risk/return profile than hedging the entire bond position. This is important to note because the goal of an overall strategy may be to retain some degree of price risk in order to gain from any upside potential.

Choosing a Hedge Instrument

Once the sources of price risk and the amount of risk to be hedged have been determined, the next step is to find a hedge instrument. The most appropriate hedge instrument is a security that has similar price movements to that of the security being hedged. By taking an opposite position in the hedge instrument, a hedge is implemented.

For example, hedging a long corporate bond position involves taking a short position in any instrument that is expected to have similar future price movements. The idea is that any loss in the long position is negated by a gain in the short position and, conversely, any gain in the long position is negated by a loss in the short position. The extent to which this perfect hedge is possible is a function of the correlation between the price movements of the two securities. Since our discussion of hedge vehicles is limited to cash-market securities, our focus will be on identifying those securities that provide the maximum correlation with the security to be hedged. While our focus is on using Treasuries, other instruments, including futures, options, interest-rate swaps and other cash-market securities, such as corporate bonds or mortgage-backed securities, also can be used as effective hedge vehicles.

Determining the Appropriate Hedge Position Using DVBP

Once a hedge instrument is identified, the next step is to determine an appropriate position in the hedge instrument. This is accomplished by calculating the dollar value of a basis point (DVBP) for both the security and the hedge instrument.

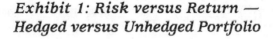

Exhibit 1: Risk versus Return —
Hedged versus Unhedged Portfolio

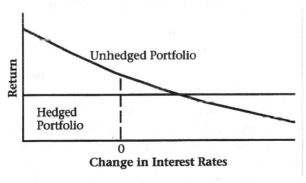

Exhibit 2: DVBP Computation for $1 Million Par Amount 10-Year Treasury Notes

Issue	Coupon (%)	Maturity	Price*	Yield (%)
10-Year Treasury Note	6.25	2/15/07	96.375	6.76

$$DVBP = \text{Dollar Par Amt.} \times (\text{Price} + \text{Accrued}) \times \text{Mod. Duration} \times \frac{1}{1,000,000}$$

$$= 1,000,000 \times (96.375 + 1.2776) \times 7.087 \times \frac{1}{1,000,000}$$

$$= \$692.06$$

* Price information as of 4/29/97.

The DVBP of a security is the security's price change for a one-basis-point change in its yield. In other words, DVBP expresses a security's dollar sensitivity to interest rates.

The following equation shows the DVBP calculation for a non-callable bond:

$$DVBP = \frac{\text{Dollar Par Amt.} \times (\text{Price} + \text{Accrued}) \times \text{Mod. Duration}}{1,000,000} \quad (1)$$

Since the price movement for a bond is different for an increase or a decrease in interest rates due to the bond's convexity, the DVBP is effectively an average price change for a one-basis-point change in interest rates.

Exhibit 2 shows the DVBP calculation for a $1 million position in a non-callable bond, in this case a 10-year Treasury note in which price and accrued interest are expressed as a percentage of par.

For an option embedded bond, the DVBP as defined in equation (1) is not appropriate because it does not account for the change in a bond's option value as interest rates change. In order for the DVBP to reflect an option-embedded bond's interest-rate sensitivity, it needs to explicitly account for the changes in both the value of the bond and the embedded option(s). The following equation shows the DVBP formula for an option-embedded bond in which the DVBP is an option-adjusted DVBP:

Option Adjusted DVBP

$$= \frac{\text{Change in Constant OAS Price}}{\text{Yield Curve Shift in BPs}} \times \frac{\text{Dollar Par Amt.}}{100} \quad (2)$$

The price changes in equation (2) have to be determined either from a theoretical model or empirically. Generally, when a model is used to generate prices under different rate scenarios, a constant-OAS pricing assumption is used, although any assumption can be used. For example, in the federal agency debt market, at the time of this writing, callable premiums currently trade at wider

OASs than callable discounts. This market reality can be readily accounted for in the DVBP computation by using the appropriate OASs in computing the respective scenario prices. Typically, option-adjusted DVBP is computed assuming parallel interest rate shifts occurring in increments of 10 to 25 basis points. Exhibit 3 shows the computation of option-adjusted DVBP for the FNMA 7.33s of 4/2/07, callable from 4/2/02.

The Hedge Ratio

Once the DVBPs of the security and the hedge vehicle are determined, they can be used to find the *hedge ratio*, which is the number of units of the hedge instrument required for the hedge strategy. The hedge ratio is calculated using the following:

$$\text{Hedge ratio} = \frac{\text{DVBP of security to be hedged per \$1 million par amount}}{\text{DVBP of hedge instrument per \$1 million par amount}} \quad (3)$$

If many units of a security are to be hedged, multiplying the hedge ratio by the number of units to be hedged will determine the position needed in the hedge instrument. Exhibit 4 shows the mechanics of a DVBP hedge for a $5 million par amount long position in Walt Disney corporate bonds using the 10-year on-the-run Treasury note as the hedging instrument.

Exhibit 3: Computation of Option-Adjusted DVBP for $1 Million Par Amount FNMA Callable Bonds

Issue	Coupon (%)	Maturity	Call Price	Call Date	Price*	Yield (%)	OAS (BPs)
FNMA	7.33	4/2/07	100.00	4/2/02	99.625	7.38	16

Constant-OAS Prices

Yield-Curve Shift	Price	Yield (%)
Up 25 BPs	98.25	7.58
Down 25 BPs	101.03	7.18

Option Adjusted DVBP

$$= \frac{\text{Change in constant} - \text{OAS price}}{\text{Yield curve shift in BPs}} \times \frac{\text{Dollar par amount}}{100}$$

$$= \frac{101.03 - 98.25}{50} \times \frac{1,000,000}{100}$$

$$= \$556.00$$

* Price information as of 4/29/97. OAS and constant-OAS prices are computed at 15% volatility.

Exhibit 4: Computation of Hedge Ratios

Issue	Coupon (%)	Maturity	Price*	Yield (%)	DVBP (Per $1MM Par Amount)
Walt Disney	6.75	3/30/06	96.942	7.22	636.56
10-Year Treasury Note	6.25	2/15/07	96.375	6.76	692.06

$$\text{Hedge ratio} = \frac{\text{DVBP of security to be hedged}}{\text{DVBP of hedge instrument}} = \frac{636.56}{692.06} = 0.92$$

Explanation: To hedge one long position in a Walt Disney bond, 0.92 10-year Treasury notes need to be shorted. To hedge a long position of $5 million par amount, $4.60 million par amount of 10-year Treasury notes need to be shorted (0.92 × $5 million).

* Price information as of 4/29/97.

Adjusted Hedge Ratio

The hedge ratio formula as given in equation (3) contains an implicit assumption that the security's yield and the hedge instrument's yield will move in equal amounts for a given change in interest rates. This is usually true for securities that are priced relative to — and are hedged with — the same instrument. Under these conditions, the hedge should provide adequate price protection against interest-rate risk. However, in many cases, a security's yield changes by a different amount or in a different direction than that of the hedge vehicle. Under these circumstances, the hedge ratio needs to be adjusted as shown in the following equation, to reflect the amount that a security's yield changes for every one-basis-point-change in the hedge instrument's yield.

$$\text{Adjusted Hedge Ratio} = \frac{\text{DVBP of Security to be Hedged}}{\text{DVBP of Hedge Instrument}} \times B \qquad (4)$$

where

B = adjustment factor equal to the yield change in the security to be hedged for a one-basis point change in the yield of the hedge instrument

The adjustment in equation (4) usually is not required for option embedded bonds in which the hedge ratio is determined using an option adjusted DVBP. An option adjusted DVBP implicitly adjusts for the change in an option embedded security's yield for a given change in the hedge instrument's yield due to the changing option cost. Therefore, an option adjusted hedge ratio, which is introduced in a later section of this chapter, does not require the adjustment as given by equation (4).

The adjusted hedge ratio is particularly useful when hedging Treasury inflation protected securities (TIPS) and zero-coupon Treasury bonds, whose yields may not necessarily move one-for-one with any hedge instrument's yield. Even if a security's yield is not perfectly correlated with the hedge instrument's yield, an estimate of the adjustment factor is still required for an effective hedge. In the end, the effectiveness of the hedge will depend heavily on how accurately the adjustment factor has been estimated. One useful starting point for estimating this adjustment factor is to use a regression model to quantify any historical relationship.

Ten-Year Treasury-Note Equivalent

The hedge ratio for a security also can be computed using the DVBP of the 10-year Treasury note as the hedge vehicle. This is also called the *10-year equivalent* and it describes a security's price sensitivity to interest rates in units of the 10-year Treasury note. The following equation shows the calculation for the 10-year equivalent.

$$\text{10-Year Equivalent} = \frac{\text{DVBP of Security to be Hedged}}{\text{DVBP of 10-Year Treasury Note}} \tag{5}$$

Calculating the 10-year equivalent of a security is useful as a benchmark for comparing the interest-rate sensitivities of different instruments. Since the hedge ratio is additive, the 10-year equivalent can be used to aggregate the different interest-rate sensitivities of securities in a portfolio to produce a portfolio 10-year equivalent that measures the entire portfolio's sensitivity to interest rates.

The 10-year Treasury note is used to calculate equivalent-risk positions because the 10-year note is used very often as a hedge vehicle for many types of fixed-income instruments, including mortgage-backed securities, long-term corporate bonds, and agency bonds. However, there is nothing unique to the 10-year Treasury note to compute an equivalent position. Theoretically, any security can be used as a reference for computing an equivalent risk position.

Although the 10-year equivalent is a useful tool for comparison purposes, this does not imply that the 10-year Treasury note should be used for hedging all securities. Clearly, a 2-year corporate bond should be hedged with a 2-year Treasury note and not with a 10-year Treasury note given that the interest-rate risk in a 2-year corporate bond is directly linked to movements in 2-year Treasury yields. Describing different securities' risk positions through the same equivalent methodology provides a way to aggregate and describe the risk of a portfolio in simple fashion.

In the next section, we will look more closely at how the hedge instrument protects a non-callable bond's price from changes in the level of interest rates, and examine the importance of the yield correlation between the security and the hedge vehicle.

HEDGING A NONCALLABLE BOND

When a non-callable bond is priced relative to a specific Treasury issue and when the yield movements are closely correlated, using that specific Treasury issue as the hedge vehicle is appropriate. In Exhibit 4, the noncallable Walt Disney 6.75s of 3/30/06 are quoted at a yield spread of +46 basis points to the 10-year Treasury note. Since yield changes in the Walt Disney issue can be attributed largely to changes in 10-year Treasury yields in the absence of any changes in spread, 10-year Treasuries are the appropriate hedge instrument. Exhibit 5 analyzes a hedge for the Walt Disney issue using 10-year Treasuries.

Comparing the unhedged position and the hedged position, we see that a 50-basis-point change in interest rates can dramatically change the value of an unhedged Walt Disney position, whereas when the position is hedged with $920,000 par amount of 10-year Treasuries, price volatility is minimal. For a $1 million par amount position, the hedged portfolio has a maximum change in value of only $140 for a 50-basis-point change in yields. In contrast, the value of the unhedged portfolio can change by as much as $32,490 for a 50-basis-point change in yields.

While the DVBP hedge in Exhibit 5 clearly limits price movements in the Walt Disney position, notice that it is not a "perfect" hedge, as the price of the hedged portfolio does change somewhat in response to interest-rate movements. There are several reasons for this. First, the hedge ratio that is used has been rounded and is not exact. Second, the prices on 10-year Treasuries have been rounded to the nearest 64th to reflect trading convention. The third reason that the hedge is not perfect is because of the effect that convexity has on DVBP.

A noncallable bond's price will change more for a given decrease in interest rates than for the same magnitude increase in rates due to its positive convexity. Since the DVBP of a bond is computed using the average price change for a one-basis-point change in interest rates, the hedge ratio will never be the exact ratio needed (although it will be very close) for a given realization of interest-rate change. If there is a strong opinion about the general direction of future interest-rate movements, then the hedge ratio could be adjusted appropriately for the given directionality in interest rates and a more efficient hedge could be constructed. Generally, however, for modest interest-rate movements, this convexity effect is not large.

Exhibit 5: Hedging a Noncallable Bond

Objective: Hedge $1 million par amount Walt Disney 6.75s of 3/30/06 priced at +46 basis points to the 10-year Treasury note. To hedge each Walt Disney bond, 0.92 10-year notes are shorted (see Exhibit 4).

Change in Portfolio Value**
The effects of a 50-basis point change in interest rates on $1 million par amount of hedged and unhedged positions are as follows.

	Unhedged Portfolio	Hedged Portfolio
Yields increase by 50 bps	= 938,230 − 969,420 = −31,190	= (938,230 − 969,420) − {0.92(930,000 − 963,750)} = −140
Yields decrease by 50 bps	= 1,001,910 − 969,420 = 32,490	= (1,001,910 − 969,420) − {0.92(999,063 − 963,750)} = 2

* Price information as of 4/29/92.
** Change in unhedged portfolio value = Change in Walt Disney position
Change in hedged portfolio value = Change in Walt Disney position − Change in 10-year Treasury position

Another important point to note about the DVBP hedge in Exhibit 5 is that it assumes that the pricing spread between the Walt Disney bond and the 10-year Treasury will remain constant. This may not be the case. In the next section, we will discuss yield-spread risk that is caused by events that are not necessarily predictable but that still may affect an issue's pricing.

Yield-Spread Risk

The Walt Disney position in Exhibit 5 is effectively hedged against interest-rate risk, but does not account for other factors that can influence pricing. The example assumes that the 46-basis-point pricing spread will not change. However, the pricing spread associated with any security can change as interest rates change or as the perceived credit risks of the issuer change.

Other event related risk also can affect the pricing spread. A good case in point is the selloff in 1997 of bonds issued by Advanta Corporation. Yield spreads on Advanta bonds widened over 100 basis points after the company announced that delinquencies and charge-offs on their loan portfolio had increased dramatically in the current quarter.

Yield-spread risk that is due to event risk, such as that in the Advanta situation, is difficult to hedge. However, general sector risks may be hedged to an extent if they are properly anticipated. Upcoming problems in particular sectors can be anticipated sometimes by examining trends in the economy or interest rates, or by anticipating the effects of upcoming changes in regulations, political structure, etc. In these scenarios, and in situations in which investors wish to continue to hold the securities, the effect of widening spreads may be mitigated by buying put options on a sector index, by shorting a basket of stocks in the sector, or by taking a position in any portfolio that will be similarly affected by such changes. These positions would be in addition to a position in the underlying interest-rate hedge instrument.

Yield-spread risk due to changing interest rates may be mitigated if there is a known correlation between the direction and magnitude of interest-rate moves and spread changes. If spreads widen when the market rallies and spreads tighten when the market sells off, then the price volatility associated with these spread changes can be reduced by shorting fewer Treasury securities than the number given by the DVBP hedge ratio. The use of the adjusted hedge ratio in equation (4) would adjust for these anticipated spread changes and provide for a more effective hedge.

In general, the effects of yield-spread changes can be accommodated into a hedging strategy. However, in the short run, pricing spreads generally are not volatile, and the risk that yield spreads will change dramatically may not be a dominating factor in the hedging issue.

The analysis so far has examined a static hedge and the effect of immediate interest-rate changes on the value of a portfolio. To examine the performance of a hedge over time, the cost of carrying the position also must be taken into account. The cost-of-carry is an integral part of the profit/loss balance of any position and the carry cost of the hedge security can be an important factor in determining if that security should be used for hedging.

Cost of Carry

The *cost of carry*, or *carry*, refers to the cash flows associated with holding a position over time, excluding those cash flows attributable to establishing or liquidating the position. Carry is simply the difference between the coupon interest cash flow received and the daily cost paid out to finance the position. A positive cost of carry means that the cost of borrowing money to finance the purchase of securities is lower than the yield on the securities themselves. A negative cost of carry results when the cost of financing is higher than the yields on the securities.

For hedging purposes, the cost of carry must be determined for both positions, since hedging involves both long and short positions. We will discuss carry from both perspectives, beginning with the long position.

Long Carry

The following equation defines the daily carry for a long position:[1]

$$\text{Long Daily Carry} = \text{Daily Coupon Income} - \text{Daily Financing Cost} \qquad (6)$$

where

$$\text{Daily Financing Cost} = (\text{Price} + \text{Accrued}) \times \frac{\text{Repo Rate}}{360}$$

The daily price accretion of a discount bond or daily price amortization of a premium bond can be included in computing the cost of carry. Accretion/amortization is factored in because a bond held to maturity will return the par amount and the price of a discount or premium bond will change gradually to approach par value by maturity. Since the price change of a discount or a premium bond is in some sense predictable, the price accretion/amortization effect can be incorporated into the cost of carry computation, as shown in the following equation:

$$\text{Long Daily Carry} = \text{Daily Coupon Income} - \text{Daily Financing Cost} \\ \pm \text{Daily Accretion/Amortization} \qquad (7)$$

Equation (7) is especially useful for determining the cost of carry of zero-coupon bonds that do not pay any coupon interest, yet accrete at the yield to maturity on a daily basis.

From the standpoint of hedging the change in portfolio value only, carry, as calculated by either equation (6) or equation (7), is acceptable as long as all of

---

[1] The formulas on carry in this section do not account for the haircut that may be involved in trying to repurchase (repo) a security. *Haircut* refers to the inability to use the entire market value of a security as collateral in a repo transaction. As a result, the carry on a long position could be decreased.

the individual components of the change in portfolio value are identified and accounted. Generally, the change in portfolio value over time is the sum of the change in the price of the portfolio and the net carrying costs excluding price accretion/amortization (i.e., net carry as defined in equation (6)). If net carry were defined to include price accretion/amortization (as in equation (7)), the change in portfolio value over time needs to be redefined as the sum of the "price change outside of any accretion/amortization effect," plus the net carry cost (which now includes the accretion/amortization). Either method provides the same change in portfolio value. Thus, from a hedging perspective only, either method of computing net carrying costs is acceptable. With this in mind, we will define carry as the difference between coupon income and financing cost (as defined in equation (6)) in our discussions.

Short Carry

The next equation shows the cost of carry for a short position. The cost of carry for a short position is the difference between the coupon interest paid out on the borrowed securities and the interest received on the reverse repurchase (repo) agreement:

$$\text{Short Daily Carry} = \text{Daily Financing Income} - \text{Daily Coupon Cost} \qquad (8)$$

where

$$\text{Daily Financing Income} = (\text{Price} + \text{Accrued}) \times \frac{\text{Reverse Repo Rate}}{360}$$

Net Carry

The sum of the cost of carry for the long and the short position is the net carry of the portfolio, as shown in the following equations.

$$\text{Net Carry} = \text{Long Daily Carry} + \text{Short Daily Carry} \qquad (9)$$

The net carry is usually positive on a long position that is hedged in the Treasury market for two reasons. First, the coupon income on the security is usually higher than the coupon on the Treasury instrument. Second, the repo/reverse-repo rates for financing are usually similar. However, this is not always the case. Using Treasuries as a hedge instrument can produce a negative net carry. If the shorted Treasury goes on special, the net carry could be negative if the reverse-repo rate is sufficiently less than the repo rate.

Negative Carry: A Treasury "Goes on Special"

A security is on *special* when it is in short supply and is difficult for short sellers to borrow, and hence is offered at lower borrowing rates when used as collateral in the repo market. As a result, lower financing income is earned from a short position in such security. For example, the 10-year Treasury note was on special at various times in the first quarter of 1997 at rates as tight as 3% versus a general collateral (not on special) rate of 5.50% for other securities.

When the net carry of a hedged position is negative, alternative hedging instruments should be considered since other hedge vehicles may be more cost effective. Alternatives include: (1) a different Treasury security; (2) a Treasury-futures contract; (3) options on Treasury securities or options on futures contracts; or, (4) interest-rate swaps. Of course, the Treasury security that is on special may be the only security that has the required similarity in price sensitivity to interest rates and hence may still be used as the hedge vehicle despite its hedging costs.

Incorporating Carry into a Hedge

Exhibit 6 reexamines the hedge from Exhibit 5 on the Walt Disney bond, incorporating carry costs into the hedge. For this example, we assume that the hedge is maintained for one week. The unhedged portfolio has very high price variation for changes in interest rates of 50 basis points. Assuming constant spreads, if interest rates increase by 50 basis points, the unhedged portfolio will suffer a one-week loss of $30,841, whereas for a 50-basis-point decrease in interest rates, portfolio value will increase by $32,739. In contrast, the hedged portfolio is insulated from these interest-rate changes and its value will change only marginally. Of course, larger interest-rate swings would further magnify the differences in value between the two portfolios.

Exhibit 6: Hedging a Noncallable Bond Incorporating Carry Costs

Objective: Hedge $1 million par amount Walt Disney 6.75s of 3/30/06 trading at +46 basis points to the 10-year Treasury note. The hedge ratio is 0.92 10-year Treasuries for each Walt Disney issue (see Exhibit 4). Maintain hedge for one week. Assume that the repo and reverse repo rates are 5.50% and 5.00%, respectively, and that they do not change during the course of the week.

Change in Portfolio Value**
The effects of no change in interest rates and a 50 basis point change in interest rates (assuming constant spreads) in one week on $1 million par of hedged and unhedged positions are as follows:

	50 BP increase	No Change	50 BP Decrease
Unhedged Position	−30,841	299	32,739
Hedged Position	−29	61	13

* Price information as of 4/29/92.
** Change in unhedged portfolio value = Change in Walt Disney position
Change in hedged portfolio value = Change in Walt Disney position − Change in 10-year Treasury position

---

Notice also that if interest rates do not change, the unhedged portfolio has a gain of $299 versus a gain of only $61 for the hedged portfolio. This difference is due to the different carry costs of the two portfolios. The unhedged portfolio has only one long position, which has large positive carry. The hedged portfolio has lower carry because the reverse-repo rate on the short position is lower than the repo rate on the long position and because interest accrual must be paid on the short position. Usually, a hedged position will have less carry than an unhedged position. The reduction in net carry income is one of the costs of hedging.

Carry cost also can be a potential source of risk in a portfolio. The repo/reverse-repo rates are reset on a daily basis and hence there is a degree of uncertainty about the costs of financing both the short and long positions of a hedged portfolio, particularly if the hedge is going to be maintained for some time. A hedged portfolio may have positive carry when the hedge is initiated and, later, as financing costs change, the carry may become negative. This can happen when a security that has been used as a hedge goes on special. One way to limit carry risk is to use term repos to finance positions.

A term repo is a repo transaction in which the rate and commitment to borrow is set for a specified period of time. While it can eliminate the risk of adverse rate changes, term repos can be expensive.

HEDGING SECURITIES WITH OFF-THE-RUN MATURITIES

Many fixed-income securities mature in years for which an on-the-run Treasury is not available for pricing. This situation is typical for many intermediate term securities and for securities that have off the run maturities of between 10 and 30 years.

These securities are priced by using:

- the specific off-the-run Treasury with a similar maturity
- the nearest on-the-run Treasury (e.g., a 15-year corporate bond priced off of the 10 year Treasury note), or
- the "blended" yield of the two on-the-run Treasuries that have maturities surrounding the maturity of the security

When a security is priced relative to an off-the-run Treasury, the hedging techniques discussed earlier in Exhibits 4 through 6 apply, and the security can be hedged by shorting the off-the-run Treasury in amounts dictated by the hedge ratio. The hedge should be effective as long as yield spreads are not volatile. One potential problem with this hedging strategy is the ability to find a sufficient number of the particular off-the-run issue to short.

For securities with off-the-run maturities that are priced off of on-the-run securities, the earlier hedging analysis still applies. The on-the-run pricing benchmark is the appropriate hedging instrument as the yield and price on the security to be hedged is going to change as the yield and price on the benchmark on-the-run Treasury changes. However, this type of hedge, in addition to being exposed to credit risk, also may be exposed to yield-curve risk. For example, a 15-year corporate bond priced off the 10-year Treasury note may see spreads widen versus the on-the-run 10-year Treasury note if the curve steepens. If yields on 15-year Treasuries increase relative to 10-year Treasury yields, then spreads on a 15-year corporate bond priced off of 10-year Treasuries will have to widen to compensate for the steeper curve.

Note that if a 15-year off-the-run Treasury is used as the hedging instrument, this risk does not exist. Generally, when on-the-run Treasuries are used to hedge off-the-run maturity bullets, this type of yield-curve risk is either not hedged or hedged by taking an additional position in another on-the-run Treasury that captures changes in the shape of the curve. For example, to hedge a 15-year corporate bond priced off of a 10-year Treasury, the hedge can be comprised of a combination of 10- and 30-year Treasury securities.

Many off-the-run securities, particularly in maturities between three and ten years, are priced off of a blend of two on-the-run Treasury notes. For these types of securities, any suitable hedging strategy needs to explicitly account for the risks that each of the Treasury instruments brings to the hedged portfolio. For example, suppose a security is priced off the 5- and 10-year Treasury blend (5-/10-year blend), where the blend is defined as the average of 5- and 10-year Treasury yields. The security's yield will change half a basis point for every basis point move in yield of either the 5-year or 10-year Treasury.[2]

To hedge this security, positions need to be established in both 5-year and 10-year Treasuries. In effect, the Treasury securities are being used to create a synthetic security that has suitable interest-rate sensitivities. The par amount of each Treasury security is found by calculating the hedge ratio as shown in equation (4), with the factor B being equal to 0.5 in this case. The following equations illustrate this

$$\text{5-Year Hedge Ratio} = \frac{\text{DVBP of Security to be Hedged}}{\text{DVBP of 5-Year Treasury}} \times 0.5 \qquad \text{(10a)}$$

$$\text{10-Year Hedge Ratio} = \frac{\text{DVBP of Security to be Hedged}}{\text{DVBP of 10-Year Treasury}} \times 0.5 \qquad \text{(10b)}$$

Exhibit 7 illustrates a hedge for a TCI corporate bond that is priced at +145 basis points off the 5-/10-year blend. For comparative purposes, a hedge using only 10-year Treasuries is included as well.

---

[2] In this discussion, the 5- and 10-year blend is defined as the average yield of two Treasury securities. However, the blend can be defined to be any linear combination of the yields of two Treasury securities. For example, a 15-year security can be priced off of the 10- and 30-year blend where the blended yield is given as:

Blend = 0.75 × 10-yr. Trsy. yield + 0.25 × 30-yr. Trsy. yield

Exhibit 7: Hedging a Security Priced off a Blended Yield

Objective: Hedge $1 million par amount TCI 8.65s of 9/15/04, priced at +145 basis points off the 5-/10-year Treasury blend, where the blend is the average of the two Treasury yields.

Issue	Coupon (%)	Maturity	Price	Yield (%)	DVBP (Per $1 MM Par Amount)
TCI	8.65	9/15/04	102.713	8.15	555.56
5-Year Treasury Note	6.625	4/30/02	99-30	6.64	419.44
10-Year Treasury Note	6.25	2/15/07	96-12	6.76	692.06

Determining the Hedge Ratios
Two different hedges are examined; Hedge 1 uses only 10-year Treasuries and Hedge 2 uses a combination of 5- and 10-year Treasuries.

Hedge 1	Hedge 2
(100% in 10-Year Treasury)	(5-Year Treasury) (10-Year Treasury)

$$\text{Hedge Ratio} = \frac{555.56}{692.06} = 0.803 \quad \text{Hedge Ratio} = \frac{555.56}{419.44} \times 0.5 = 0.662 \quad \text{Hedge Ratio} = \frac{555.56}{692.06} \times 0.5 = 0.401$$

Change in Portfolio Value**
The change in portfolio value for parallel and non-parallel shifts of the yield curve. The effect of carry is not included.

	Unhedged Position	Hedge 1 (100% in 10-Yr. Treasury)	Hedge 2 (Both 5- and 10-Yr. Treasuries)
Parallel shift: All rates increase 50 BPs	999,820–1,027,130 = –27,310	(999,820–1,027,130) –0.803×930,000–963750) = –209	(999,820–1,027,130) –0.662×(978,750–999,375) –0.401×(930,000–963,750) = –123
Parallel shift: All rates decrease 50 BPs	1,055,390–1,027,130 =28,260	(1,055,390–1,027,130) –0.803×(999,063–963,750) = –96	(1,055,390–1,027,130) –0.662×(1,020,625–999,375) –0.401×(999,063–963,750) =32
Curve steepens: 5-Year rates unchanged 10-Year rates increase 50 BPs	1,013,360–1,027,130 = –13,770	(1,013,360–1,027,130) –0.803×(930,000–963,750) =13,331	(1,013,360–1,027,130) –0.662×(0) –0.401×(930,000–963,750) = –236
Curve flattens: 5-Year rates unchanged 10-Year rates decrease 50 BPs	1,041,140–1,027,130 =14,010	(1,041,140–1,027,130) –0.803×(999,063–963,750) = –14,346	(1,041,140–1,027,130) –0.622×(0) –0.401×(999,063–963,750) = –150

* Price data as of 4/29/97.
** Change in unhedged portfolio value = Change in TCI position
Change in hedged portfolio value = Change in TCI position – Change in Treasury position

In Exhibit 7, both hedges provide effective price protection from parallel changes in interest rates because both hedges are duration matched hedges. Any duration matched hedge will provide price protection from interest-rate movements for parallel shifts in the Treasury yield curve. In fact, a duration matched hedge using 2-year, 30-year or any other Treasury will provide effective and similar price protection from parallel interest-rate swings.

However, when the shape of the curve changes, the type of hedge strategy employed is critical. As Exhibit 7 demonstrates, when the curve flattens or steepens, only the combination hedge using both 5- and 10-year Treasuries provides price protection. In the scenario where the curve flattens with 10-year yields falling 50 basis points and 5-year rates remaining unchanged, the combination hedge loses only $150, while the hedge using just 10-year Treasuries loses $14,346. In fact, in this scenario, the unhedged position gains $14,010, an amount similar to what is lost in the 10-year only hedge. The 10-year only hedge is not an effective hedge because only half of the 10-year Treasury note position is a hedge for the TCI corporate bond, while the other half is a speculative short position.

Given that the shape of the yield curve is continually changing, using a combination of securities is essential for hedging securities priced off a blend. Using only one security as a hedging instrument exposes the portfolio to yield-curve risk that may be undesirable.

One of the drawbacks of using a blended yield to price off-the-run fixed-income securities is that market participants may define the blend in various ways, basing price quotes on different weighted averages. The result can be a range of different price quotes for the same security. In such cases, the security usually ends up being priced to the nearest on-the-run Treasury, even though there may be a noticeable maturity gap between the security and the on-the-run Treasury.

HEDGING OPTION EMBEDDED BONDS

Option embedded securities, such as callable bonds, put bonds, or mortgage-backed securities can be hedged using basically the same approach used for bullet bonds. However, special care must be taken in computing the DVBP for option embedded bonds. The yield spread on an option embedded bond is highly dependent on interest-rate movements and, unlike a similar "option-free" bond, the yield spread changes with interest-rate movements. First, we will discuss hedging option embedded corporate and agency bonds and then we will focus on mortgage-backed securities.

Option Embedded Corporate Bonds

Many corporate and agency bonds have embedded call and/or put options. In a callable bond position, an investor is long a bullet bond and short a call option to the issuer, which gives the issuer the right to call this bond at some date(s) prior to maturity. Since an option has been sold by the investor, the yield spread on a callable bond is higher than the yield spread on a similar-maturity bullet bond.

For callable bonds, spreads widen as the market rallies and tighten as interest rates rise. The spread on a callable bond reflects compensation for both credit risk and for the short option position embedded in the bond. As interest rates move, even marginally, the value of the option position can change significantly. For example, when the market rallies, the value of the call option increases, which in turn widens the spread on a callable bond to account for the more valuable embedded option. Conversely, when rate rises, the value of the call option declines, which is reflected by a tighter spread on a callable note.

In a put bond, the investor is long the put option, which provides the right to put the bond back to the issuer at some date(s) prior to maturity. Since the investor is long the put option, spreads on put bonds are tighter than spreads on comparable-maturity bullet bonds to reflect the value of the put option. When rates rally, the yield-to-maturity spread on a put bond will widen to reflect the lower put option value. When rates rise, the yield-to-maturity spread on a put bond tightens to reflect the higher option value in this environment.[3]

Any hedging strategy for an option embedded bond has to take into account the effects of changing yield spreads in different rate environments. If the magnitude of yield-spread changes is known empirically, then equation (4) can be used to compute an adjusted hedge ratio that takes into account the effects of changing yield spreads. However, empirically estimating the magnitude of yield-spread changes for option embedded bonds is imprecise. Usually, more technically precise means are used to determine a hedge ratio. One such method that incorporates the effects of changing embedded option values is the option adjusted approach.

In such an approach, the option adjusted DVBP for an option embedded bond is computed by calculating the constant-OAS prices for increasing and decreasing interest-rate levels (typically plus and minus 10 or 25 basis points), as given in equation (2).

The following equation shows the formula for a hedge ratio that incorporates option adjusted analysis to determine the option adjusted DVBP:

Hedge Ratio for Option Embedded Bonds

$$= \frac{\text{Option Adjusted DVBP of Option Embedded Bond}}{\text{DVBP of Hedge Security}} \qquad (11)$$

The option adjusted approach requires the use of a stochastic option valuation model to compute constant-OAS prices. A stochastic option valuation model enables a proper valuation of the different cash flows that will be received under different interest-rate environments. Implicitly, such valuation technology

---

[3] For more information on the sensitivity of option embedded bond spreads, see David Audley, Richard Chin, and Shrikant Ramamurthy, "OAS and Effective Duration," Chapter 40 in Frank J. Fabozzi (ed.), *Handbook of Fixed-Income Securities* (Burr Ridge, Il; Irwin Professional Publishing, 1997).

accounts for any yield-spread changes that accompany the change in option value as a result of interest-rate movements.[4]

Typically with option embedded bonds, the hedging instrument is usually the reference Treasury that is used for pricing.[5] The required par amount of the hedge instrument is determined by the hedge ratio, as given in equation (11). Exhibit 8 illustrates the process of building a hedge for the callable FNMA note described in Exhibit 3 and compares the effectiveness of an option adjusted hedge to a constant-spread hedge. A constant-spread hedge is the hedge that is constructed if an option embedded bond is treated as if it were a similar-maturity bullet bond and does not take into account the yield-spread changes that accompany interest-rate movements. A constant-spread hedge is computed as described in equation (3).

In Exhibit 8, the option adjusted hedge is the most effective hedge. This hedge reduces the price volatility over a 50-basis-point range in rates from over $27,000 for the unhedged portfolio to less than $725. The option adjusted hedge is also more effective than the constant-spread hedge, which sustains price movements of over $6,000 for a 50-basis-point shift in rates. The constant-spread hedge actually over hedges the callable bond position. Recall that when rates rally, callable spreads widen, which dampens any price appreciation on a callable bond. Similarly, when rates rise, spreads tighten, which limits the price depreciation of a callable bond. As a result, a callable bond's price is less volatile than the price on a similar-maturity bullet for similar interest rate moves. To account for this type of price sensitivity, the effective hedge ratio for a callable bond should be less than that for a bullet. The option adjusted hedge in Example 7 is more effective than the constant-spread hedge because it explicitly takes into account the effects of spread widening and tightening.

Mortgage Pass-Through Securities

A mortgage pass-through security represents a share in the cash flows from a pool of mortgages. Essentially, a pass-through security is a portfolio of bonds in which each bond has a call option embedded in its structure. Each call option represents the right of a mortgagor to prepay their individual mortgage in the mortgage pool.

The embedded options in mortgage pass-throughs are similar to those of currently callable corporate bonds, and both options are affected by interest rates in a similar fashion. Yield spreads on pass-throughs generally widen when interest rates fall and generally tighten as interest rates rise. The amount of spread change, however, is not as pronounced in mortgage pass-throughs because the prepayment option (held by homeowners) is typically not as rationally exercised as a call option held by a corporation.

---

[4] As an alternative to an option-model determined hedge ratio (also know as a theoretical hedge ratio), the hedge ratio also can be determined empirically. Empirical hedge ratios typically are determined by regressing recent price changes on the security to be hedged on price changes on the hedging instruments.

[5] An alternate hedging instrument is the Treasury instrument that has the same maturity as the effective maturity of the security to be hedged. Although this hedging instrument would have the appropriate price sensitivity to interest rates, the hedged portfolio will face the risk that yield movements between the two securities may be nonsynchronous and in differing magnitudes.

Exhibit 8: Hedging a Callable Bond

Objective: Hedge $1 million par amount FNMA 7.33s of 4/2/07, callable at par from 4/2/02, trading at +62 basis points to the 10-year Treasury note.

Issue	Coupon (%)	Maturity	Call Date	Call Price	Price (32nds)	YTM (%)	YTM Spread (BPs)	OAS (BPs)	DVBP (Per $1 MM Par Amount)
FNMA	7.33	4/2/07	4/2/02	100	99-20	7.38	+62 BPs	16	556.00*
10-Year Treasury Note	6.25	2/15/07	—	—	96-12	6.76		0	692.06

Determining the Hedge Ratios

Two different hedges are examined; Hedge Ratio 1 is a constant-OAS hedge and Hedge Ratio 2 is a constant-spread hedge that assumes that the FNMA callable bond reacts like a similar-maturity bullet bond with a DVBP = 693.29.

$$\text{Hedge Ratio 1 (Option Adjusted)} \quad \text{Hedge Ratio} = \frac{\text{Option adjusted DVBP of FNMA}}{\text{DVBP of 10-Year Treasury}} = \frac{556.00}{692.06} = 0.803$$

$$\text{Hedge Ratio 2 (Constant Spread)} \quad \text{Hedge Ratio} = \frac{\text{DVBP of FNMA Bullet}}{\text{DVBP of 10-Year Treasury}} = \frac{693.29}{692.06} = 1.002$$

Explanation: To hedge $1 million par amount FNMA bonds, $803,000 par amount of 10-year Treasury notes need to be shorted utilizing a constant-OAS hedge, and $1,002,000 par amount of 10-year Treasuries need to be shorted utilizing a constant-spread hedge.

Change in Portfolio Value**

The change in portfolio value for parallel and non-parallel shifts of the yield curve. The effect of carry is not included.

	Rates Rise 50 Basis Points	Rates Fall 50 Basis Points
Unhedged Position	= 968,438–996,250	=1,024,219–996,250
	= –27,812	=27,969
Hedge 1	=(968,438–996,250)	=(1,024,219–996,250)
(option adjusted)	–0.803×(930,000–963,750)	–0.803×(999,063–963,750)
	= –711	= –387
Hedge 2	=(968,438–996,250)	=(1,024,219–996,250)
(constant spread)	–1.002×(930,000–963,750)	–1.002×(999,063–963,750)
	=6,006	= –7,415

* See Exhibit 3.
** Change in unhedged portfolio value = Change in FNMA position
Change in hedged portfolio value = Change in FNMA position – Change in Treasury position
*** Price data as of 4/29/97.

Hedging a mortgage pass-through security is similar to hedging other option embedded bonds, such as a corporate callable bond, which was just discussed. Since yield spreads on pass-throughs change as interest rates change, an option adjusted approach can be used and a hedge ratio can be computed using an option-adjusted DVBP, as in equation (11). DVBP again is computed using constant-OAS prices for different interest-rate scenarios.

Since a pass-through security's cash flows are a function of the prepayment levels that will occur in different interest-rate scenarios, proper valuation under different interest-rate environments requires the use of a general prepayment model in conjunction with a general stochastic valuation model. The effectiveness of a hedge will critically depend on how accurate these models are in forecasting prices in different rate environments.

The choice of a hedging instrument for a mortgage pass-through generally should be the reference Treasury that is used for pricing. As with corporate option embedded securities, a mortgage pass-through security can be hedged by using a portfolio of two Treasuries that, in combination, have the same DVBP as the mortgage pass-through. The mechanics of hedging with a combination of instruments is the same as discussed earlier. Since most mortgage pass-throughs are priced to their average lives, the on-the-run Treasury that is nearest to the average life of the pass-through is typically used for hedging. Exhibit 9 outlines a strategy for hedging FHLMC Gold 7.5s using the 10-year on-the-run Treasury.

As Exhibit 9 illustrates, an option adjusted hedge provides price protection from interest-rate risk for FHLMC 7.5% pass-through securities under the constant-OAS pricing assumption. The unhedged portfolio fluctuates between a gain of $20,000 and a loss of $23,000 for a 50-basis-point change in rates. In contrast, the hedged portfolio fluctuates a maximum of only $2,200. Although the hedge is effective in providing price protection, it is not as effective as the hedges in previous examples. This is mainly because the hedge is constructed for a 25-basis-point change in interest rates, whereas the hedge is evaluated for a 50-basis-point change in interest rates, which implies different prepayment rates and hence, different pricing yield spreads. These different movements have not been anticipated in the hedge ratio, resulting in the hedged portfolio showing higher price variation than in the earlier examples.

Hedging Considerations for Option Embedded Notes

In general, for any option embedded security, including corporate callable notes and mortgage pass-through securities, the hedge ratio will change as interest rates change. For example, as the market rallies and continues to rally, callable spreads will continue widening and the hedge ratio for a callable note will decline. If rates rise, then the hedge ratio will increase.

The hedge ratio using Treasury notes is not static because callable notes are negatively convex instruments, while Treasuries are positively convex instruments. As rates rally, Treasury prices rise at a faster rate than callable bond prices and, consequently, the position in the hedge instrument needs to be reduced. For example, if rates rally 25 basis points, the hedge needs to be reduced by buying back some of the short position in the hedging instrument. If this adjustment is not made, then the hedge will not provide absolute price protection and, in fact, may over or under hedge a position.

Exhibit 9: Hedging a Mortgage-Backed Pass-Through Security

Objective: Hedge $1 million par amount FHLMC Gold 7.50s.

Issue	Coupon (%)	Average Life/ Maturity (Yrs.)	Price* (32nds)	Yield (%)	OAS (BPs)	PSA (%)	DVBP (Per $1 MM Par Amount)
FHLMC Gold 7.50s	7.50	8.9	99-16	7.66	58	160	see below
10-Year Treasury Note	6.25	2/15/07	97-02	6.66	0	—	697.38

Option Adjusted DVBP Computation for FHLMC Gold 7.50s

	Constant OAS Price (BPs)	
Issue	25 Basis Point Rate Rise	25 Basis Point Rate Fall
FHLMC 7.50s	98.375	100.563

Option adjusted DVBP

$$= -\frac{\text{Change in constant} - \text{OAS price}}{\text{Yield-curve shift}} \times \frac{\text{Dollar par amount}}{100}$$

$$= \frac{100.563 - 98.375}{50} \times \frac{1,000,000}{100}$$

$$= \$437.60$$

Determining the Hedge Ratio

$$\text{Option adjusted hedge ratio} = \frac{\text{DVBP of FHLMC 7.50s}}{\text{DVBP of 10-Year Treasury}}$$

$$= \frac{437.60}{697.38} = 0.627$$

To hedge a long position of $1 million par amount of FHLMC 7.50% pass-throughs, $627,000 par amount of 10-year Treasury notes need to be shorted.

*Change in Portfolio Value***

A 50 basis point change in interest rates has the following effects on the hedged and unhedged portfolios.

	Rate rise 50 basis points	Rates fall 50 basis points
Unhedged position	=972,031−995,000 =−22,969	=1,015,156−995,000 =20,156
Option Adjusted Hedge Position	=(972,031−995,000) −0.627×(936,563−970,625) =−1,612	=(1,015,156−995,000) −0.627×(1,006,250−970,625) =−2,181

* Price information as of 5/5/97. OAS and constant-OAS prices are computed at 15% volatility.
** Price change for unhedged position = Change in FHLMC position.
Price change for hedged position = Change in FHLMC position − Change in 10-year Treasury position

As an alternative to using only Treasuries to hedge option embedded notes, Treasuries can be used to hedge only the bullet component and options to hedge the option component. This type of hedge will not need to be monitored as frequently and the hedge ratio will be less volatile as like securities are being hedged with like securities. However, for hedging an option embedded security for short time horizons like a week or a month, the use of options in a hedging strategy can be expensive given the reduced liquidity in the options markets. Typically, individual option embedded bonds are hedged using only Treasuries, with the hedge ratio adjusted periodically for interest-rate movements.

A second consideration in the hedging analysis presented herein is the assumption of constant OAS in determining the option adjusted DVBP and associated hedge ratio. The use of a constant-OAS assumption in this chapter was made more for simplicity. OASs are not constant in the marketplace and may change as rates change. For example, in the federal agency debt market, OASs for similar-duration premiums are much wider than for discounts. This market dynamic can be accounted for explicitly in the DVBP approach by using different OASs to compute the scenario prices in equation (2). Also, the use of an empirical hedge ratio, where historical data are used to compute a hedge ratio, implicitly would account for changing OASs in different environments.[6] However, to the extent that history may not be a gauge for the future trading characteristic of a security, an empirical hedge ratio may be less useful.

Another consideration to keep in mind is that any option embedded bond's price is dependent on factors other than just credit risk and changes in the yield of the pricing instrument. These other factors include the shape of the yield curve and volatility. As volatility increases, callable bond spreads widen and put bond spreads tighten, to reflect the higher cost of the embedded option.[7] The hedging analysis we have presented does not hedge this volatility risk. Effectively, the hedging examples for callable notes using Treasuries maintain a short position in volatility. If volatility rises in our examples, callable bond prices would decline with no change in the value of the Treasury positions. If volatility risk is of concern, the use of options is necessary in any hedging strategy. If changes in volatility can be anticipated as interest rates move, then this can be accounted for by under or over utilizing Treasuries in the hedge. In this scenario, the DVBP of a security can again be computed using equation (2), where scenario-based volatility levels are used to compute scenario prices.

The shape of the yield curve is also an important determinant of callable spreads. The hedge ratios described in this chapter are based on parallel interest-rate movements and do not account for the effects of a change in the shape of the curve. Generally, as the curve flattens, callable spreads widen; if the curve steep-

---

[6] See footnote 4.

[7] Callable spreads can widen from three to eight basis points for a 100-basis-point increase in volatility. For more information on the effects of volatility on callable spreads, see Shrikant Ramamurthy, "Federal Agency Debt," *Spread Talk*, Fixed-Income Research, Prudential Securities Incorporated, February 21, 1997.

ens callable spreads tighten.[8] For example, spreads on a 10-year maturity bond callable after three years (10/NC-3Y) will widen if 3-year yields rise and 10-year yields remain unchanged. The 10-year Treasury as a hedging instrument will not provide any price protection when 10/NC-3Y prices fall in this environment.

To hedge yield-curve risk for option embedded securities, it is best to use multiple hedge instruments that reflect all parts of the curve that affect the pricing of the security being hedged. In the case of the 10/NC-3Y, both the 3-year and 10-year Treasury note would be appropriate hedge instruments. The hedge ratio relative to the 3-year part of the curve can be computed by using a DVBP for the 10/NC-3Y that is computed by assuming that only Treasury yields three years and in change, while the rest of the yield curve remains unchanged. Similarly, the hedge ratio relative to the 10-year part of the curve is computed by using the DVBP of the 10/NC-3Y that is computed by assuming that Treasury yields three years and in do not change, while the yields on the longer end of the curve change. This type of a strategy would provide hedge exposure to multiple parts of the curve and will be effective for both parallel and non-parallel yield-curve shifts.

Typically, for individual bond positions, yield-curve risk generally is not accounted for in a hedging strategy. Instead, the pricing benchmark is used as a hedging instrument and the hedge ratio is adjusted to account for a particular view on the future shape of the yield curve. As is the case in hedging spread, OAS or volatility risk using only Treasury securities, this is more art than science. In the final analysis, the DVBP that is used to compute a hedge ratio needs to reflect the anticipated price behavior of a security (incorporating any views on spreads, curve and volatility) and, to that extent, should reflect both theory and market reality. These combined approaches should work together to produce a more effective hedge.

SUMMARY

Controlling the price volatility of a fixed-income security is largely a function of hedging against interest-rate movements. The basic procedure for constructing a hedge starts by correctly identifying the sources of price risk, including the effects of interest-rate movements, shape of the yield curve, volatility, and spread movements. A hedge is constructed by taking an opposite position in a hedge instrument whose price sensitivity is similar to that of the security to be hedged. This chapter focused on using Treasury instruments as hedge vehicles, although other instruments like interest-rate futures and swaps also can be used in similar fashion.

The appropriate position in the hedge instrument is a function of the DVBP of both the security being hedged and the hedge instrument. The DVBP is

---

[8] Callable spreads can widen from two to five basis points for every ten basis points of curve flattening. For more information on the effects of the shape of the curve on callable spreads, see Shrikant Ramamurthy, "Federal Agency Debt," *Spread Talk*, Fixed-Income Research, Prudential Securities Incorporated, March 21, 1997.

effectively an average price change for a one-basis-point change in rates and should incorporate any spread/OAS changes that are anticipated in different rate environments. In the context of the above framework, DVBP is a very flexible tool and can incorporate other factors that may be important in the hedge strategy.

Once a hedge is constructed and implemented, it needs to be monitored over time. The DVBP of a security, the hedge vehicle and the hedge ratio, will change over time and as interest rates change. An effective hedge strategy should reflect this dynamic behavior to the highest extent possible and may need to be adjusted periodically.

Chapter 11

Hedging Fixed-Income Securities with Interest-Rate Swaps

Shrikant Ramamurthy
Senior Vice President
Prudential Securities Incorporated

INTRODUCTION

An interest-rate swap contract is one of the many innovative financial contracts that have been introduced into the marketplace during the last two decades. Since the introduction of the first interest-rate swap in the early 1980s, this market has grown tremendously, with approximately $5 trillion in notional amount outstanding in U.S. dollar interest-rate swaps at the end of the first half of 1996. In size, the U.S. dollar interest-rate swap market is comparable to the U.S. Treasury market, which has a similar amount of securities outstanding. Exhibit 1 shows the enormous growth of the interest-rate swap market in the last decade.

Exhibit 1: Volume and Notional Outstanding of U.S. Dollar Interest Rate Swaps

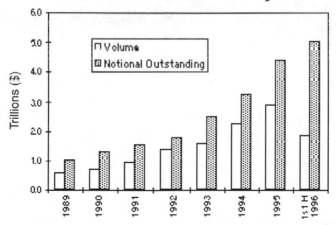

Exhibit 2: Cash-Flow Diagram of a Vanilla Interest-Rate Swap

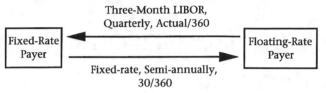

The interest-rate swap market has grown at such a phenomenal pace because swaps can be used in so many different ways by a variety of market participants. The development of the swap market also has been fueled by the growth of the Eurodollar futures market, which has developed into an efficient market for hedging swaps. Today, swaps are used by issuers to match their funding requirements while still tailoring bonds to match investor demand; they are also used by a variety of participants for asset/liability management. They can be a vehicle for speculating on a leveraged basis on interest rates and for hedging interest rate risk.

This chapter focuses on hedging applications and, in particular, how fixed-income securities can be hedged using interest-rate swaps. Although different types of interest-rate swaps exist, including vanilla swaps, basis swaps, indexed-amortizing swaps, and callable swaps, to name a few, this chapter focuses on generic interest-rate swaps as hedge instruments.

The discussion begins with a brief description of the characteristics of interest-rate swaps and how a swap can alternatively be viewed as a leveraged bond position. This alternate view is particularly useful in the hedging context. We then focus on the valuation and interest-rate sensitivity of swaps and go on to develop hedge ratios and hedge strategies using swaps. As we shall illustrate, hedging with swaps is very similar to hedging with Treasuries and interest-rate futures contracts. Several examples of constructing hedges for corporate bonds and mortgage-backed securities are included. We conclude by comparing the effectiveness of interest-rate swaps as hedge instruments with alternate hedge instruments like Treasuries and interest-rate futures.

CHARACTERIZING INTEREST-RATE SWAPS

In its most basic form, an interest-rate swap is an agreement between two parties to exchange cash flows periodically. In a plain-vanilla swap, one party pays a fixed rate of interest based on a notional amount in return for the receipt of a floating rate of interest based on the same notional amount from the counterparty. These cash flows are exchanged periodically for the life (also known as the *tenor*) of the swap. Exhibit 2 shows a pictorial example of an interest-rate swap. Typically, no principal is exchanged at the beginning or end of a swap.

The fixed rate on a swap is ordinarily set at a rate such that the net present value of the swap is zero at the start of the swap contract. This type of swap is also known as a *par swap*, and the fixed rate is also called the *swap rate*. The difference between the swap rate and the yield on an equivalent-maturity Treasury is called the *swap spread*.

The floating rate on a swap is typically benchmarked off London Interbank Offered Rates (LIBOR)[1] or constant-maturity Treasury (CMT) rates. In a plain-vanilla swap, the floating rate is 3-month LIBOR, which resets and pays quarterly in arrears[2] on an actual/360 daycount basis. The fixed-rate is paid semiannually on a 30/360 daycount basis, which is similar to the convention in the corporate bond market.

Interest-rate swaps also can be callable prior to maturity by one of the parties in the swap. These types of swaps are called *callable swaps* and the fixed rate is adjusted to reflect the value of the call option and the nature (long or short) of the option position.

There is no standard convention regarding which party is long or short in a swap agreement. For the purposes of this chapter, we will define the party receiving the fixed-rate payment as having a long swap position.[3] Conversely, we will consider the counterparty who pays the fixed rate and receives the floating rate to be short the swap. This terminology is analogous to that used in the bond market, in which a long bond position commonly implies the receipt of fixed-rate cash flows.

Swaps as Financed Bond Positions

Conceptually, a long position in an interest-rate swap can be viewed as a long fixed-rate bond position that is 100% financed at short-term interest rates, such as term repurchase (repo) rates or LIBOR. In a fully financed long bond position, fixed-rate interest payments are received and floating-rate financing costs are paid periodically, with the final principal payment from the bond used to repay the initial financing of the bond purchase. On a net basis, a fully leveraged bond position has zero cost, like a swap, and the periodic cash flows replicate the cash flows on a swap. In fact, a swap is a fully leveraged bond position where the financing rate is equivalent to the floating rate on a swap. This alternate view of an interest-rate swap is appealing because it implies that a swap can be used as an alternative hedging vehicle to Treasury securities and futures contracts to manage interest-rate risk.

---

[1] LIBOR is the rate that banks offer other banks for term deposits in the Euro-markets and is a common reference rate for floating-rate loans in the international marketplace.

[2] Paid in arrears means that the floating rate for a particular quarter is set at the beginning of the quarter and the associated cash flow is exchanged at the end of the quarter.

[3] The International Swap and Derivatives Association (ISDA) does not define a long swap position or a short swap position. Instead, the ISDA defines the fixed-rate payer and the floating-rate payer in a swap. See *1991 ISDA Definitions*, International Swap and Derivatives Association, Inc., 1991.

PRICING OF INTEREST-RATE SWAPS

The pricing of a swap requires the same financial tools that are used in the pricing of debt instruments. Essentially, the value of a generic swap is the present value of a series of uncertain net cash flows that are dependent on interest rates. In a generic interest-rate swap, the cash flows on the fixed component are known at the inception of the swap. However, the future cash flows on the floating component are unknown.

The future floating rates for purposes of valuing a swap are derived from forward rates that are embedded in the current yield curve. For floating rates based off of LIBOR benchmarks, forward rates also can be determined from the various Eurodollar futures contracts. Eurodollar futures contracts trade with four maturities each year for approximately ten years and each contract is settled into the 3-month spot LIBOR rate at the maturity of the contract.[4] Although forward rates may or may not be good predictors of future rates,[5] forward rates can be realized in future time periods via simple hedging strategies. As a result, the uncertainty associated with floating-rate cash flows in a swap can be addressed and hedged.

By utilizing forward rates, a swap net cash flow can be derived throughout the life of a swap. The sum of these cash flows discounted at the corresponding forward rate for each time period is the current value of the swap. Mathematically, the value of a long swap position is:

$$\text{Swap} = \sum_{i=1}^{n} PV_i[\text{Fixed cash flow}(i) - \text{Floating cash flow}(i)] \tag{1}$$

The discount rates used to value the future cash flows from a swap are typically forward LIBOR rates irrespective of the counterparties involved. The counterparty risk in a swap is usually accounted for through collateral arrangements that guarantee future net cash flows, and these collateral amounts vary depending on each counterparty's credit risk. As a result, swap rates are generic and do not vary between differently rated counterparties.

Equation (1) also can be used to determine swap rates. Recall that the swap rate is the fixed rate on a par swap. Fair swap rates for specific maturities can be computed by finding the fixed rate in equation (1) that provides a swap value of zero. Exhibit 3 illustrates the cash flows for a hypothetical 2-year swap and utilizes equation (1) to determine the value of the swap. At a fixed rate of 6.225%, the swap has zero value and is a fair swap.

---

[4] For more information on Eurodollar futures contracts and their role in determining forward rates and synthetic swap rates, see David Audley, Richard Chin, and Shrikant Ramamurthy, *The Interest Rate Swap Market: Valuation, Applications and Perspectives*, April 1994, Prudential Securities Incorporated.

[5] If there is a liquidity premium associated with interest rates of different maturities, forward rates are not the market's current expectation of future spot rates.

Exhibit 3: Pricing of a 2-Year Interest-Rate Swap

Maturity	2 Years			
Fixed Rate	6.225%, Semiannually, 30/360			
Floating Rate	3-Mo. LIBOR, Quarterly, 30/360			
Notional Amount	$100			

Time (Yrs.)	Implied 3-Mo. LIBOR (%)	Cash Flows ($) Fixed	Cash Flows ($) Floating	Net Cash Flows ($)	Present Value of $1 ($)	Present Value of Net Cash Flows ($)
0.00	5.750				1.0000	0.0000
0.25	5.875	0.0000	1.4375	−1.4375	0.9858	−1.4171
0.50	6.000	3.1125	1.4688	1.6438	0.9716	1.5970
0.75	6.125	0.0000	1.5000	−1.5000	0.9572	−1.4358
1.00	6.250	3.1125	1.5313	1.5813	0.9428	1.4907
1.25	6.375	0.0000	1.5625	−1.5625	0.9283	−1.4504
1.50	6.500	3.1125	1.5938	1.5188	0.9137	1.3877
1.75	6.625	0.0000	1.6250	−1.6250	0.8991	−1.4610
2.00	6.750	3.1125	1.6563	1.4563	0.8844	1.2880
					Value of Swap (Equation 1) = 0.00	

Note: Typically, the following rate on a swap is paid on an Actual/360 day-count basis. In this exhibit, the floating rate is assumed to be paid on a 30/360 day-count basis for convenience

---

The value of a swap can be computed alternatively by viewing the swap as an equivalent bond portfolio as discussed earlier. In this approach, the value of a swap is simply the difference between the value of a fixed-rate bond with a coupon equal to the fixed rate on the swap and a floating-rate bond that pays a coupon equal to the floating rate on the swap. Again the bonds and each of their cash flows are priced against LIBOR discount rates in keeping with the convention of the swap market. In this approach, the value of the swap is given mathematically by:

Swap = Fixed-rate bond − Floating-rate bond   (2)

In a plain-vanilla swap, the value of the floating rate bond on each reset is equal to par. This is because, going forward from each reset date, the interest cash flows on the floating-rate bond are equal to LIBOR rates and the discount rates used to present value future interest and principal cash flows are also LIBOR rates. Essentially, going forward from each reset date, the floating-rate note provides a coupon equal to what is expected by the marketplace. As a result, by definition, on these dates the value of the floating-rate bond should be equal to par. Incorporating this into equation (2), we can restate the value of a generic swap on a reset date to be equal to:

Swap on reset date = Value of fixed-rate bond − 100   (3)

Any of these equations (1, 2, or 3) can be used to value a swap. Typically, on a reset date, it is easier to value a swap using equation (3) given that forward floating-rate coupons need not be determined. Between reset dates, equation (2) can be a simple way to value a swap given that the value of the floating-rate component can be estimated as a fixed-rate bond that matures at par on the next reset date. In this approach also, forward floating-rate coupons do not have to be determined.

Interest-Rate Sensitivity of a Swap

Although the value of a swap is a function of both long- and short-bond positions, it is still very sensitive to interest rates. Exhibit 4 shows the price profile of a currently par-priced swap to changes in interest rates. The swap in Exhibit 4 is the same as the swap in Exhibit 3. For comparison purposes, the values of the fixed-rate and floating-rate bonds that make up the equivalent portfolio are shown as well.

The swap currently has no value and both the fixed- and floating-rate bonds are priced at par. As rates decline, the value of the swap increases as the fixed-rate cash-flow receipts become more valuable in the lower-rate environment. The value of the swap does not increase as much as that of the fixed-rate bond because the increase in the value of the swap in declining-rate scenarios is constrained by the increase in the value of the floating-rate bond. However, given that the increase in the floating-rate bond is minimal, the change in the value of the swap is similar to the change in the value of the fixed-rate bond. In environments where rates rise, the value to the swap falls like that of the fixed-rate bond; however, the decline in value is slightly reduced by the short floating-rate position.

Exhibit 4: Price Sensitivity of a 2-Year Interest Rate Swap

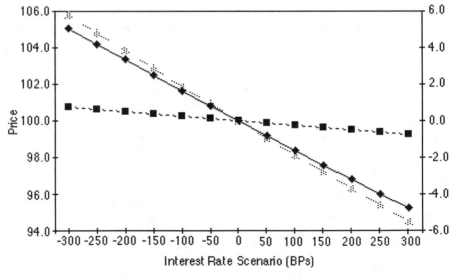

Note: The pricing on the floating-rated bond assumes that the coupon for the first period has already been set.

Like a fixed-rate bond, an interest-rate swap displays positive convexity, which means that the increase in the value of a swap for a decline in rates is larger than the loss associated with a similar increase in rates. The similar price profile between a fixed-rate bond and a swap is important to note because it is this similarity that makes swaps an efficient and alternate hedge instrument for fixed-income securities.

DVBP of a Swap

The *dollar value of a basis point* (DVBP) of a swap measures the dollar sensitivity of a swap for changes in interest rates. The DVBP of a swap is the change in the value of a swap for a 1-basis-point change in rates. In the hedging context, DVBP is the key measure in developing a hedge ratio when using interest-rate swaps.[6] Mathematically, the DVBP is defined as:

$$\text{DVBP (Swap)} = \frac{d\text{Swap}}{dr} = \frac{\text{Change in swap value}}{\text{Rate change in basis points}} \qquad (4)$$

Alternatively, the DVBP of a swap can be computed using equation (2) as follows:

$$\text{DVBP (Swap)} = \frac{d(\text{Change in fixed-rate bond value})}{dr}$$

$$- \frac{d(\text{Change in floating-rate bond value})}{dr}$$

$$= \text{DVBP(Fixed-rate bond)} - \text{DVBP(Floating-rate bond)} \qquad (5)$$

The DVBP using either equation (4) or equation (5) is usually computed on a notional amount of $1 million. Implicitly, the DVBP computation assumes that rate movements are parallel, with the entire yield curve shifting in equal fashion. Typically, DVBP is computed using increments of 10 to 25 basis points. Since DVBP is computed using scenarios where rates rise and fall, the DVBP computation is an average sensitivity measure and will not measure exactly the sensitivity in either scenario.

Exhibit 5 shows the DVBP computation for the 2-year swap example used in Exhibits 3 and 4. The DVBP of the swap is $160.71 — slightly less than the DVBP of a 2-year fixed-rate bond at $185.36. The DVBP of a swap is slightly less than that of a fixed-rate bond to account for the short position in the floater, which has a DVBP of $24.65. Either equation (4) or equation (5) provides the same DVBP for a swap, as it should by definition.

In general, the DVBP of a swap is approximately equal to the DVBP of a fixed-rate bond with maturity spanning from the next reset date to the maturity date of the swap. The DVBP of a 5-year swap is similar to the DVBP of a 4.75-year fixed-rate bond; the DVBP of a 2.25-year swap is similar to the DVBP of a 2-year fixed-rate bond.

---

[6] For more information on the DVBP approach to hedging fixed-income securities, see Chapter 10.

Exhibit 5: DVBP Computation for a Swap

Maturity	2 Years
Fixed Rate	6.225%, Semiannually, 30/360
Floating Rate	3-Month LIBOR, Quarterly, 30/360
Notional Amount	$1 Million

	Total Value ($)		
	Rates Down 10 BPs	No Change	Rates Up 10 BPs
Swap	1,609.25	0.00	−1,604.95
Fixed-Rate Bond	1,001,855.77	1,000,000	998,148.65
Floating-Rate Bond	1,000,246.52	1,000,000	999,753.60

DVBP Computation Using Equation (4)

$$\text{DVBP}_{SWAP} = \frac{\text{Change in Swap Value}}{\text{Change in Rates}} = \frac{1,609.25 - (-1,604.95)}{20} = \$160.71$$

DVBP Computation Using Equation (5)

$$\text{DVBP}_{SWAP} = \text{DVBP}(\text{Fixed-Rate Bond}) - \text{DVBP}(\text{Floating-Rate Bond})$$

$$= \frac{1,001,855.77 - 998,148.65}{20} - \frac{1,000,246.52 - 999,753.60}{20}$$

$$= 185.36 - 24.65$$

$$= \$160.71$$

Although the DVBP of a swap is similar to that of a slightly shorter fixed-rate bond, the DVBP of a swap will change differently over time from the DVBP on a fixed-rate bond. This is important to note in the hedging context. The DVBP of a swap just prior to a reset date will be identical to the DVBP of a fixed-rate bond because, at this time, the DVBP of the floater is zero. However, just after the reset date, the floater will have a DVBP that is similar to the DVBP of a fixed-rate bond to the next reset date. As a result, just after the reset date, the DVBP on a swap will immediately decline by the DVBP of the floater. Between reset periods, the DVBP of the swap will not change much as both the DVBP of the fixed-rate bond and the floater will decline in similar fashion. This is very different from the DVBP of a fixed-rate bond that declines steadily over time.

Exhibit 6 graphically displays, over time, the DVBP for the swap and fixed-rate bond used in Exhibits 3 through 5. As the exhibits illustrate, the DVBP of the fixed-rate bond declines as a function of time, while the DVBP of the swap declines in a jump fashion around the reset date of the floating rate on the swap. The DVBP is relatively stable between reset dates and actually increases incrementally as the next reset date approaches. The DVBP of a swap actually increases slightly between reset dates because the DVBP of a floating-rate note declines slightly faster than the DVBP of a fixed-rate note during these time periods.[7]

HEDGING WITH INTEREST-RATE SWAPS

Hedging fixed-income securities with interest-rates swaps is similar to hedging securities with Treasury notes or futures contracts. To hedge a long position in a fixed-income security, the hedger needs to establish a short-swap position since changes in the value of a swap are inversely related to changes in the value of the security being hedged. Recall that in a short-swap position, which is analogous to a short-bond position, the hedger pays a fixed rate to receive a floating rate. In designing a hedge using interest-rate swaps, the maturity of the interest-rate swap should match the maturity of the instrument that is used as the pricing reference for the security being hedged. This is analogous to hedging in the Treasury market.

Exhibit 6: DVBP of a 2-Year Swap and Fixed-Rate Bond over Time

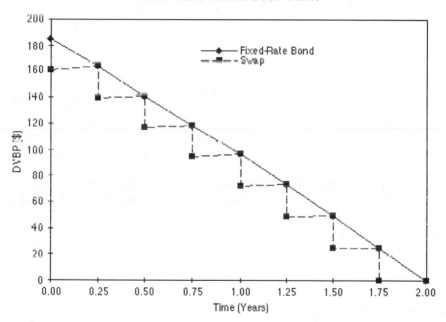

[7] The modified duration and DVBP of a bond is a concave monotonic function of maturity, i.e., the duration and DVBP increase at a decreasing rate as a function of maturity. As a result, the DVBP of a floating-rate bond, which essentially behaves like a short dated fixed-rate bond, decreases faster over time than the DVBP of a long dated fixed-rate bond.

For example, if a 2-year corporate bond is priced relative to the 2-year Treasury, the corporate bond's price changes as yield spreads change and as the yield on the 2-year Treasury changes. The appropriate swap hedge for this corporate bond is a 2-year swap since it is also priced relative to the 2-year Treasury. A 2-year swap's value changes as swap spreads change and as the 2-year Treasury's yield changes. As a result of using a 2-year swap to hedge the corporate bond, the interest-rate risk of the 2-year corporate bond that is attributable to movements in 2-year Treasury yields can be mitigated. To the extent that the 2-year corporate bond's yield spread is correlated to 2-year swap spreads, spread risk also may be mitigated.

Hedge Ratio

The hedge ratio for hedging a fixed-income instrument using interest-rate swaps is a function of the DVBPs of the swap and the security to be hedged, and is expressed as:

$$\text{Hedge ratio} = \frac{\text{DVBP of security to be hedged}}{\text{DVBP of swap}} \qquad (6)$$

Recall that the DVBP of an interest-rate swap is similar to that of a fixed-rate bond with a maturity from the swap's next reset date to the swap's maturity date. Thus the hedge ratio using interest-rate swaps generally will be slightly higher than the hedge ratio using Treasuries.

Corporate Bond Hedge

Exhibit 7 describes a hedge for a long position in TCI Corporation 9.25s of 4/15/02. Since the TCI notes are priced off 5-year Treasury rates, the appropriate hedge instrument using swaps is a 5-year interest-rate swap, which is similarly affected by movements in 5-year yields. The hedge ratio using swaps is 1.061, implying that approximately $1.061 million notional amount of 5-year swaps need to be sold in order to hedge $1 million TCI corporate notes. If 5-year Treasuries are used as a substitute, the hedge ratio will be slightly smaller because the 5-year Treasury has a higher DVBP.

If the TCI position is not hedged, the portfolio can gain or lose approximately $21,000 if rates move 50 basis points. In contrast, the hedged portfolio provides substantial protection against interest-rate movements. If rates move 50 basis points, the hedged portfolio moves minimally in value. This analysis assumes that yield spreads are unchanged and does not account for any bid/offer spread in the markets. If spread changes on the corporate bond position are accompanied by similar spread changes on the 5-year swap, the swap hedge will also eliminate spread risk. If corporate spreads are negatively correlated with swap spreads, then a swap based hedge will increase the exposure to spread risk. Generally though, swap spreads move in the same direction as corporate spreads and provide protection against general movements in corporate spreads. Of course, given the generic nature of swap spreads, they will never provide protection against the idiosyncratic risk of any particular corporate credit.

Exhibit 7: Hedging a Corporate Bullet Bond Using Interest-Rate Swaps

Objective: Hedge $1 million par amount TCI Corp 9.25s of 4/15/02 using 5-year interest-rate swaps.

Issue	Coupon/Swap Rate (%)	Maturity	Price*	Yield (%)	Spread (BPs)	DVBP per $1 million par amount ($)
TCI Corp	9.25	04/15/02	107.915	7.27	+100	420.27
5-Year Swap	6.53	06/19/02	0.000	—	+26	396.20

$$\text{Hedge Ratio} = \frac{420.27}{396.20} = 1.061$$

Change in Portfolio Value*

	Unhedged Portfolio	Hedged Portfolio
Rates increase by 50 Basis Points	=1,058,390–1,079,150 =−20,760	=(1,058,390–1,079,150) −1.061(−19,550) = 17.45
Rates decrease by 50 Basis Points	=1,100,420–1,079,150 =21,270	=(1,100,420–1,079,150) −1.061(20,080) =−34.88

* Prices as of June 16, 1997.

One point to note when using swaps as a hedge instrument is that the DVBP of a swap declines on a reset date (see Exhibit 6). This implies that on swap reset dates, the existing swap position may need to be adjusted by shorting additional swaps with the same remaining term-to-maturity to match the DVBP of the security being hedged.

Mortgage-Backed Security Hedge

Exhibit 8 illustrates the mechanics of using 5-year interest-rate swaps to hedge $1 million par amount of 15-year FNMA 7.50% pass-throughs. The FNMA 7.50s have an average life of 5.5 years and are priced relative to the 5-year Treasury note. The DVBP of the pass-through is $289.07 and is computed using a constant option adjusted spread (constant OAS) methodology, which accounts for the changing yield spread on the pass-through security as interest rates change. The hedge ratio using equation (6) is 0.73, which implies that $730,000 notional amount of 5-year swaps are required to hedge $1 million of 15-year FNMA 7.50s.

As Exhibit 8 shows, the interest-rate swap provides some price protection as rates change, but the hedge is not as effective as the corporate bond hedge discussed earlier. If the FNMA 7.50s are not hedged, the position can decline in value by approximately $16,000 if rates rise by 50 basis points or increase in value by $12,000 if rates rally by 50 basis points. The interest-rate swap provides some price protection and caps losses on the hedged portfolio to approximately $2,000 if rates change by 50 basis points.

Exhibit 8: Hedging a Mortgage Pass-Through Security Using Interest-Rate Swaps

Objective: Hedge $1 million par amount FNMA Dwarf 7.50s using 5-year interest-rate swaps.

Issue	Coupon/Swap Rate (%)	Average Life/ Maturity (Yrs.)	Price*	Yield (%)	Spread (BPs)	DVBP per $1 million par amount ($)
FNMA Dwarf	7.50	5.5	101-20	7.10	+83	289.07
5-Year Swap	6.53	5.0	0.000	—	+26	396.20

$$\text{Hedge Ratio} = \frac{289.07}{396.20} = 0.730$$

Change in Portfolio Value*

	Unhedged Portfolio	Hedged Portfolio
Rates increase by 50 Basis Points	=1,000,156–1,016,250 =–16,094	=(1,000,156–1,016,250) –0.73(–19,550) =–1,822.50
Rates decrease by 50 Basis Points	=1,028,438–1,016,250 =12,188	=(1,028,438–1,016,250) –0.73(20,080) =–2,470.40

* Prices as of June 16, 1997.

The interest-rate swap hedge is not as effective for mortgages as it is for corporate bullet bonds because of the embedded optionality in mortgages. A mortgage pass-through security consists of a series of underlying mortgages that can be prepaid or called at par prior to maturity. Essentially in a pass-through, like in other callable structures, the investor is short a call option. This creates an asymmetric payoff profile for the pass-through. As rates rally, the likelihood of increased prepayments at par increases, which limits the price appreciation potential of the pass-through once it starts trading above par. The price appreciation potential is much smaller than the price depreciation potential for the same magnitude change in rates. This phenomenon can be seen in Exhibit 8 by examining the changes in the unhedged portfolio's value.

Since the DVBP of the mortgage pass-through is based on an average price change, the DVBP never exactly captures the change in value in any particular scenario. As a result, the hedge ratio is not sufficiently large when rates rise and prices fall, and the hedge ratio is too large when rates fall and prices rise. By hedging to an average DVBP, the hedge strategy will provide ample price protection, but will never provide complete protection in any scenario.[8]

---

[8] This is true even if Treasuries are used as hedge instruments.

The hedge in Exhibit 8 can be improved upon by dynamically adjusting the hedge ratio as rates move. The analysis in Exhibit 8 assumes that the hedge is static and is maintained for a 50-basis-point move in rates. Typically, when hedging option embedded bonds, the hedge ratio should be constantly monitored and adjusted to account for the changing value of the option. As rates rally, the DVBP and hedge ratio of a callable security decline, which implies that the hedge should be reduced by buying back some of the short hedge position. If rates rise, the DVBP and hedge ratio increase, which implies that the hedge should be increased by selling more swaps. This type of dynamic adjustment will improve the efficiency of the hedge strategy. Of course, there may be costs associated with this improvement in efficiency.

An alternative way to hedge callable securities is to use callable swaps as hedge instruments. A *callable swap* is a swap in which one party has the right to terminate the swap prior to maturity. Since a callable swap has an embedded long position in a call option, this may be a more natural and efficient way to hedge a callable instrument that has an embedded short call option position. Essentially, the option position embedded in the swap will hedge the option position in the security being hedged. A callable swap is particularly useful when dynamic hedging is not cost efficient and a static hedge is desired. Callable swaps are not as liquid and the bid/offer cost to terminate these types of swaps can be high. As a result, callable swaps should be utilized only when a hedge will be maintained for a long period of time.

Swaps Versus Other Hedge Instruments

Fixed-income securities usually are hedged in the cash market using Treasuries or in the futures markets with interest-rate futures. The Treasury market can provide effective and similar protection as interest-rate swaps when hedging against interest-rate risk. The advantage of the Treasury market is that it is a highly liquid market with very small bid/offer costs, especially in on-the-run maturities. It is also easy to enter into and liquidate Treasury positions quickly and efficiently. In contrast, interest-rate swaps, although liquid, have higher bid/offer costs (typically one to two points in yield) and are more time consuming to enter and exit. Since swaps are customized contracts between two parties and are not exchange traded, they cannot be sold and actually have to be terminated, which is time consuming and can be less efficient. Alternatively, a swap position can be effectively terminated by entering into an opposite position in another interest-rate swap; however, this strategy also can be expensive. For short-term hedging purposes, Treasuries may be more desirable hedge instruments.

Many times in the hedging context, however, hedging in the Treasury market may be expensive. This may happen if the hedge instrument is a Treasury that is on "special" or if an off-the-run Treasury needs to be utilized in the hedge. In these cases, the cost of establishing a position in Treasuries may be expensive because of low reverse-repo rates or wide bid/ask spreads. Interest-rate swaps can be cheaper alternatives in these cases. Swaps can be structured for any off-the-run maturity and supply is never an issue given the liquidity in the Eurodollar market, especially five years and in.

Swaps have other advantages over Treasury securities. Swaps are off-balance-sheet instruments, unlike Treasury securities, and therefore should not affect the capital structure. In addition, to the extent that swap spreads are correlated with the spread/OAS of the security being hedged, an interest-rate swap will provide some protection against spread risk, unlike both Treasuries and futures contracts. Another advantage of an interest-rate swap is that, because it is a structured agreement, call options and amortization can be embedded into a swap. This is particularly useful when hedging amortizing and/or callable securities.

The behavior of the DVBP of a swap can be both an advantage and disadvantage versus other hedge instruments. Recall that the DVBP of a swap is fairly constant between the reset dates of the swap. This is unlike a Treasury security whose DVBP declines continuously over time. Thus, when hedging a constant-duration portfolio (e.g., an indexed bond portfolio or the bond portfolio of a dealer), an interest-rate swap is an attractive hedging instrument as the hedge ratio does not change as a function of time between reset dates.

In comparing futures contracts with swaps, futures do not have any liquidity constraints. However, the use of futures in the hedging context exposes the hedged portfolio to basis risk. Basis risk refers to the scenario in which movements in futures prices do not exactly correspond to movements in cash Treasury prices. A futures contract's price movements generally are related to price movements in the Treasury security that is the cheapest to deliver into the futures contract, which typically is not an on-the-run Treasury. Thus, when hedging a security that is priced relative to an on-the-run Treasury with a futures contract, there is the risk that movements in futures prices will not fully hedge price movements in the asset. An interest-rate swap does not have the basis risk that is inherent in a futures contract since on-the-run swaps are priced relative to on-the-run Treasuries. From a basis risk standpoint, interest-rate swaps are better hedging instruments than futures contracts.

CONCLUSION

The interest-rate swap market has grown at a rapid pace in the 1990s and today it is one of the largest markets in the fixed-income marketplace. An interest-rate swap, when broken into its individual components, can be shown to be equivalent to a 100% financed fixed-rate bond position. Given this view, swaps can be utilized like other fixed-income securities and have hedging applications. This chapter has discussed the use of interest-rate swaps to hedge fixed-income securities. Interest-rate swaps are similar to Treasuries as hedge instruments, although the DVBP of a swap can differ over time from the DVBP of a similar-maturity Treasury.

Like Treasury and futures contracts, interest-rate swaps can be used effectively to manage the interest-rate risk in bullet bonds. Unlike Treasury securities, swaps are off-balance-sheet agreements and, to the extent that fixed-income spreads are correlated to swap spreads, they can also provide protection from spread risk. For callable securities, swaps also can be used either by utilizing a dynamic hedge strategy or by embedding options in a swap. Given that swaps are customized agreements, they offer tremendous flexibility as hedge instruments. Interest-rate swaps are most appropriate for hedging portfolios rather than individual bond positions, especially if the hedge will be maintained for an intermediate or extensive period of time.

Chapter 12

Hedging Mortgage Passthrough Securities

Kenneth B. Dunn, Ph.D.
Portfolio Manager
Miller Anderson & Sherrerd, LLP

Roberto M. Sella
Portfolio Manager
Miller Anderson & Sherrerd, LLP

INTRODUCTION

With the exception of the Treasury market, the mortgage passthrough market is the most liquid bond market in the United States. Mortgage-backed securities (MBSs) make up about 30% of broad bond-market indices. Because mortgage securities often outperform government securities *with the same interest-rate risk,* they can be used to generate excess returns in client portfolios when the yield advantage of mortgages is attractive.

To execute this strategy successfully, the prepayment risk of mortgages must be managed carefully; when interest rates decline, most homeowners exer-cise their option to prepay their mortgages,[1] and, as a result, the duration of a mortgage portfolio (its price sensitivity to changes in interest rates) decreases. In other words, when interest rates decline, prepayments cause the value of a mort-gage portfolio to increase less than that of a Treasury portfolio with the same ini-tial duration. For this reason, many consider mortgages to be market-directional investments that should be avoided when one expects interest rates to decline. This perception is exacerbated by the common practice of comparing the returns of the mortgage index with the returns of the government and corporate indices *without adjusting for differences in duration.* Because the mortgage index typically has less duration than either the corporate or government index, it generally has better relative performance when interest rates rise than when interest rates fall.

We do not believe that mortgages, when properly managed, are market-directional investments. Proper management begins with separating mortgage valua-

---

[1] One can think of holding a mortgage passthrough security as equivalent to owning a fixed-rate bond and selling a prepayment option to the homeowner.

tion decisions from decisions concerning the appropriate interest-rate sensitivity of the portfolio. In turn, this separation of the value decision from the duration decision hinges critically on proper hedging. Without proper hedging to offset the changes in mortgage durations caused by interest rate movements, the portfolio's duration would drift adversely from its target. In other words, the portfolio would be shorter than desired when interest rates decline and longer than desired when interest rates rise.

Proper hedging requires understanding the principal risks of MBSs. In the next section, we provide a brief description of these risks. We then review how interest rates change over time, explain why our proprietary calculation of interest-rate risk is a better measure than duration for hedging mortgages, and describe our method of hedging mortgages with Treasuries and options. We conclude by showing how our hedging method is applied to a current-coupon mortgage and a "cuspy"-coupon mortgage.

MORTGAGE SECURITY RISKS

There are five principal risks in mortgage securities: spread, interest-rate, prepayment, volatility, and model risk. The yield of a mortgage security — the cumulative reward for bearing all five of these risks — has two components: the yield on equal interest-rate risk Treasury securities plus a spread. This spread is itself the sum of the option cost, which is the expected cost of bearing prepayment risk, and the option-adjusted spread (OAS), which is the risk premium for bearing the remaining risks, including model risk.

Spread Risk

We invest in mortgage securities when their spreads versus Treasuries are large enough to compensate for the risk surrounding the homeowner's prepayment option. Because the OAS can be thought of as the risk premium for holding mortgages, we do not hedge this risk. If we hedge against spread widening, we also give up the benefit from spread narrowing. Instead, we seek to capture the OAS over time, increasing the allocation to mortgages when yield spreads are wide and reducing these investments when yield spreads are narrow.

To calculate the OAS for any mortgage security, we use a prepayment model that assigns an expected prepayment rate every month — implying an expected cash flow — for a given interest-rate path. We then discount these expected cash flows at U.S. Treasury rates to obtain their present value. This process is repeated for a large number of interest-rate paths. Finally, we calculate the average present value of the cash flows across all paths. Typically, the average present value across all paths is not equal to the price of the security. However, we can search for a unique "spread" (in basis points) that, when added to the U.S. Treasury rates, equates the average present value to the price of the security. This spread is called the OAS.

Historical comparisons are of only limited use for making judgments about current OAS levels relative to the past, because option-adjusted spreads depend on their underlying prepayment models. As a model changes, so does the OAS for a given MBS. Over the past few years, prepayment models have changed significantly, making comparisons to historical OASs tenuous. We augment OAS analysis with other tools to help us identify periods when mortgage spreads are attractive, attempting to avoid periods when spread widening will erase the yield advantage over Treasuries with the same interest-rate risk. The risk that the OAS may change, or spread risk, is managed by investing heavily in mortgages only when the initial OAS is large.

Interest-Rate Risk

The interest-rate risk of a mortgage security corresponds to the interest-rate risk of comparable Treasury securities; this risk can be hedged directly by selling a package of Treasury notes or interest-rate futures. Once we have hedged the interest-rate risk of a mortgage security, we are left with the Treasury bill return plus a spread over Treasuries. We cannot capture all of this spread because some of it is needed to cover the cost of the homeowner's prepayment option.

Prepayment Risk

When interest rates decline, homeowners have an economic incentive to prepay their existing mortgages by refinancing at a lower rate. As a result, the average lives (or durations) of mortgage securities vary as interest rates change: they extend as rates rise and shorten as rates fall. Therefore, the percentage increase in price of an MBS for successive 25 basis point declines in yield becomes smaller and smaller. Conversely, the percentage decline in price becomes greater as interest rates rise. This effect, which is known as negative convexity, can be significant — particularly for mortgage securities that concentrate prepayment risk such as interest-only strips.

When interest rates change we must offset the change in mortgage durations in order to keep the overall interest-rate risk of the portfolio at its desired target. Neglecting to do so would leave the portfolio with less interest-rate risk than desired after interest rates decline and more risk than desired after rates increase. We adjust for changes in mortgage durations — or equivalently, manage negative convexity — either by buying options[2] or by hedging dynamically. Hedging dynamically requires lengthening duration — buying futures — after prices have risen, and shortening duration — selling futures — after prices have fallen. Whether we employ this "buy high/sell low" dynamic strategy, or buy options, we are bearing the cost associated with managing negative convexity, foregoing part of the spread over Treasuries.

---

[2] A viable alternative to buying options is buying mortgage derivatives with positive convexity, such as principal-only strips.

Volatility Risk

Like other options, the homeowner's prepayment option is more valuable when future interest-rate volatility is expected to be high than when it is expected to be low.[3] Because the yield spread adjusts to compensate the investor for selling the prepayment option to the homeowner, spreads tend to widen when expected volatility increases and narrow when volatility declines.

We manage volatility risk by choosing whether to buy options or to hedge dynamically. When the volatility implied in option prices is high and we believe that future realized volatility will be lower than implied, we hedge dynamically. When implied volatility is low and we believe that actual future volatility will be higher than implied, we hedge the mortgage position by purchasing options.[4] Because implied volatilities have tended to exceed subsequent realized volatility, we have generally hedged dynamically to a greater extent than we have hedged through the use of options.

Model Risk

Mortgage prepayment models generate cash flows for a given set of interest-rate paths. But what happens when the models are wrong? In the rally of 1993, premium mortgages prepaid at much faster rates than predicted by most prepayment models in use at that time. Investors who had purchased interest-only strips (IOs) backed by premium mortgages, and had relied on the prepayment predictions of those mortgage models, sustained losses. It is important to note that prior to the rally, the OAS on IOs seemed attractive on a historical basis. However, the *model* OAS assumed a prepayment rate of 40% per annum for premium mortgages; the actual prepayment rate for premium mortgages was as high as 60%, causing the *realized* OAS to be negative. Current models, having been calibrated to the 1993 experience, predict much faster prepayments than those used in 1993. Although *we do not know the magnitude of model error going forward*, we can measure sensitivity to model error by increasing the prepayment rate assumed by the model for securities that are hurt by prepayments.

Over time it has become cheaper to refinance mortgages as technological improvements have reduced the costs associated with refinancing. We expect this type of prepayment innovation to continue in the years ahead. Models calibrated to past behavior will understate the impact of innovation. Therefore, when we evaluate securities that are vulnerable to this type of risk, we carefully consider the likelihood and the effect of prepayment innovation in determining the size of our investments. Although we cannot hedge model risk explicitly, we can measure it and manage it by keeping our portfolios' exposure to this risk in line with that of the broad indices.

---

[3] Higher interest-rate volatility increases the likelihood of lower rates in the future, making the option to refinance more valuable.

[4] Any bond option can be "replicated" dynamically by a portfolio of bonds and cash. If future volatility turns out to be less (greater) than that initially implied in option prices, the replicating portfolio will have cost less (more) than buying the option.

Exhibit 1: Yield Curve Shifts: Changes in the Overall Level of Interest Rates

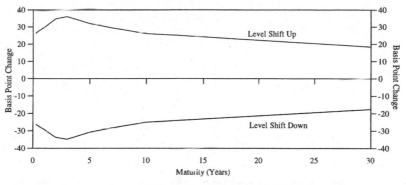

Source: Miller Anderson & Sherrerd, LLP

HOW INTEREST RATES CHANGE OVER TIME

To hedge mortgage securities effectively, we need to understand how interest rates change over time. In Chapter 7, Scott Richard and Benjamin Gord introduced the concept of "interest-rate sensitivity" (IRS) and discussed why it is a better measure of interest-rate risk than modified or effective duration. Very briefly, duration measures of interest-rate risk assume that the yield curve moves up or down by the same amount at every maturity. Empirically, we have found that yield-curve changes are not parallel. Rather, when the level of interest rates changes, 2-year yields move about twice as much as 30-year yields, which is why the yield curve typically steepens in a bond market rally and flattens in a selloff.[5] This pattern implies that duration overstates the interest-rate risk of longer-term bonds and understates the risk of shorter-term bonds. This "level" effect is shown in Exhibit 1. Empirically, we have also found that the yield curve sometimes reshapes without a meaningful change in the overall level of interest rates. We call this second factor a "twist" (Exhibit 2). Together, these two factors explain about 96% of past yield-curve reshapings.

HEDGING METHOD

With an understanding of how the yield curve changes over time — and the effect of these changes on the homeowner's prepayment option — we can estimate how mortgage prices will change as interest rates change. Since two factors (the "level" and "twist" factors discussed above) have accounted for most of the changes in the yield curve, two Treasury notes (typically the 2-year and 10-year) can hedge virtually all of the interest-rate risk in mortgage investments.

---

[5] Theoretical studies support the finding that long-term interest rates are less volatile than short-term interest rates.

Exhibit 2: Yield-Curve Twists: Flattening and Steepening

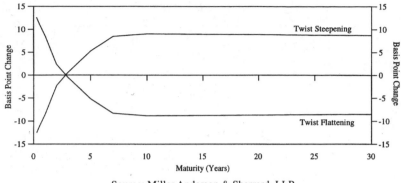

Source: Miller Anderson & Sherrerd, LLP

To hedge mortgage securities, we begin by expressing a particular security in terms of an equivalent position in U.S. Treasuries (or equivalent futures contracts). We identify this equivalent position by picking a package of 2-year and 10-year Treasuries that — *on average* — has the same price performance as the MBS under the "level" and "twist" yield-curve scenarios.[6] For hedging purposes, the direction of the change — up or down in the case of the "level" factor, flattening or steepening in the case of the "twist" factor — is not known. Assuming that either direction is equally likely, we calculate the "average" price changes of the MBS, the 2-year note, and the 10-year note for both the "level" and "twist" scenarios. In this way we calculate the unique quantities of 2-year and 10-year notes that will simultaneously hedge the mortgage's price response to both "level" and "twist" scenarios.[7] This combination is the appropriate hedge for typical yield-curve shifts and therefore defines the interest-rate sensitivity of the mortgage in terms of 2-year and 10-year notes.

The equivalent position in Treasuries will not exactly match the price performance of the MBS in the different yield-curve scenarios. This hedging error is a measure of the negative convexity[8] of the security. We choose to manage this negative convexity either by dynamically buying and selling U.S. Treasuries to adjust the hedges as interest rates change or by buying options. We base this choice on the implied volatility of option prices and on our own forecast of future realized volatility.

---

[6] We hold option-adjusted spreads constant and assume immediate yield-curve shifts when calculating horizon prices.

[7] We solve for the amount of 2-year ($H2$) and 10-year ($H10$) futures that have the same average price performance as the mortgage, assuming both level and twist movements in the yield curve. The 2-bond hedge in Exhibit 4 was determined by solving the following two equations:

   Level: $H2 \times (0.62) + H10 \times (1.69) = 1.22$

   Twist: $H2 \times (0.01) + H10 \times (0.55) = 0.25$

[8] Here, we define convexity as the price change of a security not explained by the equivalent position in Treasury futures.

Exhibit 3: Mortgage Price/Yield Curve

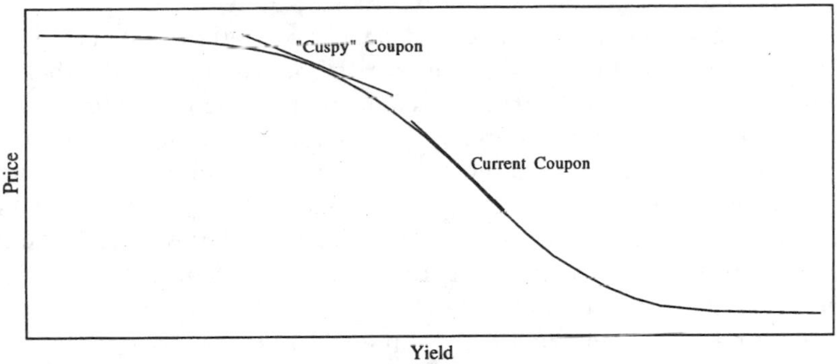

Source: Miller Anderson & Sherrerd, LLP

In many cases, the "average" price change is a good approximation of how the security's price will change for a small movement in interest rates. (See the line labeled Current Coupon in Exhibit 3.) However, some securities are very sensitive to small movements in interest rates. For example, a mortgage whose coupon is 100 basis points higher than the current coupon (often referred to as a "cuspy"-coupon mortgage) could be prepaid slowly if rates rise by 25 basis points but very quickly if rates fall by 25 basis points. Small changes in interest rates have large effects on prepayments for such securities and hence on their prices.

In this case, averaging the price changes is not a good measure of how prices will change. In other words, the tangent line (labeled "Cuspy" Coupon in Exhibit 3) is not a good proxy for the price/yield curve. At times, these types of securities trade at very attractive levels, but hedging only with Treasury notes or futures contracts may leave the investor exposed to more negative convexity than is desired. By purchasing options, the investor can shed unwanted negative convexity while benefiting from the cheapness of the security.

TWO HEDGING EXAMPLES

At the end of February 1997, the effective duration of Freddie Mac 7.5% mortgages was 4.4 years and its price was 99-25.[9] Exhibit 4 compares the results achieved using two hedging strategies. The duration hedge strategy compares the security's performance with that of an equal-duration U.S. Treasury, while the 2-bond hedge strategy uses 2-year- and 10-year-note futures. By construction, the 2-bond hedge dominates because the amount in 2-year-note ($76 per $100 of MBSs) and 10-year-note ($44 per $100 of MBSs) futures is determined from price changes derived from the assumed level and twist yield-curve scenarios.

---

[9] All numerical calculations are based on closing prices as of 3/4/97.

However, Exhibit 4 demonstrates that duration is not a good measure of interest-rate risk because typical yield-curve shifts are not parallel.

If the duration hedge is used, it appears that mortgages do better in market selloffs and worse in rallies — apparently confirming a market belief that mortgages are "market-directional" investments (see the two bolded values in Exhibit 4). However, evidence using the 2-bond hedge suggests otherwise: because the yield curve seldom moves in a parallel fashion, properly hedged mortgages are not market-directional. When "likely" changes in the yield curve are accounted for, virtually all of the market-directionality is removed. The IRS of the 7.5% mortgage — 4.0 years — is derived from the IRS of the equivalent position in 2- and 10-year note futures. Assuming a "likely" yield-curve shift, mortgage passthroughs have about 10% less interest-rate sensitivity than duration measures imply.

The "error" in the 2-bond hedge is a measure of the negative convexity of the Freddie Mac 7.5% mortgage. For a 26 basis point move in the 10-year — assuming no rebalancing — the mortgage would underperform its Treasury hedge by two basis points (or two cents per $100 of face value). This loss is more than offset by the carry advantage of mortgages over Treasuries: over a 1-month holding period, this incremental yield would be worth about nine basis points. In practice, because more frequent rebalancing lowers the hedging error, we adjust our hedges daily.[10]

"CUSPY"-COUPON MORTGAGES

At times, "cuspy"-coupon mortgages offer attractive risk-adjusted expected returns. However, they have more negative convexity than current-coupon mortgages. Using options enables us to offset some or all of this negative convexity. Exhibit 5 presents the same 2-bond hedge information (we have dropped the duration hedge) as Exhibit 4 for 8.5% Freddie Mac mortgages (duration = 3.3 years, IRS = 3.0 years, price = 103.50).

Exhibit 4: Alternative Hedging Methods

Yield Curve Change	Price Change			Error	
	FHLMC 7.5	Duration Hedge	2-Bond Hedge	Duration Hedge	2-Bond Hedge
"Level" Up	−1.27	1.36	1.25	**0.09**	−0.02
"Level" Down	1.18	−1.34	−1.20	**−0.16**	−0.02
"Twist" Flat	0.24	−0.24	−0.25	−0.00	−0.01
"Twist" Steep	−0.26	0.24	0.25	−0.02	−0.01

Source: Miller Anderson & Sherrerd, LLP

[10] Over the past three years the daily standard deviation of the 10-year yield has been 6.7 basis points.

Exhibit 5: Hedging Negative Convexity with Options

Yield Curve Change	Price Change		Error		Options+
	FHLMC 8.5	2-Bond Hedge	2-Bond Hedge	Option Pay-Off	2-Bond Hedge
"Level" Up	−0.98	0.93	−0.05	0.05	0.00
"Level" Down	0.85	−0.90	−0.05	0.05	0.00
"Twist" Flat	0.11	−0.12	−0.01	0.01	0.00
"Twist" Steep	−0.12	0.11	−0.01	0.01	0.00

Source: Miller Anderson & Sherrerd, LLP

Because the prepayment option of the 8.5s is closer to the refinancing threshold than that of the 7.5s at the time of this analysis, the 2-bond-hedge error is greater. Buying calls and puts eliminates this drift. In Exhibit 5, we add two option positions[11] on the 10-year note that offset the 2-bond-hedge error, making the total package (MBS + 2-bond-hedge + options) insensitive to likely interest-rate movements. Of course, buying these options requires paying a premium which amounts to about seven basis points per month. Since the yield advantage of the 8.5s versus Treasuries is about 11 basis points, the expected excess return over Treasuries is about four basis points per month after we hedge out the negative convexity.

CONCLUSION

Successful MBS investing requires the ability both to find value and to extract it. Extracting value requires proper hedging of attendant risks. Understanding how the yield curve changes over time and how these changes affect mortgage prices allows a portfolio manager to use mortgages in client portfolios when mortgage spreads are attractive, thereby enhancing long-term returns. Careful hedging is the linchpin for separating the value decision from the duration decision so that mortgages can be used to construct attractive total-return portfolios without compromising the appropriate interest-rate sensitivity of the portfolio.

---

[11] Per $100 of MBS, $18 6-month call on 10-year U.S. Treasury (UST), strike = 99.5; $17 6-month put on 10-year UST, strike = 95; 10-year UST priced at 97-15.

Chapter 13

Measuring Plausibility of Hypothetical Interest Rate Shocks

Bennett W. Golub, Ph.D.
Managing Director
Risk Management and Analytics Group
BlackRock Financial Management, Inc.

Leo M. Tilman
Associate
Risk Management and Analytics Group
BlackRock Financial Management, Inc.

INTRODUCTION

Many areas of modern portfolio and risk management are based on portfolio managers' view on the way the U.S. yield curve will evolve in the future. These predictions are often formulated as hypothetical *shocks* to the spot curve that portfolio managers expect to occur over the specified *horizon*. Via key rate durations as defined by Thomas Ho[1] or as implied by principal component durations,[2] these shocks can be used to assess the impact of implicit duration and yield curve bets on a portfolio's return. Other common uses of hypothetical interest rate shocks include various what-if analyses and stress tests, numerous [duration] measures of portfolios' sensitivity to the slope of the yield curve, etc.

The human mind can imagine all sorts of unusual interest rate shocks, and considerable time and resources may be spent on investigating the sensitivity of portfolios to these interest rate shocks without questioning their *historical plausibility*. Our goal in this chapter is to define what historical plausibility is and how to measure it quantitatively. In order to achieve that, we will employ the approaches suggested by principal component analysis. We will introduce the framework which derives statistical distributions and measures historical plausibility of hypothetical interest rate shocks thus providing historical validity to the corresponding yield curve bets.

[1] T. S. Y. Ho, "Key Rate Durations: Measures of Interest Rate Risks," *Journal of Fixed Income* (September 1992), pp. 29-44

[2] B.W. Golub and L.M. Tilman, "Measuring Yield Curve Risk Using Principal Component Analysis, Value-at-Risk, and Key Rate Durations," *Journal of Portfolio Management* (Summer 1997).

The authors would like to thank Yury Geyman, Lawrence Polhman, Ehud Ronn, Michael Salm, Irwin Sheer, Pavan Wadhwa, and Adam Wizon for their helpful comments and feedback.

We start with a brief overview of the principal component analysis and then utilize its methods to directly compute the probabilistic distribution of hypothetical interest rate shocks. The same section also introduces the notions of *magnitude plausibility* and *explanatory power* of interest rate shocks. Then we take the analysis one step further and introduce the notion of *shape plausibility*. We conclude by establishing a relationship between the shape of the first principal component and the term structure of volatility and verify the obtained results on the historical steepeners and flatteners of U.S. Treasury spot and on-the-run curves.

PROBABILISTIC DISTRIBUTION OF HYPOTHETICAL INTEREST RATE SHOCKS

The U.S. Treasury spot curve is continuous. This fact complicates the analysis and prediction of spot curve movements, especially using statistical methods. Therefore, practitioners usually *discretize* the spot curve, presenting its movements as changes of key rates — selected points on the spot curve.[3] Changes in spot key rates are assumed to be random variables which follow a multivariate normal distribution with zero mean and the covariance matrix computed from the historical data. There exist different ways to estimate the parameters of the distribution of key rates: equally-weighted, exponentially-weighted, fractional exponentially-weighted, etc. Although extensive research is being conducted on the connection between the appropriate estimation procedures and different styles of money management, this issue is beyond the scope of this chapter. Ideas presented below are invariant over the methodology used to create the covariance matrix ($\mathfrak{I}$) of key rate changes. We assume that the covariance matrix $\mathfrak{I}$ is given.

Principal component analysis is a statistical procedure which significantly simplifies the analysis of the covariance structure of complex systems such as interest rate movements. Instead of key rates, it creates a new set of random variables called principal components. The latter are the special linear combinations of key rates designed to explain the variability of the system as parsimoniously as possible. The output of the principal component analysis of the RiskMetrics[TM] monthly dataset is presented in Exhibit 1.

The data in Exhibit 1 can be interpreted as follows: over 92% of the historical interest rate shocks are "explained" by the first principal component, over 97% by the first two, and over 98% by the first three. Also note that the "humped" shape of the first principal component is similar to that of the term structure of volatility of changes in spot rates. Later in this chapter we will demonstrate that this is a direct implication of the high correlation between U.S. spot key rates.[4]

---

[3] See Ho, "Key Rate Durations: Measures of Interest Rate Risks."

[4] For a detailed discussion of principal components and their use in portfolio and risk management see Golub and Tilman, "Measuring Yield Curve Risk Using Principal Component Analysis, Value-at-Risk, and Key Rate Durations."

Exhibit 1: Principal Components Implied by JP Morgan RiskMetrics^{TM} Monthly Dataset (9/30/96)

		3Mo	1Yr	2Yr	3Yr	5Yr	7Yr	10Yr	15Yr	20Yr	30Yr
Annualized ZCB Yield Vol (%)		9.63	16.55	18.33	17.82	17.30	16.62	15.27	14.25	13.26	12.09
One Std Dev of ZCB Yields (bps)		52	96	113	112	113	11	104	101	97	83
Correlation Matrix	3Mo	1.00	0.80	0.72	0.68	0.65	0.61	0.58	0.54	0.51	0.46
	1Yr	0.80	1.00	0.91	0.91	0.89	0.87	0.85	0.81	0.78	0.76
	2Yr	0.72	0.91	1.00	0.99	0.97	0.95	0.93	0.89	0.85	0.84
	3Yr	0.68	0.91	0.99	1.00	0.99	0.97	0.96	0.92	0.90	0.88
	5Yr	0.65	0.89	0.97	0.99	1.00	0.99	0.98	0.96	0.93	0.92
	7Yr	0.61	0.87	0.95	0.97	0.99	1.00	0.99	0.98	0.96	0.95
	10Yr	0.58	0.85	0.93	0.96	0.98	0.99	1.00	0.99	0.98	0.97
	15Yr	0.54	0.81	0.89	0.92	0.96	0.98	0.99	1.00	0.99	0.98
	20Yr	0.51	0.78	0.85	0.90	0.93	0.96	0.98	0.99	1.00	0.99
	30Yr	0.46	0.76	0.84	0.88	0.92	0.95	0.97	0.98	0.99	1.00

PC No	Eig Val	Vol PC	Var Expl	CVar Expl	Principal Components									
					3Mo	1Yr	2Yr	3Yr	5Yr	7Yr	10Yr	15Yr	20Yr	30Yr
1	9.24	3.04	92.80	92.80	11.09	28.46	35.69	36.37	36.94	36.30	34.02	32.40	30.33	25.71
2	0.48	0.69	4.80	97.60	43.93	48.66	34.19	20.37	5.23	−9.32	−18.63	−30.09	−37.24	−36.94
3	0.13	0.36	1.27	98.87	42.43	54.93	−44.61	−35.28	−21.02	−8.43	0.31	19.59	27.12	17.76
4	0.06	0.25	0.62	99.49	76.77	−61.47	9.21	−0.18	−0.01	−2.08	−0.65	10.46	11.30	−0.31
5	0.02	0.14	0.20	99.69	12.33	−4.93	−55.03	−3.84	38.06	47.33	33.64	−21.36	−35.74	−14.98
6	0.01	0.10	0.11	99.79	8.94	0.33	18.59	−11.83	−15.02	−2.14	19.64	−44.15	−30.58	77.03
7	0.01	0.09	0.09	99.88	3.02	0.79	−38.42	49.35	45.01	−48.00	−28.08	−10.93	7.76	27.93
8	0.00	0.07	0.06	99.94	3.26	−1.14	−24.96	66.51	−66.82	17.27	13.02	−0.70	−2.46	−1.38
9	0.00	0.06	0.03	99.97	0.76	−0.46	−1.46	−0.97	0.21	60.38	−72.73	−20.12	19.52	16.59
10	0.00	0.05	0.03	100.00	0.54	0.00	−2.53	1.32	−0.42	5.15	−27.03	67.98	−64.58	21.03

ZCB	=	Zero-coupon bond
Eig Val	=	Eigenvalues (i.e., principal component variances) × 10,000
Vol PC	=	Volatility of principal components × 100
Var Expl	=	Percentage of variance explained
CVar Expl	=	Cumulative percentage of variance explained

Since key rates and principal components are random variables, any hypothetical (and, to that matter, historical) interest rate shock is a particular realization of these variables. We will use the subscripts "KR" and "PC" to indicate whether we are referring to a key rate or principal component representation of interest rate shocks. For instance,

$$\vec{X} = (x_1, \ldots, x_n)_{KR}^T$$

is an interest rate shock formulated in terms of changes in key rates. As mentioned earlier, our goal in this chapter is to analyze the shape and magnitude plausibility of hypothetical interest rate shocks and derive statistical distribution of interest rate shocks of a *given shape*. We start with the following definition.

Exhibit 2: Interest Rate Shocks of the Same Shape

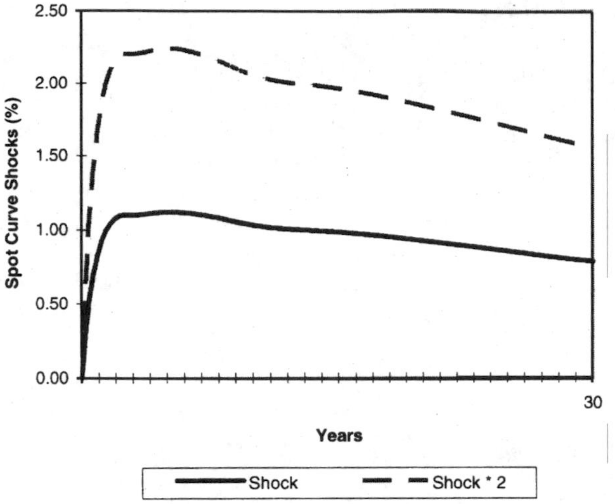

Let

$$\vec{X} = (x_1, ..., x_n)_{KR}^{T}$$

and

$$\vec{Y} = (y_1, ..., y_n)_{KR}^{T}$$

be spot curve shocks represented as vectors of key rate changes. We will say that $\vec{X}$ and $\vec{Y}$ have the *same shape* if they differ only by a factor, i.e.,

$$(y_1, ..., y_n)^{T} = (c \times x_1, ..., c \times x_n)^{T}$$

where c is a real number. (See Exhibit 2.)

As this section will show, it turns out that all interest rate shocks of a given *shape* correspond to the realizations of an underlying standard normal random variable. Once we know that, we can talk about the probability associated with a given shock (i.e., given realization). For instance, if a given interest rate shock corresponds to a three standard deviation realization of this underlying standard normal random variable, we will conclude that it is improbable. While deriving the probabilistic distribution of hypothetical interest rate shocks, we will utilize approaches used while constructing principal components. Namely, we will start with the discussion of how to compute *one standard deviation principal component shocks* used in a variety of instances including principal component durations. Relationships discussed below apply to random variables and their realizations alike.

Let

$$\vec{X} = (x_1, ..., x_n)^T_{KR}$$

be a spot curve shock formulated in terms of changes in key rates. Let

$$\vec{X} = (p_1, ..., p_n)^T_{PC}$$

be a representation of the *same* interest rate shock $\vec{X}$ corresponding to the coordinate system of principal components (x_i and p_i are the particular realizations of key rates and principal components respectively). Then the relationship between the two representations of the same vector $\vec{X}$ is given by

$$
\begin{bmatrix} p_1 \\ ... \\ p_n \end{bmatrix} =
\begin{bmatrix} pc_{1,1} & \cdots & pc_{1,n} \\ ... & ... & ... \\ pc_{n,1} & \cdots & pc_{n,n} \end{bmatrix} \times
\begin{bmatrix} x_1 \\ ... \\ x_n \end{bmatrix}
\tag{1}
$$

where $\Omega = \{pc_{i,j}\}$ is a matrix whose rows are principal component coefficients. They are the unit vectors of the form

$$\begin{bmatrix} pc_{i,1} & \cdots & pc_{i,n} \end{bmatrix}$$

If K_i are [random] changes in key rates, then the principal components are defined as the following linear combinations

$$pc_{i,1} \times K_1 + \quad + pc_{i,n} \times K_n$$

of key rate changes. From the linear algebra viewpoint, the matrix Ω allows us to translate the representation of an interest rate shock in one coordinate system (key rates) into another (principal components) The matrix Ω is orthogonal by construction, i.e., $\Omega^{-1} = \Omega^t$. Therefore, we can rewrite equation (1) as follows:

$$
\begin{bmatrix} x_1 \\ ... \\ x_n \end{bmatrix} =
\begin{bmatrix} pc_{1,1} & \cdots & pc_{n,1} \\ ... & ... & ... \\ pc_{1,n} & \cdots & pc_{n,n} \end{bmatrix} \times
\begin{bmatrix} p_1 \\ ... \\ p_n \end{bmatrix}
\tag{2}
$$

or simply

$$
\begin{bmatrix} x_1 \\ ... \\ x_n \end{bmatrix} =
\sum_{i=1}^{n} \begin{bmatrix} pc_{i,1} \\ ... \\ pc_{i,n} \end{bmatrix} \times p_i
\tag{3}
$$

Equation (3) allows us to interpret an arbitrary interest rate shock $\vec{X}$ as a *sum of principal component coefficients which are multiplied by a realization of the appropriate principal component.*

Exhibit 3: Principal Component Shocks to Spot Curve Smoothed Via Cubic Splines

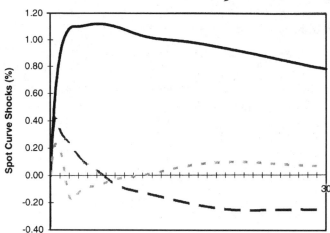

For example, consider a one standard deviation shock corresponding to the first principal component (PC_1). The realization of such event in terms of principal components is given by

$$(\sqrt{\lambda_1}, 0, ..., 0)^T_{PC}$$

where $\sqrt{\lambda_1}$ is the one standard deviation of PC_1. In terms of key rate changes, however, via equation (3) this shock has the following familiar representation

$$(\sqrt{\lambda_1} \times pc_{1,1}, ..., \sqrt{\lambda_1} \times pc_{1,n})_{KR}$$

The splined shapes of the first three principal components are presented in Exhibit 3.

Principal components constitute an orthogonal basis PC in the space of spot curve movements. By definition, the i-th principal components is obtained from the covariance matrix $\Im$ of key rate changes via the following optimization problem:

- compute the remaining variability in the system not explained by the first $i - 1$ principal components;
- find a linear combination of key rates which explains as much of the remaining variability as possible;
- the i-th principal component should be orthogonal to all the previously selected $i - 1$ principal components.

Clearly, in an n-dimensional linear space of spot curve movements, there exist orthogonal *bases other than the one consisting of principal components*. Surprisingly, this fact will help us derive the distribution of interest rate shocks of a given shape.

Suppose $\vec{Y} = (y_1, ..., y_n)_{KR}$ is a hypothetical interest rate shock defined in terms of key rate changes. We claim that $\vec{Y}$ corresponds to a particular realization of some standard normal random variable y. In other words, all interest rate shocks of a given shape are in one-to-one correspondence with the set of realizations of y. Therefore, we can speak about the probability of $\vec{Y}$ occurring. We will now construct y and establish its relationship with $\vec{Y}$.

Let

$$\vec{y} = (\hat{y}_1, ..., \hat{y}_n)_{KR}$$

be a unit vector whose shape is the same as that of $\vec{Y}$, i.e.,

$$\hat{y}_i = y_i / \sqrt{\sum_{i=1}^{n} y_i^2}$$

Similarly to the way we define principal components, define a new random variable Y to be the linear combination

$$Y = \sum_{i=1}^{n} \hat{y}_i \times K_i$$

where $\hat{y}_i$ are real numbers and K_i are changes in key rates (random variables). Then the variance of Y is given by

$$\sigma^2(Y) = (\hat{y}_1, ..., \hat{y}_n) \times \mathfrak{Z} \times (\hat{y}_1, ..., \hat{y}_n)^T \qquad (4)$$

We will now construct a new coordinate system in the space of spot curve changes. It will correspond to the new orthogonal basis B (different from principal components) such that Y is the first element in B. We modify the principal component optimization problem as follows:

- on the first step, instead of selecting a linear combination of changes in key rates which explains the maximum amount of variance, select Y.
- on each following step, find a linear combination of key rates which explains the maximum of the remaining variability in the system
- every newly selected element of the basis B should be orthogonal to all previously selected elements of B.

As a result, we have selected a set of n orthogonal variables which explain the total historical variability of interest rate movements. Moreover, Y is the first element in this basis. Define $y = Y/\sigma(Y)$, then y is a standard normal variable. The analog of equation (3) in this new coordinate system is given by

$$
\begin{bmatrix} x_1 \\ ... \\ x_n \end{bmatrix} = \begin{bmatrix} \hat{y}_1 \\ ... \\ \hat{y}_n \end{bmatrix} \times Y + ... \tag{5}
$$

or simply

$$
\begin{bmatrix} x_1 \\ ... \\ x_n \end{bmatrix} = \begin{bmatrix} \sigma(Y) \times \hat{y}_1 \\ ... \\ \sigma(Y) \times \hat{y}_n \end{bmatrix} \times y + ... \tag{6}
$$

where

$$
(\sigma(Y) \times \hat{y}_1, ..., \sigma(Y) \times \hat{y}_n)^T_{KR}
$$

is the one standard deviation shock corresponding to Y. Therefore, due to orthogonality, *every interest rate shock whose shape is the same as that of $\vec{Y}$ (and $\vec{\hat{y}}$) corresponds to a particular realization of the standard normal variable y.*

For example, consider 10 key rates ($n = 10$) and suppose $\vec{Y}$ is a 200 bps parallel spot curve shock:

$$
\vec{Y} = (200, ..., 200)_{KR}
$$

Then

$$
\vec{\hat{y}} = (1/\sqrt{10}, ..., 1/\sqrt{10})_{KR}
$$

is the corresponding unit vector which has the same shape as $\vec{Y}$. Using the Risk-Metrics^{TM} dataset, we can compute the standard deviation of the corresponding random variable Y. It can be shown that the "one standard deviation parallel shock" on 9/30/96 was 92 bps. Therefore, since we started with a parallel 200 bps spot curve shock, it implies a 200/92 = 2.17 standard deviation realization in the underlying standard normal variable. Then the probability of an annualized parallel shock over 200 bps is 0.015.

The magnitude of a one standard deviation parallel shock varies with the total variability in the market. Thus, on 2/4/97 the one standard deviation parallel shock was 73 bps and the probability of a parallel shock being over 200 bps was 0.003.

Ability to derive the distribution of interest rate shocks of a given shape leads us to the following important concepts.

Parallel First Principal Component

Many practitioners believe that it is convenient and intuitive to force the first principal component duration to equal effective duration.[5] To acheive this, we need to

---

[5] Ram Willner,"A New Tool for Portfolio Managers: Level, Slope, and Curvature Durations," *Journal of Fixed Income* (June 1996), pp. 48-59.

assume that the first principal component is a parallel spot curve shock. However, unlike the first principal component, a parallel spot curve shock is correlated with steepness and curvature (second and third principal components, respectively). Therefore, immunization and simulation techniques involving principal components become more complicated. Via the method introduced above, we can create a new coordinate system which has a parallel shock as the first basis vector. In this case, since we need to maintain orthogonality in the new coordinate system, the shapes of steepness and curvature will change. Nevertheless, the first three factors will still explain a vast majority of the total variability in the system. We believe, however, that the humped shape of the first principal component should not be ignored. As discussed below, it is meaningful and can be used as a tool while placing yield curve bets.

Explanatory Power of a Given Curve Shock

Among all interest rate shocks, the first principal component has the maximum explanatory power by construction. For instance, Exhibit 1 indicates that the first principal component "explains" 92% of the recent historical spot curve movements. The number 92% is the ratio of the variance of the first principal component to the total variance in the system (sum of all principal components' variances). We now know how to compute a "one standard deviation shock" of a given shape as well as its variance via equation (4). The ratio of the variance of the parallel shock to the total variance in the system in the above example is 87%. This means that on 9/30/96 a parallel spot curve shock "explained" 87% of the historical spot curve movements. We will call the ratio of the percentage of total variability explained by a given shock to the percentage of total variability explained by the first principal component the *explanatory power* of the given shock. The explanatory power of the first principal component is 1; that of a parallel spot shock in the given example is 95%.

Magnitude Plausibility of a Given Curve Shock

Once we know how many standard deviations k of the underlying standard normal variable a given interest rate shock Y implies, we can talk about the historical magnitude plausibility $mpl(Y)$ of this shock. Let Ψ denote the event "we guessed the direction of change in rates." We define the magnitude plausibility of a given interest rate shock $\vec{Y}$ as

$$mpl(\vec{Y}) = \text{Prob}(y > |k| \mid \Psi) \tag{7}$$

We can simplify equation (7) as follows:

$$mpl(\vec{Y}) = 2 \times \text{Prob}(y > |k|) \tag{8}$$

For example, the magnitude plausibility of a 200 bps spot curve shock is 3% whereas the magnitude plausibility of a 25 bps parallel spot curve shock is 78%.

Exhibit 4: SEDUR Shock Applied to OTR Curve as of 9/30/96

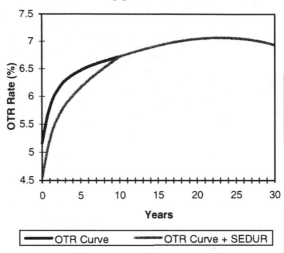

The interest rate shock used by Klaffky, Ma, and Nozari to compute what they call short-end duration (SEDUR) is defined as a 50 basis point steepener at the short end.[6] (See Exhibit 4.) It can be shown that the explanatory power of SEDUR is 38% and the magnitude plausibility is 54%.

SHAPE PLAUSIBILITY

The previous section deals with the quantitative measurement of the *magnitude plausibility* of a given spot curve shock. Thus we start with an interest rate shock of a *given shape* and then derive its distribution which is used to determine if the magnitude of the given shock is reasonable given the recent covariance of interest rates. However, the issue of whether the shape of the shock is plausible from the historical perspective is never considered. This section deals with an independent assessment of the *shape plausibility* of interest rate shocks.

Principal components are the latent factors which depict the historical dynamics of interest rates. Therefore, we have a specific notion of plausibility at hand. The "most plausible" or "ideal" shock is the one whose "decomposition" into principal components is exactly that of the system (Exhibit 1):

$$\hat{\lambda} = \{92.80, 4.80, 1.27, \ldots 0.03\}$$

---

[6] T.E. Klaffky, Y.Y. Ma, and A. Nozari, "Managing Yield Curve Exposure: Introducing Reshaping Durations," *Journal of Fixed Income* (December 1992), pp. 5-15. Note that SEDUR shock is applied to the OTR curve. To perform principal component decomposition, we first need to analytically transform it into a shock to the spot curve.

In other words, the first principal component should "contribute" 92.8% to the "ideal" shock, the second should contribute 4.8%, the third 1.3%, etc. The measure of plausibility should be defined in a way that the plausibility of an "ideal" shock is 1. On the other hand, it is natural to consider "the least plausible" shock to be the last principal component which has the least explanatory power and therefore is the least probable one. Clearly, the decomposition of the least plausible shock into principal components is $\hat{\gamma} = \{0, ...0, 100\}$. Thus, the measure of plausibility should be defined in a way that the plausibility of the least plausible shock is 0. Any other shock $\vec{X}$ will be somewhere in between the "ideal" and "the least plausible" shocks, and will have plausibility $spl(\vec{X})$ between 0 and 1. Below we present one such measure of plausibility.[7]

Write a hypothetical interest rate shock $\vec{X}$ in terms of principal components:

$$\vec{X} = (p_1, ..., p_n)_{PC}$$

Since $\vec{X}$ is a vector, it is reasonable to define the "contribution" of the i-th principal component in $\vec{X}$ based on the percentage of the squared length of $\vec{X}$ due to p_i, i.e.,

$$\hat{p}_i = p_i^2 / \sum_{i=1}^{n} p_i^2$$

Hence, to measure the shape plausibility of $\vec{X}$ is equivalent to measuring *how different the vector $\hat{p} = \{\hat{p}_i\}$ is from the "ideal" shock*. Let $D(\hat{p}, \hat{\lambda})$ be the "distance" between $\vec{X}$ and the ideal shock. Since the maximum distance between any two vectors is the distance $D(\hat{\lambda}, \hat{\gamma})$ between an "ideal" and "the least plausible" shocks, there is a way to normalize the measure of plausibility and present it as a number between 0 and 1.

We define the shape plausibility of $\vec{x}$ as

$$spl(\vec{X}) = 1 - \frac{D(\hat{p}, \hat{\lambda})}{D(\hat{\gamma}, \hat{\lambda})} \tag{9}$$

where

$$D(\hat{a}, \hat{\lambda}) = D(\{\hat{a}_i\}, \{\hat{\lambda}_i\}) = \sum |\hat{a}_i - \hat{\lambda}_i| \tag{10}$$

The functional form of the "distance" measure in equation (10) is not unique. We have experimented with several other functional representations only to discover that they fail to effectively differentiate between shapes of interest rate shocks, thus making the mapping $spl: \vec{X} \rightarrow [0, 1]$ almost a step function.

[7] For alternative approaches, see "measures of consistency" introduced by P.M. Brusilovsky and L.M. Tilman ("Incorporating Expert Judgement into Multivariate Polynomial Modeling," *Decision Support Systems* (October 1996), pp. 199-214). One may also think of the explanatory power of a shock as an alternative measure of shape plausibility.

Exhibit 5: Shape Plausibility and Principal Component Decomposition

Shock	Spl (.)	Principal Component Decomposition (%)									
		1	2	3	4	5	6	7	8	9	10
Ideal	1.00	92.80	4.80	1.27	0.62	0.20	0.11	0.09	0.06	0.03	0.03
Least Plausible	0.00	0.00	0.00	0.00	0.00	0.00	0.00	0.00	0.00	0.00	100.00
SEDUR	0.41	34.67	59.58	0.67	1.87	0.17	0.30	1.08	0.02	1.62	0.02

For example, to measure the shape plausibility of SEDUR, write its decomposition into principal components along with that of the "ideal" and "least plausible" shocks (Exhibit 5). It can be shown via equations (9) and (10) that $spl(SEDUR) = 0.41$. This means that from the historical perspective, the shape of SEDUR shock is not very plausible. Therefore, one may question the meaningfulness of the corresponding duration.

It remains to note that all characteristics of a given interest rate shock, such as "explanatory power," "magnitude plausibility," and "shape plausibility" depend on historical data and may vary dramatically over time.

FIRST PRINCIPAL COMPONENT AND THE TERM STRUCTURE OF VOLATILITY

Changes in U.S. Treasury spot rates are generally highly correlated. This fact has significant implications in interpreting the shape of the first principal component. This section deals with this issue. We claim that when spot rates are highly correlated, the shape of the first principal component resembles the shape of the term structure of volatility (TSOV) of changes in spot rates. The above statement provides the intuition behind the reason why, according to Ehud Ronn, "large-move days reflect more of a level [first principal component] shift in interest rates."[8] It also enables us to conclude that on days when the market moves substantially (e.g., more than two standard deviations) the relative changes in spot rates are almost solely a function of their historical volatilities. We now provide the informal proof of the above claim.

Let r_i and r_j be spot rates of maturities i and j respectively. Let σ_i and σ_j be the volatilities of *changes* of r_i and r_j respectively, while $pc_{1,i}$ and $pc_{1,j}$ be the coefficients of the first principal component corresponding to r_i and r_j. The statement *"the shape of the first principal component resembles that of TSOV of spot rate changes"* is equivalent to the following identity:

$$\frac{\sigma_i}{\sigma_j} \approx \frac{pc_{1,i}}{pc_{1,j}} \tag{11}$$

---

[8] E.I. Ronn, "The Impact of Large Changes in Asset Prices on Intra-Market Correlations in the Stock and Bond Markets," Working Paper, University of Texas in Austin, 1996.

Our argument is based on the following representation of the principal component coefficients:[9]

$$pc_{1,i} = \frac{\rho_{1,i} \times \sigma_i}{\sqrt{\lambda_1}}; \quad pc_{1,j} = \frac{\rho_{1,j} \times \sigma_j}{\sqrt{\lambda_1}} \tag{12}$$

where $\rho_{1,i}$ and $\rho_{1,j}$ are the correlations between the first principal component and the rates r_i and r_j respectively. Note that since all spot key rates are highly correlated, they will be also highly correlated with the principal components, i.e., $\rho_{1,i} \approx \rho_{1,j}$, and then equation (11) yields

$$\frac{pc_{1,i}}{pc_{1,j}} = \frac{\rho_{1,i} \times \sigma_i}{\sqrt{\lambda_1}} \Big/ \frac{\rho_{1,j} \times \sigma_j}{\sqrt{\lambda_1}} = \frac{\rho_{1,i}}{\rho_{1,j}} \times \frac{\sigma_i}{\sigma_j} \approx \frac{\sigma_i}{\sigma_j} \tag{13}$$

There are a number of interesting implications of the above result. For instance, *when the market rallies, the long end of the spot curve steepens, and when the market sells off, the long end of the spot curve flattens* To see that just notice that since the historical volatility of the 10-year rate is higher than the historical volatility of the 30-year rate, therefore, the changes in the former are generally larger than those in the latter. Therefore when the market rallies, according to the shape of the first principal component, the 10-year rate should decrease more than the 30-year rate; hence the spot curve should steepen.

U.S. Treasury bond market data seems to support this result:[10] over the 4-year period November 1992-November 1996, the ratio of bull steepenings to bull flattenings of the spot curve was 2.5:1, and the ratio of bear flattenings to bear steepenings was 2.75:1. If we study the steepeners/flatteners of the OTR Treasury curve instead, we will notice that while bull steepening and bear flattening patterns dominate, the proportions are different: over the same time period, the ratio of bull steepenings to bull flattenings of the OTR Treasury curve was 1.6:1, and the ratio of bear flattenings to bear steepenings was 6.5:1.

CONCLUSION

One of the advantages of key rate durations is the ability to estimate the instantaneous return on a portfolio given a hypothetical curve shift. The latter does not require us to do any additional simulations. Until now, sensitivity analysis was

---

[9] See R.A. Johnson and D.W. Wichern, *Applied Multivariate Statistical Analysis* (Englewood Cliffs: Prentice-Hall, 1982).

[10] Monthly changes in the level and steepness of the U.S. spot and OTR curves were considered. We define the market as "bull" if the 10-year spot (OTR) key rate fell more that 5 bps, "bear" if it rose more that 5 bps, and "neutral" otherwise. Likewise, a change in the slope of the spot (OTR) curve is defined as a "steepening" if the spread between the 2-year and 30-year increased by more than 5 bps, "flattening" if it decreased by more than 5 bps, and "neutral" otherwise.

never concerned with the issue of whether the utilized hypothetical shocks were plausible from a historical perspective. The measures of plausibility of interest rate shocks introduced in this chapter constrain interest rate shocks used in sensitivity analysis and portfolio optimization. They provide discipline to the scenario analysis by excluding historically implausible interest rate shocks from the consideration. The framework which allows us to compute the distribution of interest rate shocks of a given shape is important by itself. In another study,[11] we utilize the knowledge about these distributions to simulate interest rate shocks and make conscious trade-offs between the value surface and the yield curve dynamics while computing value-at-risk.

[11] B.W. Golub and L.M. Tilman, "Value-at-Risk Methodological Trade-Off: Value Surface, Yield Curve Dynamics, and Computational Costs," BlackRock Financial Management, Inc. Working Paper 97_03, 1997.

Chapter 14

Yield Curve Risk Management

Robert R. Reitano, Ph.D., F.S.A.
Vice President
John Hancock Mutual Life Insurance Company

INTRODUCTION

Yield curve risk management pertains to the general discipline of controlling the sensitivity of a portfolio of fixed-income securities to changes in one or more interest rates or yield curves. In general, the purpose for wanting control can be defensive or offensive, strategic or tactical, but in virtually all such cases, the sensitivity of the given portfolio is being controlled relative to the sensitivity of a second "target" fixed-income portfolio. For example, in asset/liability management, one controls the sensitivity of assets relative to fixed-income liabilities. In total-return fixed income management, one typically controls the sensitivity of the asset portfolio relative to a fixed-income benchmark index which defines the performance objective of the portfolio. Finally, in fixed-income market-neutral portfolios, one manages the sensitivities of a long portfolio of fixed-income assets relative to a short portfolio of fixed-income derivatives, such as interest rate futures contracts.

Defensive yield curve risk management means controlling interest rate sensitivity with the primary objective of protecting against losses relative to the target portfolio; in contrast, the primary objective of offensive or opportunistic management is to capitalize on perceived opportunities for gains. Defensive risk management can be strategic or tactical. A strategic implementation involves risk management in light of longer term models of the behavior of interest rates, while a tactical implementation is in response to shorter term expectations for such behavior. Offensive risk management is by definition tactical.[1] Asset/liability management and market-neutral portfolio management tend to be primarily strategic and defensive but with perhaps a tactical leaning, while total-return management tends to be strongly tactical but with perhaps a defensive leaning. Exceptions are not rare.

---

[1] One documented example of a strategic offensive management approach pertains to portfolios at the very short (under 1 year) end of the yield curve, where longer portfolios enjoy a "liquidity premium" relative to shorter portfolios. See for example, Robin Grieves, and Alan J. Marcos, "Riding the Yield Curve: Reprise," *Journal of Portfolio Management* (Summer 1992), pp. 67-76.

The author dedicates this chapter to his mathematics advisor and mentor, Professor Alberto P. Calderón, on the occasion of his 75th birthday.

Independent of the objective of the yield curve risk management program, the first fundamental problem is one of quantifying the interest rate sensitivities of a given fixed-income portfolio. The next fundamental problem is either one of developing defensive risk management strategies from a longer term model of yield curve movements, or developing opportunistic tactics to capitalize on shorter term expectations. The last fundamental problem relates to the development of yield curve models, both strategic and tactical.

The purpose of this chapter is to provide a detailed survey of various approaches to the problem of quantifying interest rate sensitivity, emphasizing both the theoretical merits and practical shortcomings, and to discuss the implications of these approaches for defensive and opportunistic portfolio management. As for models of yield curve movements, useful strategic approaches will be outlined. Tactical models of yield curve expectations will not be surveyed because practitioners are silent both on the methodologies utilized, and especially on all but selective reports of the efficacy of such models.

SINGLE FACTOR YIELD CURVE MODELS[2]

Mathematical Framework

A single factor model is a model for which all of the uncertainty in the future movement of all interest rates is reduced to uncertainty about a single factor, which is typically thought of as a statistical entity, i.e., random variable. There are many such models, as will be seen, because there are many reasonable ways in which this unique factor can be specified. We suspend for now the question of whether or not *any* one factor is sufficient, and simply note that given the assumption of adequacy, many possibilities for a factor can be evaluated. Moreover, independent of any such adequacy assumption, it seems reasonable to expect that there must be a "best" such factor, which might in fact work very well.

Given this factor, which we denote as i even though in some models this variable may not be an interest rate in the usual sense, we can now model the price of the security or portfolio of interest as a function of this variable, $P(i)$, and inquire into the sensitivity of price to changes in this variable. Luckily for portfolio managers, Leibnitz and Newton developed calculus centuries earlier, so this inquiry has a fruitful conclusion. Specifically, it is well known that:

$$P(j) = P(i) + P'(i)(j-i) + 0.5P''(i)(j-i)^2 + \dots \qquad (1)$$

where $P'(i)$ and $P''(i)$ denote the first and second derivatives of $P(i)$, respectively.

---

[2] For more technical details on these models and their properties, and additional historical references, see Robert R. Reitano, "Multivariate Duration Analysis," *Transactions of the Society of Actuaries*, XLIII (1991), pp. 335-91.

Equation (1), which is recognizable to math aficionados as a Taylor series expansion, states that by knowing the value of a function and its derivatives at a point i, it is possible to determine the exact value of the function at a point j. While this equation is not valid for all functions in theory, it is valid for the fixed-income price functions encountered in practice. Besides providing an identity for the exact value of $P(j)$, equation (1) also provides a basis for approximating $P(j)$: simply stop after the first two or three terms. Just how well a given number of terms works depends on the security and the size of the "shift" implied by the factor shift, $j-i$. In general, the approximation of any given security will deteriorate as $j-i$ increases, while for a given value of $j-i$, a given approximation will deteriorate for securities which are more "exotic;" i.e., contain more embedded optionality.

For finance applications, equation (1) is always restated by factoring out $P(i)$; that way, the units of the derivative terms are relative, so for a given security they are independent of the dollar amount held. Special notation and terminology for these "relative" derivatives have evolved, so that rewritten in the common finance fashion, and omitting terms beyond the second derivative, equation (1) becomes.

$$P(j) \approx P(i)[1 - D(i)(j-i) + 0.5C(i)(j-i)^2]$$ (2)

The "duration," $D(i)$ or D for short, has picked up a mysterious negative sign compared to equation (1), but this is because duration is defined as a negative derivative to be more compatible with the "Macaulay duration"[3] which was developed earlier and outside a calculus context. While apparent by comparison, the definitions of duration and convexity are:

$$D(i) = -\frac{P'(i)}{P(i)}; \; C(i) = \frac{P''(i)}{P(i)}$$ (3)

Of course, in finance as in any application of mathematics, derivatives must often be approximated since there may be no simple closed formula for the function of interest which allows an exact differentiation. In these cases, derivatives can be approximated by:

$$P'(i) \approx \frac{P(i + \Delta i) - P(i - \Delta i)}{2\Delta i}$$ (4)

$$P''(i) \approx \frac{P(i + \Delta i) - 2P(i) + P(i - \Delta i)}{(\Delta i)^2}$$ (4b)

In equation (4a), the so-called "central difference" formula is given. An alternative method, though typically biased because of the price function's convexity, is the forward difference formula which uses $P(i)$ in the numerator, instead of $P(i-\Delta i)$, and Δi in the denominator. For any approximation application, there is no

---

[3] Frederick R. Macaulay, *Some Theoretical Problems Suggested by the Movements of Interest Rates, Bond Yields, and Stock Prices in the United States Since 1856* (New York: Columbia University Press, 1938).

useful rule of thumb as to how small Δi must be to give a good numerical approximation. Perhaps using trial and error, the objective is to determine a value so that the approximation produced "stabilizes," and changes little if smaller values are used. This is not as inefficient as it seems, as once the necessary tolerance is calibrated for a given asset class, it tends to remain stable so further testing is unnecessary.

Equation (3) has as a simple consequence the fact that duration and convexity have the "portfolio" property. That is, given the durations or convexities of a collection of securities, the corresponding measure of the portfolio is easily calculated as a weighted average of the individual measures, with weights equal to the "relative" prices of the securities, and where relative price is the ratio of security price to portfolio price. Specifically:

$$D^P = \frac{\sum P_j D^{P_j}}{\sum P_j}; \quad C^P = \frac{\sum P_j C^{P_j}}{\sum P_j}$$

These identities have numerous applications. For example, one can calculate measures for surplus given values for assets and liabilities; embedded option characteristics can be determined from those of a security with options and its "optionless" counterpart; portfolio effects of a given trade can be predicted, and, desired effects at the portfolio level can readily be translated to the trade required; etc.

Yield to Maturity Approach

The simplest and most natural one factor model is based on the yield to maturity (YTM) of a security. This value, of course, equals the unique interest rate i, so that the present value of the cash flows equals the price, $P(i)$. That is: $P(i)=\Sigma c_t v^{mt}$, where c_t equals the time t cash flow (t is usually denominated in yearly time increments, by convention), and $v=(1+i)^{-1}$ for annual YTMs, $v=(1+0.5i)^{-1}$ for semi-annual YTMs, and $v=(1+i/m)^{-1}$ in general. Equation (3) now produces the familiar:

$$D = \frac{\sum t c_t v^{mt+1}}{P}; \quad C = \frac{\sum t(t+1/m)c_t v^{mt+2}}{P} \tag{5}$$

The Macaulay duration of a security, D^M, equals: D/v. While not actually derived within a calculus context, nor as a result of a pursuit of a measure of price sensitivity, it was soon realized that D^M provided such a measure as long as it was first multiplied by v. Macaulay duration remains popular despite this numerical shortcoming because it has the intuitive interpretation as a weighted-average-time-to-receipt of the cash flows: $D^M=\Sigma t w_t$, where $w_t=c_t v^{mt}/P$. Consequently, for a zero-coupon bond, D^M equals the maturity. Interpreting the weights as probabilities, since they sum to one (though need not be all positive), D^M equals the average or "expected" value of t, $E[t]$. Extending the analogy, if we define the Macaulay convexity, C^M, as C/v^2, this measure equals $E[t^2]+E[t]/m$, which can in turn be expressed in terms of the variance of t, and hence has the intuitive appeal as a measure of cash flow dispersion.

Unfortunately, besides the minor inconvenience of having to scale the Macaulay measures to use for an approximation formula given by equation (2), these measures have limited use in securities with embedded options where the basic formulas make little sense. In addition, when the durations of such securities are calculated in terms of equations (3) and (4), and converted into the Macaulay counterpart, the value often defies interpretation in terms of measures of t and implied cash flows. For example, interest-only strips (IOs) have negative durations, and principal-only strips (POs) have duration values far in excess of the time to receipt of the last cash flow. Nonetheless, Macaulay advocates persist and often refer to D and C in equation (3) as "modified" duration and convexity to avoid confusion.

Beyond the Macaulay shortcomings, the YTM one factor formulation itself suffers a fatal flaw. That is, YTMs of fixed cash-flow securities cannot satisfy *any* one factor relationship, except under the most restrictive model for the shape and movement of the term structure of interest rates (i.e., the "yield curve"). This restrictive model is that the yield curve is flat, and can only move in parallel.

For example,[4] the assumption that all YTMs move by equal amounts readily implies this conclusion. However, this result leaves open the possibility that YTMs may satisfy a more complicated one factor relationship. That is, perhaps there is a function, $Y(i,y)$, where $Y(0,y)=y$, or today's YTMs, so that as the factor i changes, each y-value changes according to $Y(i,y)$. For the above classical result, it was assumed that $Y(i,y)=y+i$. As it turns out, even the general one factor model requires the yield curve to be flat and move only in parallel.

Even more generally, it can be shown that the above conclusion also extends to general multi-factor models. That is, if $Y(i,y)$ is a given model with $Y(0,y)=y$, and i denotes the factor vector, it turns out that the YTM shift model, $y \rightarrow Y(i,y)$, can never be consistent if the yield curve is not flat. The proof of this result is technical and tedious, and beyond the scope of this chapter.

Consequently, even though YTMs are a natural factor framework for single security analysis, they provide a hopeless dead end for portfolio analysis and management. This is because to perform portfolio analysis, one must be able to calculate the one factor sensitivity of the total portfolio from the sensitivities of the individual securities. To do that, one needs in essence a model which specifies how the individual YTMs move as a collective. But as was noted, no such model can in general exist.

Other Single Factor Models

The problem with YTM is that it summarizes too much information; many cash flow structures can have the same YTM. Therefore, based on virtually any example of how the underlying term structure moves, these initially equal YTMs will move to different values. In fact, this observation underlies the proofs of the results noted above. But within this observation of the problem with YTMs lies an alternative potential solution to the single factor problem: simply model the

---

[4] See Jonathan E. Ingersoll, Jr., Jeffrey Skelton, and Roman L. Weil, "Duration Forty Years Later," *Journal of Financial and Quantitative Analysis* (November 1978), pp. 627-650.

movement of the term structure of interest rates directly as a one factor model. The price and price sensitivity of all assets can then be related to today's yield curve and the single factor proposed for its movement.

Of course, there are any number of ways of doing this. First off, one must choose the initial term structure. The most common models are the "par bond" curve, and "spot rate" models, typically denominated in semi-annual equivalent units, although a forward rate model is equally serviceable. The obvious starting points for these models are the "on-the-run" Treasury bond and Treasury strip (i.e., zero coupon bond) curves. Typically, various levels of "quality spreads" are added to these "risk-free" rates to allow the market pricing of securities with default risk.

The next step is to define the manner in which these underlying term structures move, assuming a single factor format. Many models have evolved,[5] among them:

Parallel (Additive) Shift:	$i_t \rightarrow i_t + i$
Multiplicative Shift:	$i_t \rightarrow i_t (1+i)$
Lognormal Shift:	$i_t \rightarrow i_t \, e^i$
Log-Additive Shift:	$i_t \rightarrow i_t + i \ln(1+\alpha t)/\alpha t$
Directional Shift:	$i_t \rightarrow i_t + n_t i$

where in each of the above specifications, i_t denotes the initial (pre-shift) value of the term structure utilized at maturity t, i denotes the single factor, α is a parameter, and n_t a maturity-specific shift parameter. The first such model introduced was the additive shift by Fisher and Weil, then multiplicative by Bierwag and Kaufman, log-additive by Khang, who also devised a log-multiplicative model, and directional by Reitano.[6] Of course, many other specifications have been studied as well.

While not initially obvious, the directional shift model is the most general specification possible for the purpose of defining a duration measure. To see this, consider the specification: $Y(i,i_t)$, where $Y(0,i_t)=i_t$. It is easy to check using equation (3) that this specification gives the same duration value as the directional model with $n_t = \partial_1 Y(0,i_t)$, where ∂_i denotes differentiation with respect to i.

Using any single factor specification, it is not difficult to prove the following identity [compare to equation (2)]:

$$P(j) = P(i) \exp\left[-\int_i^j D(s)ds\right] \tag{6}$$

---

[5] In addition to the references in footnotes 2 and 3, see G. O. Bierwag, *Duration Analysis* (Cambridge, MA: Ballinger Publishing, 1987), and the references therein.

[6] Lawrence Fisher and Roman L. Weil, "Coping with the Risk of Interest Rate Fluctuations: Returns to Bondholders from Naive and Optimal Strategies," *Journal of Business* (October 1971), pp. 408-31; G.O. Bierwag and George Kaufman, "Coping with the Risk of Interest Rate Fluctuations: A Note," *Journal of Business* (July 1977); Chulson Khang, "Bond Immunization when Short-Term Interest Rates Fluctuate More Than Long-Term Rates," University of Oregon Working Paper (1977); Reitano, "Multivariate Duration Analysis."

In contrast to equation (2), this identity states that the price on factor value j is completely determined by the price on factor value i and the duration values at all factor values between i and j. On the surface, it indicates that all higher order derivatives of the price function are irrelevant, and to control price, one only needs to control duration. While this observation is formally valid, it does not carry with it the practical significance one might expect for yield curve management. In short, one cannot manage duration with the precision required by equation (6) without also managing convexity.

While this will also be discussed below in the context of time dynamics, it is easy to understand this point in the current context. To determine the "manageability" of duration, we need to understand the sensitivity of duration to changes in the factor. Applying equation (1) to the function $D(i)$, we get:

$$D(j) \approx D(i) + [D^2(i) - C(i)](j - i) \tag{7}$$

Consequently, even for the smallest of factor shifts, $j-i$, the change in duration will reflect the magnitude of convexity relative to duration squared.

When convexity is relatively large, duration will decrease with increases in the factor; for example, noncallable bonds and insurance and annuity contracts with long embedded put options have this property. When convexity is relatively small or negative, duration will increase with increases in the factor; for example, callable bonds, mortgage-backed securities, and collateralized mortgage obligations have this property. Finally, when convexity equals duration squared, such as is nearly true for zero coupon bonds, duration is relatively insensitive to factor changes.

Equation (6) also provides a new approximation basis for price sensitivity, which in many situations is superior to the approximation basis derived above in equation (2) for a given "order" in terms of j i. For example, the first order approximation:

$$P(j) \approx P(i) \exp[-D(i)(j - i)] \tag{8}$$

is often superior to the first order approximation implied by equation (2). In addition, these two approximations can often be used together to provide upper and lower bounds for the exact value of $P(j)$.

Beyond the formal mathematics underlying equations (6) and (8), a relatively simple and intuitive explanation can be given. Imagine dividing the factor shift interval, $[i,j]$, into a large number of subintervals, $[t_j, t_{j+1}]$, and on each, approximating the relative change, $P(t_{j+1})/P(t_j)$, by $1-D(t_j)\Delta t$ reflecting equation (2). Of course, the total relative change, $P(j)/P(i)$, is just the product of the subinterval changes. As can be shown, if all the intermediate duration values used are exact, equation (6) is produced in the limit, whereas setting all to $D(i)$ produces equation (8). Approximating the intermediate durations based on equation (7) provides the second order exponential approximation.

Single Factor Yield Curve Management

The opportunistic, i.e., tactical, implications of any one factor model are quite obvious. Given an expectation for the "sign" of the factor change, i.e., positive or negative, one simply trades to the maximum feasible value of duration of the opposite sign. For example, a negative shift expectation motivates a maximum positive duration, as is easily seen from any of the above approximations. Convexity can be ignored for this purpose since in any one factor model, $j-i$ will quite small so the duration effects on price will overwhelm the convexity effects; that is, $j-i$ will be very large compared to $(j-i)^2$. Of course, this aggressive strategy carries the risk that if the realized factor shift has the opposite sign, large losses are possible.

When less certain of the sign of the factor shift, tactical management becomes more subtle. For example, given a likely range for the shift, say: -0.01 to 0.02, a probability distribution, say rectangular, and a personal utility function for wealth, $u(w)$, one would seek a duration value which maximized one's expected utility, $E[u(P(j))]$, which is approximated by: $P(i)E[u(1-D(i)(j-i))]$. Equating the first derivative with respect to D to zero, one must solve: $E[(j-i)u'(1-D(j-i))]=0$, for $D=D(i)$. If the solution exists, it is easy to see that this must be an expected utility maximizing duration value when the manager is risk averse (i.e., $u''(w)<0$). This analysis could be further refined by considering the duration-income relationship over the period modeled.

In defensive yield curve management, one seeks to find conditions which will minimize factor exposure of the managed portfolio relative to a target portfolio. As noted above, asset/liability and market-neutral portfolio management are examples of this, but so is active management of a fixed-income portfolio to match a benchmark index. In each such case, one can create an "objective" portfolio equal to a long portfolio of assets and a short position in the target portfolio. In market-neutral strategies, this objective portfolio is actively managed on both the long and short (i.e., futures, for example) positions, where in general active management only occurs in the long position.

For example, in ALM the objective portfolio is surplus, $S(i)$, and the objective price function is given by: $S(i)=A(i)-L(i)$. Using equation (2), although this result can be derived more formally, it seems apparent that to minimize surplus sensitivity to factor changes, one must have $D^S(i)=0$, since otherwise one will have first order exposure to "unfavorable" shifts. Furthermore, once this is done, one can in theory make surplus favorably exposed to all factor shifts by making $C^S(i)>0$. Using equation (3) to convert these conditions to conditions on assets and liabilities, we get:

$$D^A = \frac{L}{A}D^L; \quad C^A > \frac{L}{A}C^L \qquad (9)$$

While one must assume that $S(i)\neq0$ to derive these "immunization" conditions, they remain valid if $S=0$.

The conditions in equation (9) can be interpreted in two ways. First, consistent with equation (2), the equivalent conditions $D^S=0$ and $C^S>0$, create a surplus function which has the graph of an upright parabola with equation:

$$S(j) \approx S(i)[1 + C^S(j-i)^2] \tag{10}$$

where this statement is approximately correct with error magnitude: $(j-i)^3$, which is usually quite small.

Secondly, using equation (7), these conditions assure that the duration of surplus will always have the "right" sign. That is, with error magnitude $(j-i)^2$:

$$D^S(j) \approx -C^S(i)(j-i) \tag{11}$$

so duration will become positive for negative factor shifts, and conversely. That this is a favorable factor sensitivity for surplus duration stems from the identity in equation (6), since this in turn assures that the exponent of "exp" will be positive, and surplus will always grow.

One of the troubling implications of equation (10) is that perhaps immunization works too well; we have now created a portfolio which is instantaneously riskless, and with real opportunities for a profit due to a change in the factor value. This is, in theory, the holy grail of finance, but in practice, it is usually an indication that a mistake has been made. But has one? Does equation (10) really imply a risk-free arbitrage? On close examination, the answer is an unambiguous not necessarily.

First, the real world is not constrained by our single factor representation of it. If the term structure shifts in a way that is outside that anticipated by the model used, this immunization equation is no longer valid. Second, even if the real world were constrained by our model, what does "instantaneously" immunized really mean? If it means we are immunized against instantaneous factor shifts, what is that? Does anything really happen "instantaneously," without the passage of any time? Of course not! Even within the realm of our single factor world, every shift in the factor corresponds to some shift in time, which the above analysis ignores. This time dynamic will be addressed below, but for now, suffice it to note that equation (10) does not imply the possibility of untold riches.

The above development centered on the objective of immunizating today's surplus value, but can readily be applied to market-neutral portfolios, with $L(i)$ denoting the short portfolio, and to actively managed indexed portfolios, with $L(i)$ denoting the benchmark index. In the surplus context, one may also be interested in immunizing other objective functions, such as the surplus ratio: $S(i)/A(i)$, or the time T forward value of surplus: $S(i)/Z_T(i)$, where $Z_T(i)$ denotes the price of a T-period zero-coupon bond.[7] In these cases, analogous conditions to those in equation (9) can be developed (see equation (34) in the multi-factor development below).

Single (and Multi-)Factor Yield Curve Management Failure

Unfortunately, single and multi-factor yield curve management can fail, and at times fail seriously. Fortunately, these failures are always explainable; indeed,

---

[7] See Robert R. Reitano, "Multivariate Immunization Theory," *Transactions of the Society of Actuaries* XLIII(1991), pp. 392-438 for more details on these objective functions.

they are predictable. Specifically, it is always the case that such failures are traceable to the failure of one or more of the assumptions required in the development of the management strategy. While we illustrate this in the context of single factor models, the validity of these comments in the more general case will be obvious.

As a simple example, it is implicit in the above development that prices, and the associated durations and convexities, are calculated accurately, properly, and consistently. The need for accuracy is self evident. As an example of an improper calculation, consider the pricing of a callable bond or MBS as the present value of noncallable or best-guess callable cash flows at a given spread to Treasuries. Such a spread can always be found, of course, so that today's price is accurately reproduced. However, such a valuation scheme will provide erroneous durations because it ignores the sensitivity of cash flows to changes in the factor. More subtly, even for option-adjusted valuations, it is important that the prepayment model utilized be calibrated as closely as feasible to that underlying traded prices.

Inconsistent calculations occur primarily due to inconsistencies in the manner in which the term structure and shift factor are specified. For example, a yield curve can be specified in par bond, spot, or forward rates; in continuous, semi-annual, monthly, etc., nominal units; and as a credit quality specific curve, Treasuries plus credit spreads, or Treasuries plus option-adjusted spreads. Besides consistency between all valuation yield curves, it is equally important that the shift factor be consistently modeled in terms of both the parameters above, and the manner in which the factor is applied. For example, any multiplicative factor model will provide one set of price sensitivities if applied to the Treasury curve underlying the credit-adjusted valuation curves, and a different set if applied directly to the credit-adjusted curves.

Consistency problems also occur when using stochastic yield curve generators for price valuations. In theory, the exact price is produced only when an infeasible number of "yield curve paths" is generated, where each path is usually generated by first generating a binomial "bit string" of 0s and 1s. To utilize such systems, one typically samples several hundred to several thousand such bit strings, and uses the resulting price as an approximation to the theoretically correct result. The consistency problem occurs in the application of equation (3) which requires three such price estimates. If three sets of bit strings are generated, the resulting D and C values will reflect both price sensitivities and the errors in the estimated prices. To avoid this inconsistency, it is better to generate only one set, and use it for all three valuations.

The major challenge today in achieving correct calculations from practitioner-developed pricing systems stems from the complexity of the finance theory, computer programs, and data manipulations required. For vendor-developed software, assuming correct calculations, the primary challenge is producing valuations which are consistent with the results of practitioner-developed and other vendor supplied systems. In general, when working with more than one system it is better to calculate all price sensitivities directly using equation (4) than use vendor supplied sensitivities, since one can then control consistency through the term structure specifications.

Beyond inaccurate, improper and inconsistent valuations, failure of a yield curve management strategy can also be due to unanticipated higher order effects, model risk, and most importantly, what has been called factor risk or stochastic process risk.

A *higher order effect* means the effect of the first term of the Taylor series in equation (1) that is ignored. For example, it is not uncommon to only partially implement the immunization conditions of equation (9) by balancing durations, but ignoring convexities. This strategy is typically justified by the commitment to rebalance duration frequently, and the belief that this will imply that rebalancing will occur only after small shifts, for which the convexity implications are minor. Unfortunately, the yield curve can occasionally move quickly and significantly, and generate substantial losses.

As a simple example, consider duration balancing mortgage-backed securities and single premium deferred annuities using equation (9). The convexities of these portfolios violate the immunizing condition since as is obvious, MBSs lengthen when rates rises due to the short call option, and SPDAs shorten due to the long put (i.e., surrender) option. Consequently, the duration of surplus moves in exactly the wrong direction — positive for rate increases and conversely. For small shifts, this "tracking" error may seem minor, but large losses have been realized in periods of large shifts.

Model risk means using the wrong pricing model. The simplest example is the improper valuation of a callable bond discussed above. More common examples include using a different option pricing model (i.e., different yield curve dynamics) or most seriously, a different option election behavior function than those used underlying traded prices. The behavior function risk is by far the most serious since it is standard practice to assume, say, that the mortgagors underlying MBSs are relatively inefficient in the election of their call (i.e., refinancing) options. Unfortunately, these assumptions are regularly updated as experience emerges, with major updates not uncommon. In essence, immunization fails because the sensitivity of the prepayment model to a change in factor values was not modeled for the calculated D and C values from equation (3).

Finally, and perhaps most obvious, is *stochastic process risk*. This is the risk that the yield curve shift experienced is inconsistent with the factor assumed.[8] For example, one may immunize against parallel shifts, but experience a steepening shift.

While using a multi-factor model mitigates stochastic process risk more or less, depending on the number and quality of the factors used, the other causes

---

[8] For theoretical estimates and illustrations of this risk, see Robert R. Reitano, "Nonparallel Yield Curve Shifts and Durational Leverage," *Journal of Portfolio Management* (Summer 1990), pp. 62-7; Robert R. Reitano,"Nonparallel Yield Curve Shifts and Spread Leverage,"*Journal of Portfolio Management* (Spring 1991), pp. 82-7; Robert R. Reitano, "Nonparallel Yield Curve Shifts and Convexity," *Transactions of the Society of Actuaries*, XLIV (1992), pp. 479-507; Robert R. Reitano,"Nonparallel Yield Curve Shifts and Immunization,"*Journal of Portfolio Management* (Spring 1992), pp. 36-43. See also: G.O. Bierwag, G.C. Kaufman, and A. Toevs, "Bond Portfolio Immunization and Stochastic Process Risk," *Journal of Bank Research* (Winter 1983) for the first formal analysis of this risk.

of management failure discussed above apply equally well in these more general models, and will not be repeated below.

Single Factor Yield Curve Management: The Time Dynamic

The above discussion ignored the fact that a price function modeled as $P(i)$ can only represent the price sensitivities of a portfolio to an immediate shift in interest rates; that is, to a shift which occurs before the passage of time has a material effect on the portfolio and its price sensitivities. Such shifts are also called *instantaneous shifts*. In reality, price would be better modeled as an explicit function of time, as would the factor value, that is, $P=P(t,i(t))$.

To this end, we use the methods of Ito stochastic calculus.[9] To begin with, we need a model for the evolution of the factor $i(t)$ in time, where this factor will also be denoted i_t. A tremendously important and general model is that of an Ito process, whereby the "instantaneous" change in i_t, denoted di_t, satisfies:

$$di_t = \mu(t, i_t)dt + \sigma(t, i_t)dz_t \tag{12}$$

where z_t denotes Brownian motion. This "differential" expression is shorthand for the notion that i_T, or the value of the factor at time T, is a random variable that is a stochastic integral, and that i_T is given by:

$$i_T = i_0 + \int_0^T \mu(t, i_t)dt + \int_0^T \sigma(t, i_t)dz_t \tag{13}$$

One of the critical contributions of Ito was introducing the manner in which the integrals in equation (13) could be interpreted, and determining properties of the functions μ and σ that were sufficient to make these integrals, and functions of these integrals, well defined in that context.

For our purpose, it is sufficient to think of equation (12) as describing how i_t changes in a very short time increment. Specifically, this equation can be interpreted as stating that $i_{t+\Delta t} - i_t$, or Δi_t for short, is approximately normally distributed with mean (i.e., expectation) and variance given by:

$$E(\Delta i_t) \approx \mu(t, i_t)\Delta t; \text{Var}(\Delta i_t) \approx \sigma(t, i_t)^2 \Delta t \tag{14}$$

where the approximations are good to the order of $(\Delta t)^2$. Because of equation (14), $\mu(t,i_t)$ is generally referred to as the "drift" coefficient, and $\sigma(t,i_t)$ as the "diffusion coefficient."

Returning to the subject of primary interest, if the factor i_t is assumed to follow the Ito process defined in equation (12), what can be said about a function of that process; or more specifically, what can be said about $P(t,i_t)$?

Another critically important contribution of Ito, which has come to be known as Ito's Lemma, answers this question. It states that if P is a fairly smooth

---

[9] See John C. Hull, *Options, Futures and Other Derivative Securities* (Englewood Cliffs, New Jersey: Prentice Hall, 1993), second edition.

function (i.e., twice differentiable with continuous second derivatives), then P_t $\equiv P(t,i_t)$ is also a stochastic integral with drift and diffusion coefficients definable in terms of the coefficients in equation (12) and the derivatives of P. Applying this result and dividing the Ito expression for dP_t by P_t produces:

$$\frac{dP_t}{P_t} = \left(\frac{\partial_t P_t}{P_t} - D_t\mu_t + \frac{1}{2}C_t\sigma_t^2\right)dt - D_t\sigma_t dz_t \tag{15}$$

where D_t, C_t, μ_t, and σ_t denote $D(t,i_t)$, etc., and ∂_t denotes differentiation with respect to t.

While initially imposing, equation (15) has a relatively simply interpretation in terms of single factor yield curve management. Before discussing this, let's first look at what equation (15) reduces to for the simply example of a T-period zero-coupon bond, and where i_t denotes the $(T-t)$-period spot rate at time t. For this example, $P(t,i_t)=\exp[-(T-t)i_t]$, and a calculation produces:

$$\frac{dP_t}{P_t} = \left(i_t - (T-t)\mu_t + \frac{1}{2}(T-t)^2\sigma_t^2\right)dt - (T-t)\sigma_t dz_t \tag{16}$$

These equations state that the relative price change (i.e., dP_t/P_t) has three components of drift at time t. The first component reflects the relative time-derivative, also known as the security's earnings rate, which for time zero is just the $(T-t)$-period spot rate at that time. The second drift component is the "expected" factor gain or loss reflecting the security's duration at that time and the expected change in the factor, and is reminiscent of equation (2). The third component is perhaps unexpected based on the earlier analysis which ignored time drift, and represents the "expected" factor gain or loss reflecting half the security's convexity and the variance of the factor. The surprise is that in these equations, convexity is first order in time as is duration, in contrast to the implication of equation (2), where convexity was a second-order adjustment in factor units. That such a convexity adjustment is appropriate can be inferred by treating j in equation (2) as a random variable and taking expectations. The convexity term then is multiplied by $\sigma^2+\mu^2$ instead of just σ^2 as in equation (15), but this is a start. Just what happens to the μ^2 term, not to mention all the other terms of the Taylor series, must remain a mystery for now, with a resolution contained in the theory of stochastic calculus.

The diffusion coefficient in equations (15) and (16) is no surprise. Specifically, these terms state, due to the interpretation in equation (14), that the standard deviation of a portfolio equals the standard deviation of the factor times the duration of the portfolio. That is, duration acts like a lever when $|D|>1$, and like a buffer when $|D|<1$, in translating factor volatility into portfolio volatility. Of course, $|D|$ denotes the absolute value of D.

While providing an elegant and complete framework for representing the time dynamic of a portfolio, equation (15) does not generally alter the conclusions developed earlier using the naive, time-static model. For example, applying this equation to the surplus function $S_t=S(t,i_t)$, it becomes clear that the conditions of equation

(9), that $D^S=0$ and $C^S>0$, are again necessary. These immunization conditions then force dS_t/S_t to have only the earnings rate and convexity drift terms, and *no* stochastic term; but only for an instant! At any time $t+\Delta t$, the D^S and C^S values change (see below) and immunization is certainly lost because the stochastic term in equation (15) depends on D^S. That is, having $D^S=0$ and $C^S>0$ initially does not protect surplus even a moment later as in the static model, where these conditions assured that D^S would move in the right direction relative to the factor move. Here, as soon as D^S strays away from 0, immunization is lost due to the diffusion term in equation (15).

So how can we be sure that duration will immediately drift away from zero? The answer can be found in a second application of Ito's Lemma, this time to $D_t \equiv D(t,i_t)$, the duration of surplus, to get:

$$dD_t = (\partial_t D_t + (D_t^2 - C_t)\mu_t + 0.5[D_t(D_t^2 - C_t) - \partial_i C_t]\sigma_t^2)dt$$
$$+ (D_t^2 - C_t)\sigma_t dz_t \qquad (17)$$

While the drift term in equation (17) is complicated, it need not concern us for the question at hand. Looking to the diffusion coefficient, at time zero this term is equal to $-C_0\sigma_0$, which is strictly negative by the immunization condition and the assumption that the factor is not deterministic (i.e., $\sigma_t >0$). Consequently, even though initially zero, the duration of surplus will immediately change in an unpredictable way due to the non-zero diffusion coefficient, and hence, the immunization property will be immediately lost.

While the above derivation and conclusion was based on the simple model in equation (12), with only one Brownian motion term, dz_t, it holds equally well if it is assumed that the single factor, i_t, depends on several such terms, $dz_t^{(k)}$, $k=1, 2, ..., n$. Moreover, with still more effort and advanced Ito calculus, this conclusion holds for the general vector valued Ito process, di_t, where $\mathbf{i}_t$ denotes the vector of factors in the multi-factor model discussed below, and each depends on the collection of Brownian motions above; i.e., on the vector valued Brownian motion, $d\mathbf{z}_t$.

Of course, this does not imply that immunization is not effective in managing yield curve risk. It simply implies that immunization does not create the risk-free arbitrage implied by equation (10), above, or in the multi-factor counterpart in equation (32) below.

Is There a "Best" Single Factor Model?

Before exiting the realm of single factor models, it makes sense to at least consider the question: Is there a best factor to use when you are using only one factor? Before answering this, it makes sense to first contemplate in what way do we mean "best." Of course, the best single factor model is the one which exactly predicts the "nature" of the yield curve shift which occurs over the period of interest. For example, during a period of parallel shifts, one can hardly do better than the Fisher-Weil model. Unfortunely, since such predictions seem to be impossible to make with confidence, we abandon this notion of "best."

At the other extreme, what if we not only did not possess perfect foresight, but we had no knowledge at all? That is, what if it were the case that any yield curve shift that was possible was equally likely and that historical data were of no value in determining shifts to come. In a sense, yield curve shifts were just a random walk limited only to the extent that shifts which allowed riskless arbitrage were "banned." In such a world, it is hard to imagine by what paradigm we could evaluate whether a given single factor model was best.

Consequently, we pose the question and propose an answer within the framework of an informational "middle-ground," as it were, whereby we assume that we have good information on the "necessary" structure of yield curve moves, but that past experience suggests that there are random components in these moves which preclude perfect predictions. That is, using a sample of historical shifts and the assumption that future shifts will be selected from the same statistical "urn," we pose the question: Is there a single shift, which when used to underlie a single factor model, will provide the best predictor of yield curves to come? This model of shifts is also called a "stationary" model, in the sense that all of the statistics of the series are assumed to be fixed in time.

We now investigate an answer to this question under the additional assumption that sequential shifts have no autocorrelation structure and can be assumed to be independent. The approach to be taken is known as the *method of principal components*.[10] To begin, assume that we are given a collection of historical yield curve shifts: $\{\mathbf{Y}_j\}$, where each shift is a vector: $\mathbf{Y}=(y_1, y_2, ..., y_m)$, of changes at selected points on the term structure. Our goal is to find a vector, $\mathbf{P}$, so that its multiples approximate the original shifts as closely as possible. We use multiples of $\mathbf{P}$ because in the context of a single factor model, $\mathbf{P}$ represents the "shape" of the term structure shift, while the multiples equal values of the factor modeled.

One method for simultaneously approximating all shifts is the method of principal components, which seeks to minimize the sum of the squared lengths of the residual terms: $\sum |\mathbf{Y}_j - a_j \mathbf{P}|^2$, where the multiples, a_j, are chosen optimally, and $|\mathbf{P}|^2$ denotes the length of $\mathbf{P}$ squared, $|\mathbf{P}|^2 = \sum p_j^2$. It is sometimes convenient to express this value in the notation of the dot or inner product of vectors $|\mathbf{P}|^2 = \mathbf{P} \bullet \mathbf{P}$, where in general this product is defined as $\mathbf{X} \bullet \mathbf{Y} = \sum x_j y_j$, and will also be denoted: $(\mathbf{X}, \mathbf{Y})$. In order to simplify the interpretation of results later, it is standard practice to first normalize the yield curve shifts to have a mean of zero. That is, we seek to approximate $\{\mathbf{Y}_j'\} = \{\mathbf{Y}_j - E[\mathbf{Y}_j]\}$ with multiples of $\mathbf{P}$, where $E[\mathbf{Y}_j]$ denotes the mean or average shift vector.

As it turns out, given any value of $\mathbf{P}$ it is straightforward to determine the optimal values for the multiples of $\mathbf{P}$; specifically, $a_j = (\mathbf{P}, \mathbf{Y}_j') / |\mathbf{P}|^2$, which geomet-

---

[10] For the traditional derivation of this approach, see Henri Theil, *Principles of Economics* (New York: John Wiley & Sons, 1971), and, Samuel S. Wilks, *Mathematical Statistics* (New York: John Wiley & Sons, 1962). For an application of this method in the multi-factor context to yield curve management, see Robert Litterman and Jose Scheinkman, "Common Factors Affecting Bond Returns," *The Journal of Fixed Income* (June 1991), pp. 54-61.

rically represents the "projection" of Y_j' onto P. This can be readily derived by defining $f(a)=\sum|Y_j-E[Y_j]-a_j P|^2$, with $a=(a_1,...., a_n)$, and setting the partial derivatives equal to zero. This derivation is simplified by rewriting the terms in the summation as inner products $|X|^2=(X, X)$, and rewriting each term as $|Y_j'|^2-2a_j(Y_j',P)+a_j^2|P|^2$. That this value of a identifies a minimum of $f(a)$ follows from the positive definiteness of the (diagonal) matrix of second derivatives. Below, we assume that P is a unit vector, i.e., $|P|=1$, to simplify this expression for a_j.

The problem of identifying the "best" single factor model now becomes:

$$\text{Minimize: } \sum|Y_j' - (Y_j', P)\, P|^2 \qquad (18)$$

over all unit vectors, P. Unfortunately, methods of calculus quickly produce a mess here because unlike the search for the a_j, setting these partial derivatives to zero produces difficult nonlinear equations. We need a trick!

Rewriting the terms in the summation in equation (18) as inner products, and rearranging, we get:

$$\text{Minimize: } \sum|Y_j'|^2 - \sum(Y_j', P)^2 \qquad (19)$$

which is equivalent to maximizing the second summation since the first is independent of P. This second summation can be rewritten as a matrix product $P^T VP$, where V is $n-1$ times the variance/covariance matrix of the sample $\{Y_j\}$, justifying the normalization of the sample above; P^T is the row vector transpose of the column vector P; and n is the sample size. Since this matrix has the special property of positive semi-definiteness (which is in fact usually the stronger condition of positive definiteness in practice), finding the maximum of this "quadratic form" is easy. Specifically, it is well-known[11] that this expression is maximized when $P=E_1$, the unit "eigenvector" or "characteristic vector" of V associated with the largest (eigen)characteristic value, e_1.

As an aside, let's recall some linear algebra. First, an eigenvector of a matrix, V, is a vector, E, so that $VE=eV$ for some constant, e. That is, multiplying by the matrix just "stretches" the vector if $e>1$, "compresses" the vector if $0<e<1$, and zeros it out if $e=0$. If e is negative, matrix multiplication first "flips" the vector $180°$, then stretches or compresses. In general, e can also be a complex number. Because V is a symmetric matrix, $V=V^T$, it is well known that all eigenvalues are real, and that there exists a complete set of orthogonal (i.e., $(E_i,E_j)=0$ for $i \neq j$) eigenvectors. Because V is also positive semi-definite, i.e., $E^T VE \geq 0$, for all E, the eigenvalues satisfy: $e_j \geq 0$. Finally, for the typical case of V positive definite, i.e., $E^T VE=0$ only when $E=0$, the eigenvalues are strictly positive.

Now that we have P, just how good is it? Returning to equation (19), the "total variation" of the original sample $\sum|Y_j'|^2$ equals $\sum e_j$, where $e_2, ..., e_m$, denote the remaining characteristic values of V in descending order (all are non-

---

[11] See any linear algebra textbook that discusses quadratic forms: for example, Gilbert Strang, *Linear Algebra and Its Applications* (New York: Academic Press, 1976).

negative because $\mathbf{V}$ is positive semi-definite). This assertion follows from the observation that both equal the "trace," or sum of the main diagonal components, of $\mathbf{V}$. In addition, the second term in equation (19) is easily seen to equal e_1, since it can be rewritten as $\mathbf{E}_1{}^T\mathbf{V}\mathbf{E}_1 = e_1|\mathbf{E}_1|^2$, and $\mathbf{E}_1$ has unit length. Consequently, the total variation of the sample *net* of the first principal component is $\Sigma e_j - e_1$, for a relative reduction of $e_1/\Sigma e_j$, which is often 60-80%.

As for the "shape" of $\mathbf{E}_1$, what can be said? As noted by an associate,[12] since $\mathbf{V}$ is a "positive" matrix, i.e., all components are positive, it must be the case by the Perron-Frobenius Theorem that all of the components of $\mathbf{E}_1$ are also positive. Of course, that does not imply that this is a parallel shift, but only that it is a yield curve shift for which all points move in the same direction. In practice,[13] however, the first principal component looks somewhat linear, but decreases from the short to long maturities; that is, short rates have a tendency to move more than long rates.

MULTI-FACTOR YIELD CURVE MODELS

Mathematical Framework

As expected, it is relatively straightforward to generalize the mathematics underlying single factor model risk analysis to its multi-factor counterpart since once again, only calculus is required. Given a collection of factors, $i_1, i_2, ..., i_m$, assumed to capture the statistical drivers of yield curve movements, and which will often be denoted as a vector, $\mathbf{i} = (i_1, i_2, ..., i_m)$, it is natural to model the price of a security or portfolio as a function of these factors $P(\mathbf{i})$. Generalizing the single factor case, there is a multivariate version of the Taylor series expansion which gives the value of the price function on $\mathbf{j}$, $P(\mathbf{j})$, in terms of the value of the price function and its various derivatives on $\mathbf{i}$. Specifically:

$$P(\mathbf{j}) = P(\mathbf{i}) + \Sigma \, \partial_k P(\mathbf{i})(j_k - i_k) + 0.5 \,\Sigma\Sigma\, \partial_{kl}P(\mathbf{i})(j_k - i_k)(j_l - i_l) + \ldots\ldots \quad (20)$$

where ∂_k and ∂_{kl} denote first and second order partial derivatives.

Restating equation (20) analogously to equation (2), one identifies natural generalizations of the notions of duration and convexity in this multi-factor framework:[14]

$$P(\mathbf{j}) \approx P(\mathbf{i})[1 - \Sigma D_k(\mathbf{i}) \, (j_k - i_k) + 0.5 \,\Sigma\Sigma\, C_{kl}(\mathbf{i}) \, (j_k - i_k)(j_l - i_l)] \quad (21)$$
$$= P(\mathbf{i})[1 - \mathbf{D}(\mathbf{i}){\bullet}\Delta\mathbf{i} + 0.5\Delta\mathbf{i}^T\mathbf{C}(\mathbf{i})\Delta\mathbf{i}]$$

---

[12] Benjamin Wurzburger, personal communication. See Marvin Marcus and Henryk Minc, *A Survey of Matrix Theory and Matrix Inequalities* (New York: Dover Publications, 1992), for properties of positive matrices.

[13] See Litterman and Scheinkman, "Common Factors Affecting Bond Returns."

[14] See Reitano "Multivariate Duration Analysis" for a more complete treatment of risk analysis based on multi-factor (i.e., multivariate) models.

where $\Delta i = j - i$. In equation (21), the first approximation is in terms of "partial" durations, $D_k(\mathbf{i})$, and "partial" convexities, $C_{kl}(\mathbf{i})$, while the second uses the more compact vector and matrix notation of the "total duration vector," $\mathbf{D}(\mathbf{i}) \equiv (D_1(\mathbf{i}),....,D_m(\mathbf{i}))$, and "total convexity matrix," $\mathbf{C}(\mathbf{i}) \equiv (C_{kl}(\mathbf{i}))$, where:

$$D_k(\mathbf{i}) = -\partial_k P(\mathbf{i}) / P(\mathbf{i}), \qquad C_{kl}(\mathbf{i}) = \partial_{kl} P(\mathbf{i}) / P(\mathbf{i}) \qquad (22)$$

$\mathbf{C}$ is a "symmetric" matrix, i.e., $C_{kl} = C_{lk}$, reflecting a well-known analogous property of second-order partial derivatives.

Just as for the single factor model and equation (4), equation (22) has as a consequence that all of the above duration and convexity measures enjoy the portfolio property, in that the corresponding measure for a portfolio equals the price-, or market-value-weighted average of the component security measures.

Analogous to equation (4), it is also the case that partial durations and convexities can be approximated by finite difference methods. For example:

$$\partial_k P(\mathbf{i}) \approx [P(\mathbf{i} + \Delta i \mathbf{E}_k) - P(\mathbf{i} - \Delta i \mathbf{E}_k)] / [2\Delta i] \qquad (23)$$

$$\partial_{kl} P(\mathbf{i}) \approx [P(\mathbf{i} + \Delta i(\mathbf{E}_j + \mathbf{E}_k)) - P(\mathbf{i} + \Delta i(\mathbf{E}_l - \mathbf{E}_k)) - P(\mathbf{i} + \Delta i(\mathbf{E}_k - \mathbf{E}_l))$$
$$+ P(\mathbf{i} - \Delta i(\mathbf{E}_k + \mathbf{E}_l))] / [2\Delta i]^2 \qquad (23b)$$

where $\mathbf{E}_k$ is a vector with all 0's except for the kth component, which is a 1. Although these equations at first seem imposing, they are easily programmed and simply require calculated prices on the original term structure, $\mathbf{i}$, as well as on a host of term structures where one or two of the factors is shifted up or down by a "small" amount.

In all, given m factors, equation (23a) requires $2m$ calculated prices in addition to the price on the original term structure, or only m additional prices if the "forward" difference approach is taken. Equation (23b) requires a good deal more effort, requiring in addition to the prices used in equation (23a), a total of $2(m^2 - m)$ additional valuations.

Analogous to equation (6), there is an identity for multi-factor models which relates the price on $\mathbf{j}$, $P(\mathbf{j})$, to the price on $\mathbf{i}$, and values of the total duration vector "between" $\mathbf{j}$ and $\mathbf{i}$. To this end, let $\gamma(t)$ denote a parametrization of term structures so that $\gamma(0) = \mathbf{i}$, and $\gamma(1) = \mathbf{j}$. For example, a simple linear shift could be defined as $\gamma(t) = \mathbf{i} + (\mathbf{j} - \mathbf{i})t$. The identity is then:

$$P(\mathbf{j}) = P(\mathbf{i}) \exp(-\int \mathbf{D}(\gamma(t)) \bullet \gamma'(t) dt) \qquad (24)$$

where the integral is taken over $[0,1]$, and $\gamma'(t)$ denotes the derivative of this vector valued function, which in the case of the above simple example is $\gamma'(t) = \Delta \mathbf{i}$. This identity gives rise to an alternative approximation approach, similar to equation (8), which in its first order version replaces the integral with $\mathbf{D}(\mathbf{i}) \bullet \gamma'(0)$, in general, or with $\mathbf{D}(\mathbf{i}) \bullet \Delta \mathbf{i}$ in the linear case.

Multi-Factor Models

With the first general single factor term structure model introduced in 1971 by Fisher and Weil, multi-factor models have been investigated since 1976.[15] The first such model was:

Mixed Additive-Multiplicative Shift: $i_t \to (1 + i)i_t + j$

$$\mathbf{i} \to (1 + i)\mathbf{i} + j\mathbf{M}$$

where i and j denote the two factors, and i_t denotes the term structure at maturity t. Letting $\mathbf{i}$ denote the term structure in vector notation, and $\mathbf{M}$ the vector with all 1's, this multi-factor model can also be represented as in the second expression above, where the various operations are by convention to be interpreted component by component.

Another model, generalizing the directional model earlier, is the:

Multi-Directional Model: $\mathbf{i} \to \mathbf{i} + \sum j_k \mathbf{N}_k$

where $\{\mathbf{N}_k\}$ are a collection of fixed vectors, and the various j_k are the factors. One implementation of this model is derived from a principal component analysis, whereby the various direction vectors used represent some or all of the principal components of term structure movements (see below).

Another example of this model is the key (spot) rate model of Ho.[16] Here, $\mathbf{i}$ denotes the risk-free term structure of 360 monthly spot rates from 1 month to 30 years, derived from a procedure which reflects the prices of all traded Treasuries, subject to various smoothness criteria. From this vector, "key" rates are selected at maturities: 1, 2, 3, 5, 7, 10, 20, and 30 years, and each rate has associated with it a "pyramid" direction vector defined to be 1 at the key rate maturity, 0 at maturities equal to or greater than the next key rate, and maturities equal to or smaller than the prior key rate, and with all other values linearly interpolated. Consequently, the collection $\{\mathbf{N}_k\}$ so defined forms a "partition of unity" in that $\sum \mathbf{N}_k = \mathbf{M}$, the parallel shift vector of all 1's.

Another convenient parametrization of the term structure was introduced by Reitano as part of the first general study of these models, and called the "yield curve driver" model.[17] Here, $\mathbf{i}$ denotes the term structure of "on the run" treasury bond yields, at maturities 0.25, 0.5, 1, 2, 3, 5, 7, 10, 20, and 30 years, with other maturities developed using interpolation by spline or other methods, and the entire term structure is then converted to spot rates for valuations in the usual

[15] See G.O.Bierwag, "Measures of Duration," University of Oregon, working paper, 1976. Other historical references can be found in Bierwag, *Duration Analysis*. See also D.R.Chambers, W.T. Carleton, and R.W. McEnally, "Immunizing Default-Free Bond Portfolios With a Duration Vector," *Journal of Financial and Quantitative Analysis* (March 1988), pp. 89-104; T.S.Y. Ho, *Strategic Fixed Income Management* (Homewood, Ill.: Dow Jones-Irwin, 1990); T.S.Y. Ho, "Key Rate Durations: Measures of Interest Rate Risks," *Journal of Fixed Income* (September 1992), pp.29-44; and the various papers by Reitano referred to in this chapter.

[16] See Ho, "Key Rate Durations: Measures of Interest Rate Risks."

[17] See Reitano, "Multivariate Duration Analysis."

way. Consequently, these ten or so yields form the "drivers" of the valuation process. The shift model is then:

Yield Curve Driver Model: $\mathbf{i} \rightarrow \mathbf{i} + \Delta \mathbf{i}$

where $\Delta \mathbf{i}$ denotes the vector of factors of yield curve driver shifts $\Delta \mathbf{i} = (\Delta i_1, \Delta i_2, ..., \Delta i_m)$. Of course, the yield curve driver model can be implemented with an arbitrary number of yield curve drivers, and within any term structure basis.

Relationships Between Single and Multi-Factor Models

Once a multi-factor model is developed, it is only natural to investigate its properties relative to single factor, and other multi-factor models. For instance, assume that partial durations and convexities have been calculated as in equation (22). Next, fix a direction vector, $\mathbf{N}$, denominated in components consistent with the multi-factor model, which specifies the fixed relationship assumed to hold between the various factor movements. For instance, the original factors could be based on yield curve drivers, key rates, or a multi-factor directional model. What then is the relationship between the duration and convexity in the single factor directional model, called "directional" durations and convexities, and the "partials" of the multi-factor model?

As proved elsewhere,[18] denoting by D_N and C_N the directional duration and directional convexity calculated as in equation (3) using the directional shift model:

$$D_N = \mathbf{D} \cdot \mathbf{N} \qquad C_N = \mathbf{N}^T \mathbf{C} \mathbf{N} \tag{25}$$

where $\mathbf{D}$ and $\mathbf{C}$ denote the total duration vector and total convexity matrix of the multi-factor model as defined in equations (22) and (23). That is, the directional duration and convexity of the single factor model is easily calculated by:

$$D_N = \sum D_j n_j \qquad C_N = \sum\sum C_{jk} n_j n_k \tag{25b}$$

where $\mathbf{N} = (n_1, n_2, ..., n_m)$.

A simple consequence of equation (25) follows when $\mathbf{N}$ is set equal to the parallel shift vector, $\mathbf{M}$, which has all its components equal to 1. Specifically, the resultant duration and convexity is equal to the sum of the "partials:"

$$D = \sum D_j \qquad C = \sum\sum C_{jk} \tag{26}$$

Equations (25) and (26) are identities between exactly calculated durations and convexities (i.e., identities between the underlying derivatives). Consequently, for durations and convexities approximated using the finite difference equations (4) and (23), these identities will hold only approximately. Similarly, for measures calculated using yield curve scenario sampling techniques, the resultant values will only approximately satisfy these identities, even when the binary bit

---

[18] See Reitano, "Multivariate Duration Analysis."

strings are controlled as discussed above. To be certain that the resulting "errors" are the result of such approximations, and not calculation errors, it is important to "stress test" calculations by decreasing the finite difference interval, increasing the sample size, and verifying that the convergence assured by the theory is observed.

It is also important that equation (26) not be too hastily applied in anticipation that the "traditional" duration and convexity measures of Fisher-Weil will be produced from any multi-factor model. This equation simply states that if the individual factors of a multi-factor model are assumed to move "in parallel," that the sum of the partials will reproduce the results of the single factor model where this assumption is modeled explicitly. A few examples will clarify this point.

For the yield curve driver model, the individual factors are defined as the respective shifts of the various yield curve drivers: $\Delta i = (\Delta i_1, \Delta i_2, \ldots, \Delta i_m)$. The associated parallel shift model reflects the assumption that each shift component, Δi_j, is equal to i, say. Is this model now equivalent to the Fisher-Weil parallel shift model where each point of the term structure is shifted in parallel? A little thought reveals that this will be the case only if the interpolation algorithm used converts parallel shifts of the yield curve drivers to parallel shifts of all the interpolated points of the term structure. Linear interpolation has this property, of course. On the other hand, if the Fisher-Weil parallel shift model is "defined" in terms of the yield curve drivers, the resulting duration and convexity will satisfy equation (26), independent of the interpolation method used.

As another example, consider the multi-factor directional model, where the shift is given by $\Sigma j_k N_k$, and where the $\{j_k\}$ are the factors. Assume next that these factors are modeled to move in parallel; that is, where each j_k equals a given single factor, i. By construction, this single factor model will now be a single factor directional model, where shifts are modeled as $(\Sigma N_k)i$. Is this parallel shift model that of Fisher-Weil? Only when the sum of the direction vectors equals M, the vector of all 1's. An example of when this condition holds is the key rate model, as noted above. However, it is clear from this construction that any multi-factor directional model for which the direction vectors form a "partition of unity," $\Sigma N_k = M$, will enjoy the property that the partial durations and convexities will sum to the corresponding traditional values.

Equation (25) can be generalized to relate the total duration vectors and total convexity matrices of two multi-factor models for which the factors are functionally related. For simplicity, we assume here that this functional relationship is linear. Specifically, consider the above multi-factor directional model with shift $\Sigma j_k N_k$, and where $\{j_k\}$ are interpreted as the factors, denoted J for short, and $\{N_k\}$ are interpreted as fixed. Consider next the general multi-factor model whereby each point of the term structure is modeled as a separate factor, and parametrized in terms of the term structure vector i. What is the relationship between the total duration vectors of the two models? Letting N denote the matrix with the $\{N_j\}$ as columns, we have in matrix notation (D is interpreted as a row matrix):

$$D(j) = D(i)N \quad C(j) = N^T C(i)N \tag{27}$$

Equation (27) provides a more formal way of justifying the observations above regarding "parallel" shift relationships. By equation (25), the parallel shift duration in $\mathbf{j}$-space is equal to $\mathbf{D(j)} \bullet \mathbf{M}$, which can also be expressed in matrix notation as $\mathbf{D(j)M}$, where $\mathbf{M}=(1,1,....,1)$. Is this equal to the parallel shift duration in $\mathbf{i}$-space? Using equation (27), we see that $\mathbf{D(j)M}=\mathbf{D(i)NM}$, so the answer is in the affirmative if and only if $\mathbf{NM}=\mathbf{M}$, which is equivalent to $\sum N_k=\mathbf{M}$; i.e., $\{\mathbf{N}_k\}$ form a partition of unity. The careful reader will note that in the above argument, the symbol $\mathbf{M}$ was used with dimension equal to that of $\mathbf{j}$-space, as well as $\mathbf{i}$-space. The transition occurred in the equation $\mathbf{NM}=\mathbf{M}$, in which the $\mathbf{M}$ on the left had dimension equal to the number of columns of $\mathbf{N}$ (i.e., the number of the $\mathbf{N}_k$, or j_k), while the $\mathbf{M}$ on the right had dimension equal to the number of rows of $\mathbf{N}$ (i.e., the dimension of the $\mathbf{N}_k$, or $\mathbf{i}$).

Is There a "Best" Multi-Factor Model?

Without a great deal of thought, the obvious answer to the above question is: Yes, the model with the number of "independent" factors equal to the number of yields on the term structure being modeled. For instance, if the term structure is modeled as a vector in 360-space, describing monthly spot rates from 1-month to 30 years, one such multi-factor model is the general yield curve driver model: $\mathbf{i} \rightarrow \mathbf{i} + \Delta\mathbf{i}$, where the shift vector describes the component by component moves along the curve. Alternatively, one could use any multi-factor directional model with 360 linearly independent direction vectors. This generalizes the above general yield curve driver model which is equivalent to a multi-factor directional model with $\mathbf{N}_k=(0,..,1,0,...0)$, with 1 in the k-th component.

For the yield curve driver model described earlier, with 10 or so yields identified on a par bond curve and the rest interpolated, again it makes little difference whether one parametrizes factors as described, or in terms of a multi-factor directional model with 10 linearly independent direction vectors. While one parametrization may be more convenient to work with than the other, they will be equivalent in terms of their ability to capture all feasible shifts in the given model.

It is also clear that adding linearly dependent direction vectors to a multi-factor model in no way improves the model's descriptive ability or analytic power. More factors are only better if they are independent factors.

Returning to the title of this section, the real question is: Is there a "best" multi-factor model when the number of factors is "small," i.e., small relative to the number of parameters in the term structure model? In the single factor case discussed above, this distinction did not need to be made because all term structure models have at least one parameter, so of necessity, single factor models are relatively "sparse" in their descriptive ability. However, as was shown above, one single factor model was indeed "best" in terms of capturing the largest share of the movement in historical yield curve shifts.

Specifically, if $\{\mathbf{Y}_j{'}\}$ represents a collection of historical yield curve shifts, denominated in units compatible with the term structure model used, and normalized to have mean **0**, we saw that the "best" direction vector to use to approximate this collection was $\mathbf{E}_1$, the unit eigenvector of the variance/covariance matrix of these shifts, **V**, associated with the largest eigenvalue, e_1. In that development, the $\mathbf{Y}_j$ were assumed to have dimension m, so we next consider the generalization of this result to multi-factor models with less than m factors. In actuality, the two factor development provides the template and will be seen to be easily generalized.

To this end, we seek a direction vector, **P**, so that for optimally chosen $\{b_j\}$, the following is minimized: $\Sigma|\mathbf{Y}_j'-a_j\mathbf{E}_1-b_j\mathbf{P}|^2$, where as noted earlier, $a_j=(\mathbf{E}_1,\mathbf{Y}_j')$. Not surprisingly, the same derivation shows that the optimizing b_j equals: $(\mathbf{P},\mathbf{Y}_j'-a_j\mathbf{E}_1)/|\mathbf{P}|^2$. Before proceeding, let's simplify this expression by requiring **P** to also be a unit vector, and "orthogonal" to $\mathbf{E}_1$, i.e., $(\mathbf{P},\mathbf{E}_1)=0$. Then, mirroring the formula for a_j, we have: $b_j=(\mathbf{P},\mathbf{Y}_j')$.

Another neat consequence of this orthogonality assumption is that the objective function to be minimized reduces to:

$$\text{Minimize: } \Sigma|\mathbf{Y}_j'|^2 - \Sigma(\mathbf{Y}_j',\mathbf{E}_1)^2 - \Sigma(\mathbf{Y}_j',\mathbf{P})^2 \tag{28}$$

because $|\mathbf{X}|^2=(\mathbf{X},\mathbf{X})$, and all the mixed terms in $\mathbf{E}_1$ and **P** disappear. Comparing equation (28) to equation (19), a clear pattern emerges in the problem to be solved. Specifically, the problem is to *maximize* the last term, $\Sigma(\mathbf{Y}_j',\mathbf{P})^2$, which equals $\mathbf{P}^T\mathbf{VP}$, subject to $|\mathbf{P}|=1$, and $(\mathbf{P},\mathbf{E}_1)=0$.

As expected, the solution to this problem is well known to be $\mathbf{E}_2$, the eigenvector of **V** associated with the second largest eigenvalue, e_2. Using these first two principal components, $\mathbf{E}_1$ and $\mathbf{E}_2$, in a 2-factor directional model explains $(e_1+e_2)/\Sigma e_j$ of the total variation of the sample, which is often 80% to 90%.

Generalizing the above derivation, it is apparent that the "best" n-factor directional model uses the first n eigenvectors of **V**, corresponding to the largest eigenvalues, which need not be distinct. That is, a single eigenvalue can have multiple eigenvectors in theory. In that case, it is irrelevant in which order they are used once the given eigenvalue is brought into the model. This n-factor directional model then explains $\Sigma'e_j/\Sigma e_j$, where the sum in the numerator includes only the first n eigenvalues, and each summation includes eigenvalues up to their multiplicity (i.e., number of eigenvectors used).

Multi-Factor Yield Curve Management I

Once a multi-factor model is in place, how do we evaluate and reduce the strategic or tactical risk implied by the portfolio's durational profile, or, how do we evaluate and enhance the tactical opportunities?

To begin with, recall equation (21) which provides an approximation to the value of price on multi-factor value $\mathbf{j}\equiv\mathbf{i}+\Delta\mathbf{i}$, $P(\mathbf{j})$, based on the value of price, durations and convexities on **i**: $P(\mathbf{i})$, $\mathbf{D}(\mathbf{i})$, and $\mathbf{C}(\mathbf{i})$; and on $\Delta\mathbf{i}$. Using only the durational term, the expression $P(\mathbf{i}+\Delta\mathbf{i})/P(\mathbf{i})$ can be approximated by $R(\Delta\mathbf{i})$:

$$R(\Delta\mathbf{i}) = (1 - \mathbf{D}(\mathbf{i})\bullet\Delta\mathbf{i}) \tag{29}$$

Recalling the well known Cauchy-Schwarz inequality, that: $|X \cdot Y| \leq |X||Y|$, we have that the absolute variation of this price ratio from 1 is bounded by:

$$|R(\Delta i) - 1| = |-D(i) \cdot \Delta i| \leq |D(i)| \, |\Delta i| \tag{30}$$

Taking risk assessment first, equation (30) provides an upper bound to risk based on the total duration vector and an estimate of the maximum shift possible. For the yield curve driver model, $|D(i)|$ is equal to the square root of the sum of the partial durations squared:

$$\sqrt{\Sigma D_j^2}$$

by definition, and an estimate of $|\Delta i|$ can be made by an analysis of historical yield curve data denominated in the same units as the yield curve driver basis.

Within a multi-factor directional model, such as the key rate model, $|D(i)|$ again reflects the partial durations under this model, which in turn are directional durations to the direction vectors. For example, if the model used is: $\Delta i = \Sigma j_k E_k$, with $\{E_k\}$ defined from a principal component analysis, each partial duration to j_k, $D_k(i)$, is in fact a directional duration with respect to E_k, $D_E(i)$, which in turn is equal to, by equation (27), $D(i) \cdot E_k$, where here $D(i)$ equals the total duration vector with respect to the yield curve driver model underlying the principal components. The estimate here for $|\Delta i|$ is again based on historical data, but recognizing that for this multi-factor directional model, Δi is defined in terms of the coefficients of the principal components in the yield curve expansions. That is, since each historical yield curve can be expanded $Y_k = \Sigma(Y_k, E_j)E_j$, we have $\Delta Y_k \equiv Y_{k+1} - Y_k = \Sigma(\Delta Y_k, E_j)E_j$, and the components of the parameter vector in equation (30), Δi, are the $(\Delta Y, E_j)$ terms and hence:

$$|\Delta i| = \sqrt{[\Sigma(\Delta Y, E_j)^2]}$$

for each shift, ΔY.

Opportunistically, equation (30) can be utilized by investigating the relationship between $D(i)$ and Δi that assures the most favorable result. Besides providing an inequality for a dot product, the Cauchy-Schwarz derivation identifies the relationship between the two vectors which assures that the largest or smallest value is in fact obtained. Specifically, it turns out that the maximum value of a dot product is obtained when X equals a positive multiple of Y, denoted $X \approx Y$, while the minimum value is obtained when X is a negative multiple, $X \approx -Y$.

Consequently, referring to equation (30), to take a maximum opportunistic position on an anticipated factor shift Δi, one needs to trade to achieve a total duration vector, $D(i)$, so that $-D(i)$ is positively proportional to this anticipated shift; i.e., $D(i)$ must be positively proportional to $-\Delta i$. Hence, one wants negative durational exposure to positive anticipated factor shifts and conversely, and the more one anticipates the factor to move, the more durational exposure is sought. This generalizes the one factor opportunistic tactic in a natural way.

However, there are infinitely many vectors positively proportional to $-\Delta\mathbf{i}$, so which should be targeted? Again, the answer is analogous to the single factor case where it was clear that for negative shifts, maximize $D(\mathbf{i})$, and conversely. Here, "larger" multiples are better than smaller multiples since this strategy magnifies the effect. Specifically, if $\mathbf{D}(\mathbf{i})=-a\Delta\mathbf{i}$, where a is assumed to be positive, then by equation (30), $|R(\Delta\mathbf{i})-1|=a|\Delta\mathbf{i}|^2$, so the larger a is the better.

When making an explicit assumption about $\Delta\mathbf{i}$ is deemed imprudent, but one wishes to take advantage of beliefs about the probable range of such factor shifts, as in the single factor model, a utility based analysis is possible. To this end, assume that the likely behavior of $\Delta\mathbf{i}$ can be modeled in terms of a probability distribution, however crude, and that a utility function, $u(w)$, has been selected. Consider the expected utility objective function to be maximized: $f(\mathbf{D})=E[u(1-\mathbf{D}\bullet\Delta\mathbf{i})]$. Equating the partial derivatives with respect to the various D_j to zero, the following system of equations is produced:

$$E[\Delta i_j\, u'(1 - \mathbf{D}\bullet\Delta\mathbf{i})] = 0$$

It is easy to see that any solution, $\mathbf{D}$, to this system is a utility maximizing total duration vector for a risk averse investor, because the matrix of second degree partial derivatives $(E[\Delta i_j\Delta i_k u''(1\ \mathbf{D}\bullet\Delta\mathbf{i})])$ is positive definite.

To see this, let $\mathbf{X}$ be any vector and consider the matrix product: $\mathbf{X}^T\mathbf{A}\mathbf{X}$, where $\mathbf{A}$ is this second derivative matrix. Using properties of expectations, we get: $\mathbf{X}^T\mathbf{A}\mathbf{X}=E[(\sum\Delta i_k x_k)^2 u''(1-\mathbf{D}\bullet\Delta\mathbf{i})]$, which is positive unless the entire probability mass of $\Delta\mathbf{i}$ is concentrated on a hyperplane. In that case, there is an $\mathbf{X}$ so that $\sum\Delta i_k x_k=0$ for all $\Delta\mathbf{i}$. Of course, in this case, the number of factors can in fact be reduced by 1, and the process repeated.

We next return to a risk assessment perspective, and investigate theoretical risk "elimination" with an immunization strategy. As in the case for single factor models, we in reality eliminate risk only to factor shifts encompassed by the given model, since we can not escape stochastic process risk unless the model is full dimensional (i.e., the same dimension as the number of points on the term structure). However, even in that case, protection is compromised once the time dynamics of the portfolio are taken into consideration.

To this end, consider equation (21). In order to eliminate the risk to all factor shifts encompassed by the model, it is evident that as in the single factor case, we must have $\mathbf{D}(\mathbf{i})=\mathbf{0}$. In actuality, it is only necessary that $\mathbf{D}(\mathbf{i})\bullet\Delta\mathbf{i}=0$ for all feasible factor shifts, $\Delta\mathbf{i}$. However, this equation implies that $\mathbf{D}(\mathbf{i})=\mathbf{0}$, except in the case when all feasible shifts belong to a hyperplane of the factor space. In that case, the number of factors in the model can be reduced to the point where $\mathbf{D}(\mathbf{i})=\mathbf{0}$ is the conclusion. This vector equation is equivalent to $D_j(\mathbf{i})=0$ for all j. When the model is a multi-factor directional model, these equations are equivalent to having the directional durations with respect to the model's directions all zero; i.e., $D_E(\mathbf{j})=D(\mathbf{j})\bullet\mathbf{E}=0$ for all $\mathbf{E}$ in the model. This result follows from equation (27), where here, $\mathbf{D}(\mathbf{j})$ denotes the total duration vector on the yield curve driver model underlying the directional model.

Besides the durational constraint, immunization theory also recognizes the potential for gains and losses from the convexity term, and seeks to make them only gains. Again referring to equation (21), we seek to have: $\Delta i^T C(i) \Delta i \geq 0$, for all Δi. That is, we seek to have the total convexity matrix positive semi-definite, although the purists might require positive definiteness: $\Delta i^T C(i) \Delta i > 0$, except if $\Delta i = 0$. In the multi-factor directional model, this condition on the convexity matrix in units of direction factors, i, can also be translated to a condition on the convexity matrix in units of the yield curve driver model underlying the directional model, using equation (27).

Let j denote the yield curve driver units, $j = \Sigma i_k N_k = N i$, where N denotes the matrix with the N_k as columns. Then

$$\Delta i^T C(i) \Delta i = \Delta i^T N^T C(j) N \Delta i = (N \Delta i)^T C(j) N \Delta i$$

so the conclusion is that $C(j)$, the convexity matrix in yield curve driver units, must be positive (semi-)definite on the space generated by the collection of direction vectors used. For example, if the direction vectors used are from a principal component analysis, $\{E_j\}$, the yield curve driver convexity matrix must have this property on all yield curve shifts generated by these components.

Combining the above results, immunization criteria for a general multi-factor model can be easily stated in terms of the price function of interest, $P(i)$. When applied, the general equation (21) becomes the multi-factor counterpart to equation (10):

$$P(j) \approx P(i)(1 + 0.5 \Delta i^T C(i) \Delta i) \tag{31}$$

where $C(i)$ is at least positive semi-definite, so it is always the case that $P(j) \geq P(i)$.

However, as noted above, this price function typically represents a net portfolio such as surplus, a market-neutral account, or an asset portfolio net of a notional index portfolio, so it is more relevant to state these criteria in terms of these underlying price functions. To do this, we need to recall that as a consequence of equation (22), total duration vectors and convexity matrices enjoy the portfolio property. That is, if $\{P_k(i)\}$ are a collection of non-zero price functions with duration vectors, $\{D_k(i)\}$, and convexity matrices, $\{C_k(i)\}$, then if $P(i) = \Sigma P_k(i)$ is non-zero:

$$D(i) = \Sigma w_k D_k(i) \qquad C(i) = \Sigma w_k C_k(i) \tag{32}$$

where $w_k = P_k(i)/P(i)$.

Using equation (32) applied to a surplus portfolio, $S(i) = A(i) - L(i)$, we obtain the following conditions for immunization against yield curve shifts implied by the multi-factor model used:

$$D^A(i) = [L(i)/A(i)] D^L(i) \qquad A(i) C^A(i) - L(i) C^L(i) >> 0 \tag{33}$$

where $X >> 0$ denotes that X is a positive definite matrix.

The conditions of equation (33) provide protection for the current value of surplus against "instantaneous" shifts in the factors. One can also develop conditions which protect the value of the surplus ratio, $(A(\mathbf{i})/L(\mathbf{i}))/A(\mathbf{i})$, which turn out to be identical to those in equation (33) *except* that the values of assets and liabilities are omitted.[19] Another strategy, with applications to surplus as well as to other portfolios discussed above, is the strategy of immunizing the *forward* value of surplus against instantaneous shifts.

To make this notion precise, let $Z_k(\mathbf{i})$ denote the value of a k-period, zero-coupon bond with maturity value \$1, where as always, this value reflects the term structure implied by the factor value, $\mathbf{i}$. If $P(\mathbf{i})$ denotes the price function for a given portfolio, define the forward price function, denoted $P_k(\mathbf{i})$, by:

$$P_k(\mathbf{i}) = P(\mathbf{i})/Z_k(\mathbf{i})$$

Intuitively, $P_k(\mathbf{i})$ represents the value of the portfolio at time k that can be locked-in today by selling the portfolio and buying the zero. Strictly stated, this value is locked-in only if the zero is risk-free, but we assume that this poses no valuation problems and that the necessary term structure is also driven by the multi-factor model used.

Immunization criteria for $P_k(\mathbf{i})$ are:

$$\mathbf{D}^A(\mathbf{i}) = [L(\mathbf{i})\mathbf{D}^L(\mathbf{i}) + S(\mathbf{i})\mathbf{D}^Z(\mathbf{i})]/A(\mathbf{i})$$

$$A(\mathbf{i})\mathbf{C}^A(\mathbf{i}) - L(\mathbf{i})\mathbf{C}^L(\mathbf{i}) - S(\mathbf{i})\mathbf{C}^Z(\mathbf{i}) >> \mathbf{0}$$

(34)

where $\mathbf{D}^Z$ and $\mathbf{C}^Z$ denote the duration vector and convexity matrix of $Z_k(\mathbf{i})$. Note that the conditions in equation (34) reduce to those in (33) when $k=0$, as expected. Note also that the conditions in equation (34) are equivalent to the requirement that surplus have the same durational structure, and more convexity (i e , in the sense of positive definiteness), than the k-period zero-coupon bond.

When either equation (33) or equation (34) is utilized in equation (31), it appears that we have constructed conditions which assure a risk-free arbitrage for surplus, on the one hand, or the forward value of surplus, on the other. However, in the same way that this conclusion was overstated in the one factor case using equations (9) and (10), it is again overstated here, and for the same reason. The reason is that the multi-factor immunization conditions were developed without regard for the time dynamics of the portfolio in question. It was explicitly assumed that the portfolio's characteristics did not change as the factor shifted, so as before, the above immunization conditions can only be said to provide protection against "instantaneous" factor shifts.

In the more realistic model which explicitly recognizes the time dynamic, what was modeled as $P(\mathbf{i})$ above, would be modeled as $P(t, \mathbf{i}_t)$, where $\mathbf{i}_t$ denoted the dependence of the factor vector on time. As in the one factor case, when $\mathbf{i}_t$ is assumed to follow a multi-factor Ito process, one discovers that the

---

[19] See Reitano, "Multivariate Immunization Theory" for more details on all the immunization models discussed.

immunization condition on the duration structure can only hold instantaneously, due to the diffusion coefficients, and hence no risk-free arbitrage is created.

Multi-Factor Yield Curve Management II[20]

Once an immunization theory has been developed within a multi-factor context and implemented, two fundamental truisms are discovered: (1) the more factors that are used, the more restrictive the conditions become until virtual cash-matching is required; and, (2) the less factors that are used, the more likely immunization will fail because the model is too sparse to capture the true variability of term structure shifts.

While initially discouraging, these truisms compel a rethinking of the underlying framework for immunization theory. The classical goal of immunization theory is the virtual elimination of downside risk, but in practice, it is only to a subset of feasible shifts that the portfolio is protected. Worse yet, the typical approach completely ignores the potential for loss from shifts outside the model used. As an alternative, rather than seek complete protection from some shifts and have unknown protection from others, perhaps it would be better to have a strategy which provided a minimal amount of risk from all shifts.

The search for such a strategy lead to the development of the theory of "stochastic immunization." Its goal is to minimize the "risk," as yet to be defined, of the relative price function $P(\mathbf{i}+\Delta\mathbf{i})/P(\mathbf{i})$, which is approximated by the linear function, $R(\Delta\mathbf{i})$, defined in equation (29). More generally, its goal is to minimize risk subject to various constraints and objectives of interest.

To develop a measure of risk, first note that since $\Delta\mathbf{i}$ is fundamentally a stochastic variable, it makes sense to follow Markowitz,[21] and consider the variance of $R(\Delta\mathbf{i})$. As it turns out:

$$\mathrm{Var}[R(\Delta\mathbf{i})] = \mathbf{D(i)KD(i)}^T$$

where $\mathbf{K}$ denotes the variance/covariance matrix of the factor change vector, $\Delta\mathbf{i}$ (recall that above, $\mathbf{V}$ denoted $n-1$ times the variance/covariance matrix; i.e., $\mathbf{V}=(n-1)\mathbf{K}$). For simplicity, $\Delta\mathbf{i}$ will be referred to as if its components were in fact changes in the term structure at designated maturities, although the model applies equally well in the general multi-factor case. Recall also that $\mathbf{D(i)}$ is by convention treated as a row matrix, and hence the placement of the transpose symbol above.

Variance is an important measure to minimize because its value determines the likelihood that the random variable under consideration can assume relatively large values. For instance, when normally distributed, only 32% of the distribution is more than one standard deviation away (recall S.D.$=\sqrt{\mathrm{Var}}$), only 5% more than 2 S.D.'s, 0.2% more than 3 S.D.'s, etc. While Ito calculus assumes

---

[20] For details on the approach developed here, see Robert R. Reitano, "Multivariate Stochastic Immunization," *Transactions of the Society of Actuaries*, XLV (1993), pp. 425-484 and, "Non-Parallel Yield Curve Shifts and Stochastic Immunization," *Journal of Portfolio Management* (Winter 1996), pp. 71-78.

[21] Harry Markowitz, *Portfolio Selection: Efficient Diversification of Investments* (New York: John Wiley & Sons, 1959).

that factors are "locally" normal, i.e., over infinitesimal time increments, we cannot assume the same for Δi or $R(\Delta i)$ over finite time interval shifts. So what does variance imply in the general case?

An important result, known as Chebyshev's Inequality, provides the answer in the general case. Specifically, it states that for any constant $a>0$, the distribution of $R(\Delta i)$ satisfies:

$$Pr(\{\Delta i: |R(\Delta i) - E[R(\Delta i)]|^2 \ge a\}) \le \text{Var}[R(\Delta i)]/a$$

That is, the probability that the random variable, $R(\Delta i)$, is far from its expected value depends on the variance. Setting $a=n^2\text{Var}[R(\Delta i)]$, and rearranging, we get:

$$Pr(\{\Delta i: |R(\Delta i) - E[R(\Delta i)]| \ge n(\text{S.D.})\}) \le n^{-2}$$

which is much weaker than in the normal case. For example, the probability that the random variable is at least 3 S.D.'s away from its mean is no more than about 11% in general, compared with 0.2% for the normal.

Because of this relatively weak general upper bound, and the importance of limiting the likelihood of "outlier" values of $R(\Delta i)$, another risk measure of interest follows from equation (30), which can be restated:

$$|R(\Delta i) - E[R(\Delta i)]| \le |\mathbf{D}(i)| \, |\Delta i - E[\Delta i]|$$

That is, the difference between the approximate relative price ratio, $R(\Delta i)$, and its expected value, $E[R(\Delta i)]$, is bounded above by the length of the duration vector, $\mathbf{D}(i)$, and the length of the yield curve shift less its mean. Because that last term can be assumed to be bounded, $|\mathbf{D}(i)|$, or equivalently, $|\mathbf{D}(i)|^2$, can be viewed as a risk proxy in that by making it small, outliers in the distribution of $R(\Delta i)$ can be limited, not only in probability as is assured by Chebyshev, but completely.

Both risk proxies above, $\text{Var}[R(\Delta i)]$ and $|\mathbf{D}(i)|^2$, can be weighted and combined into a general risk proxy which provides the user with the option of giving these measures the relative weights desired. Specifically, for a general weighting parameter, w, we define a risk measure, $RM(w)$, by:

$$RM(w) = w\text{Var}[R(\Delta i)] + (1 - w)|\mathbf{D}(i)|^2$$

where we assume $0 \le w \le 1$. As it turns out, $RM(w)$ can also be written as a quadratic form in $\mathbf{D}$, similar to the above expression for variance. That is, defining $\mathbf{K}_w \equiv w\mathbf{K} + (1 - w)\mathbf{I}$, we have:

$$RM(w) = \mathbf{D}\mathbf{K}_w\mathbf{D}^T \tag{35}$$

As noted above, $\mathbf{K}$ is at least positive *semi*-definite in theory, although in practice, it will be positive definite for appropriate factor parametrizations. In any case, $\mathbf{K}_w$ is positive definite for $w<1$, so we assume that $\mathbf{K}_1=\mathbf{K}$ also has this property.

On a practical note, while the theory only requires $0 \leq w \leq 1$, in practice, w must be relatively close to 1. This is due to the fact that the units of $\mathbf{K}$ are of the order of magnitude of 10^{-5} or so, depending on the length of the period underlying $\Delta\mathbf{i}$, while the units of $\mathbf{I}$ are magnitude 1. Hence, unless w is close to 1 to offset this unit disparity, the risk minimization problem will effectively reduce to the minimization of $|\mathbf{D(i)}|^2$.

Because $\mathbf{K}_w$ is positive definite, as noted above, it is completely trivial to minimize $RM(w)$ for any w. That is, the minimum of $RM(w)$ is 0, and this value is obtained if and only if $\mathbf{D=0}$, by definition. This conclusion is equivalent to that which is obtained by applying the traditional notion of immunization to this multi-factor setting. We have not yet obtained anything of value using this new immunization paradigm.

The payoff for this model is the ability of the portfolio manager to incorporate a host of constraints and strategic objectives into the minimization problem. One such objective relates to the targeting of the term structure shift (i.e., factor shift) return, $E[R(\Delta\mathbf{i})]$. An easy calculation shows that since $R(\Delta\mathbf{i})=1-\mathbf{D}\bullet\Delta\mathbf{i}$:

$$E[R(\Delta\mathbf{i})] = 1 - \mathbf{D}\bullet E[\Delta\mathbf{i}]$$

where $E[\Delta\mathbf{i}]$ is the expected yield curve (i.e., factor) vector shift. Consequently, one can target $E[R(\Delta\mathbf{i})]=r$, using the constraint: $\mathbf{D}\bullet E[\Delta\mathbf{i}]=1-r$.

In practice, this objective can be used strategically or tactically. In the former case, one selects $E[\Delta\mathbf{i}]$ based on an analysis of historical data; in the latter case, $E[\Delta\mathbf{i}]$ represents a personal view of short-term expectations on which one seeks to take a position. Admittedly, the strategic approach has limited applicability because historical values of $E[\Delta\mathbf{i}]$ are so dependent on the period analyzed. Consequently, the selection of a value often involves a process which is fundamentally tactical in nature. As a final point, the strategic choice $E[\Delta\mathbf{i}]=\mathbf{0}$, adds nothing to the problem and can be omitted because this assumption in no way constrains the solution, $\mathbf{D}$, sought.

Another constraint of interest is the targeting of one or more directional durations. That is, based on a principal component or other analysis, or tactically selected direction vectors, one may want to target directional duration values $D_N=\mathbf{D}\bullet\mathbf{N}$, for various values of $\mathbf{N}$. For example, choosing $\mathbf{N=M}\equiv(1,1,..,1)$, allows the targeting of the parallel factor shift duration measure.

In practice, the direction vectors selected and the values of the directional durations targeted will reflect the application in hand. For example, if surplus is the object portfolio underlying the price function, one might simply target traditional duration to 0 or a small value consistent with the traditional theory. More generally, one could limit the directional duration exposures to one or several of the principal component directions. A similar approach might be taken with a market neutral portfolio, or a portfolio actively managed against an index fund where one creates an objective portfolio equal to a long position in the active portfolio and a short position in the index. Alternatively, this last application can be handled by targeting the various directional durations of the actively managed portfolio to those of the index fund.

A final constraint of interest is one which reflects the assets available for trading from the initial total durational structure to that identified as the solution to the constrained risk minimization problem. This asset collection is important since the fewer securities it contains, the less likely one will be able to achieve the desired outcome without specifically providing for the implied limitations. For example, if one can only trade 5-year and 10-year bonds, it is apparent that the portfolio's 20-year partial duration can not be changed. Hence, when developing the constrained minimization problem, it is important to have some constraint so that the solution does not require a change in this value.

In general, it turns out that the asset trading set imposes constraints by defining direction vectors for which the directional durations of the portfolio cannot be changed. That is, it defines a collection $\{N_j\}$, so that the solution to the problem, D, must satisfy $D \bullet N_j = D(i) \bullet N_j$, where $D(i)$ denotes the original portfolio total duration vector. As expected, when the asset trading set is sufficiently large, the above set of vectors is empty, implying that the duration of the portfolio can be changed in any direction.

To determine the constraining direction vectors implied by the given asset trading set, first note that any trade in the portfolio must be "cash neutral;" that is, the totality of purchases must equal the totality of sales. While one may initially reject this notion with the counterexample of a portfolio with excessive cash, a moment of thought reveals that cash neutrality is again obeyed since the purchases must be funded by the sale of short-term securities, such as commercial paper, or the "sale" of cash holdings in a STIF (i.e., short term investment fund) account. In any case, these "cash" positions are part of the initial portfolio value, and this value does not change after a trade; i.e., trades are always cash neutral.

Next, assume that there are n assets available, with total duration vectors $\{D_k(i)\}$. Form the matrix, A, with $n-1$ columns equal to: $D_1-D_n, \ldots, D_{n-1}-D_n$. It is irrelevant which asset is chosen as the nth; while the matrix A will look different, the same constraints result in the end. Finally, determine a "basis" for the null space of A^T. That is, determine any collection of independent vectors that span the vector space of solutions to $A^T N = 0$. This can be accomplished with available software, or with more effort, by reducing this system of equations to upper triangular form. The number of such solutions is called the nullity of A^T, and denoted $v(A^T)$, or v for short.

The collection of null space vectors: $N_1, N_2, \ldots, N_v$ then represent the directions in which the directional duration of the portfolio can not be changed by trading the given assets. That is, this collection of tradable assets requires the following constraints on the risk minimization problem: $D \bullet N_j = D(i) \bullet N_j$, for $j = 1, 2, \ldots, v$.

In summary, note that every constraint or strategic objective above could be represented by a linear equation for the total duration vector of the form $D \bullet N = r$, for some vector N and value r. Collecting all such constraint vectors as columns of a matrix, B, and the associated values into a vector, r, all such constraint equations can be compactly expressed as $DB = r^T$. Consequently, the constrained risk minimization problem of "stochastic immunization" can be expressed:

Minimize: $\mathbf{DK}_w\mathbf{D}^T$, subject to: $\mathbf{DB} = \mathbf{r}^T$ (36)

Before presenting a solution to equation (36) which requires conditions on $\mathbf{B}$, let's pause to understand why conditions are needed. First off, no limitation has yet been placed on the number of restrictions allowed in the equation $\mathbf{DB}=\mathbf{r}^T$. Even on an intuitive level this seems problematic since if there are too many constraints, there will likely be no solutions; i.e., we will have an empty constraint set. For example, in 2 dimensions if $\mathbf{D}=(x,y)$, the three constraints: $2x+2y=4$, $2x+3y=4$, and $2x+3y=8$, have no solution, as is easily verified. In general, the number of constraints must be no greater than the dimension of $\mathbf{D}$, or m. But is that enough to assure a "consistent" constraint set?

In general the answer is no. Returning to the above example of three equations, any one gives a consistent constraint set of a straight line, as do equations 1 and 2 together, or, 1 and 3, in each case giving a constraint set of a single point. But equations 2 and 3 produce an empty set! In this case the problem is that the constraint direction vectors agree, equalling $(2,3)$, but the constraint values do not, producing an empty intersection. Geometrically, the constraint lines are parallel. If the constraint values also agreed, the constraints would be redundant, and only one needed.

In m dimensions, the constraint set will always be problem free if the set of direction vectors, i.e., the columns of $\mathbf{B}$, are linearly independent. Automatically, this condition assures that the number of such constraints is less than the dimension of $\mathbf{D}$, but also, that inconsistent and redundant constraints illustrated above are avoided.

Assuming that $\mathbf{B}$ has linearly independent columns, i.e., that the constraint direction vectors have this property, the solution to equation (36), $\mathbf{D}_o$, is unique and given by:

$$\mathbf{D}_o^T = \mathbf{K}_w^{-1}\mathbf{B}(\mathbf{B}^T\mathbf{K}_w^{-1}\mathbf{B})^{-1}\mathbf{r}$$ (37)

Further, the value of the risk measure for this total duration vector, $RM_0(w)=\mathbf{D}_o\mathbf{K}_w\mathbf{D}_o^T$, is given by:

$$RM_0(w) = \mathbf{r}^T(\mathbf{B}^T\mathbf{K}_w^{-1}\mathbf{B})^{-1}\mathbf{r}$$ (38)

While equations (36) and (37) appear imposing because of the needed matrix manipulations, they are easily evaluated using popular computer software.

Equation (38) can be interpreted as defining an "efficient frontier" in (Risk, $\mathbf{r}$)-space, reflecting the constraint direction vectors assumed in $\mathbf{B}$. Specifically, if $\mathbf{D}'$ is any total duration vector satisfying $\mathbf{DB}=\mathbf{r}^T$, then $RM(w) \geq RM_0(w)$. It is not difficult to show that the "shape" of this frontier is a paraboloid in (Risk, $\mathbf{r}$)-space.

For example, if $\mathbf{B}$ has only one column equal to $\mathbf{M}=(1, 1, ..., 1)$, then $\mathbf{DB}=\mathbf{r}^T$ reduces to: $D=r$, where D denotes the traditional parallel factor shift duration measure. Equation (38) then reduces to $RM_0(w)=cr^2$, where $c=(\mathbf{M}^T\mathbf{K}_w^{-1}\mathbf{M})^{-1}=$ $1/\sum\sum(\mathbf{K}^{-1})_{jk}$, and $(\mathbf{K}^{-1})_{jk}$ denotes the jk^{th} element of $\mathbf{K}^{-1}$. Clearly, this efficient frontier is a parabola in (Risk, r)-space.

Once D_0 has been calculated from equation (38), the final problem is to develop the trade that will convert the current total duration vector, $D(i)=D$, into the optimum total duration vector, D_0. To this end, let $a=(a_1, a_2, ..., a_n)$ denote the "trade vector," with a_j corresponding to the amount traded of the jth asset, which as before is assumed to have total duration vector, D_j. By convention, we will interpret $a_j>0$ as denoting a purchase, and $a_j<0$ a sale (of course, $a_j=0$ means "no trade").

If $P(i)=P$ denotes the value of the portfolio pre-trade, then by equation (32), the total duration vector after a trade, D', is given by: $D'=[PD+\Sigma a_j D_j]/P$, since all trades are cash neutral (i.e., $\Sigma a_j = 0$). Of course, the goal of the trade it to make $D'=D_0$. Equating expressions, and substituting: $a_n=-\Sigma a_j$, where $j<n$, we get:

$$Aa' = P[D_0 - D]^T \qquad (39)$$

where A is the matrix used above in connection with the asset trading set constraints (i.e., with columns equal to D_j-D_n, $j=1, 2, ..., n-1$), a' is the "truncated" trade vector: $a'=(a_1, ..., a_{n-1})$, and a_n is implicitly defined by the condition of cash neutrality. Equation (39) will always be solvable with a sufficient number of assets (i.e., large enough so that A has "rank" equal to m, the dimension of D), or with fewer assets if constraints are imposed in equation (36) as discussed above. Being solvable, of course, does not mean "uniquely solvable." In general, there will be an infinite number of solutions from which to chose based on criteria outside the scope of the problem so far.

As is well known, if the solution of equation (39) is not unique, then there exists vectors a_j', $j=0, 1,...v$, so that a_0' is an arbitrary solution to this equation, and the other a_j' span the null space of A: $\{a'|Aa'=0\}$. It should be noted that here, $v=v(A)$ denotes the "nullity" of A, in contrast to the discussion on asset trading set constraints where this standard notation denoted the nullity of A^T. Consequently, any solution of equation (39) can be expressed as $a'=a_0'+\Sigma b_j a_j'$.

Once this standard expression is derived, the actual implemented solution can be required to satisfy additional constraints on current yield, average quality, amount traded, etc. Many such constraints will in themselves require the solution to a minimization/maximization problem, which can usually be solved with standard techniques.

For example, one might chose to minimize the amount traded to limit bid/asked trading costs. Using linear programming software, the problem is to: Minimize $\Sigma|a_j'|$, summing j from 1 to n, where $a'=(a_1', ..., a_{n-1}')$ solves: $a'=a_0'+\Sigma b_j a_j'$, and a_n' is defined as: $-\Sigma a_j'$, for cash neutrality. In the absence of such software, one could solve a related problem analytically: Minimize $\Sigma|a_j'|^2$, subject to the same constraints. Note that a_n' can be written as: $-a'\bullet M$, where $M=(1,1,...,1)$ as before. Consequently, $\Sigma|a_j'|^2=a'\bullet a'+[a'\bullet M]^2$.

Additional Considerations for Multi-Factor Models
Throughout the above development, the intuitive framework for the multi-factor representations was the term structure. That is, it was intuitively assumed that the

factors utilized were in one way or another, directly related to the dependence of yield on maturity. This yield could be defined on a par bond, spot, or forward basis, and be denominated in semi-annual or any nominal basis. In general then, the multiple factors related either to movements in these yields directly, as in the general yield curve driver model, or were related indirectly by assuming certain "structural" relationships in the factor movements, as in the general multi-factor directional model.

However, these multi-factor models have much wider applicability. For instance, even in the realm of a term structure, there is not a unique structure but many such structures. Risk-free yields represent the most obvious example of a term structure because of the "real time" availability of traded yields. But at every credit quality another structure exists, although generally less observable across all maturities in real time. Even different sectors of the fixed-income markets often trade at different yields for a fixed given credit quality and maturity, sometimes due to factors such as liquidity and optionality, but equally often not apparently related to any such analytic variable.

Fortunately, such sector differentials are usually relatively small, so it is not unrealistic to ignore them in a strategic model, the goal of which is to develop yield curve management strategies, even though it would be foolhardy to ignore such differentials in a tactical model, the goal of which is to develop cheap/rich insights. Consequently, for a realistic model of "term structure" movements, one needs not only the term structure of risk free rates, but also the term structure of risk spreads for the various credit qualities. Within such a multi-factor model, one could also evaluate "credit spread" durations and partial durations,[22] and evaluate the risks of immunization strategies to shifts among the various spreads. For example, multi-term structure shifts which widen quality spreads would be expected to adversely affect the real value of surplus if assets were of a lower quality than liabilities, although simple single-term structure models would not identify this risk because such models implicitly assume that all spreads move in lock-step.

Naturally, the more general and realistic multi-term structure model can be accommodated in a multi-factor framework by defining **i** to not only reflect risk-free term structure parameters, but also the term structure parameters for credit spreads at the various qualities. While the resulting multi-factor models will have more dimensions than simple single-term structure models, the various risk analyses and immunization strategies are as easily implemented using computer routines.

One real difficulty, however, is the development of statistical assumptions needed for principal component analyses, or for stochastic immunization discussed above, or any application which requires the variance/covariance matrix

---

[22] See Reitano, "Nonparallel Yield Curve Shifts and Spread Leverage," for more details on the multi-factor framework. See also Martin L. Liebowitz, William S. Krasker and Ardavan Nozari, "Spread Duration: A New Tool for Bond Portfolio Management," *Journal of Portfolio Management* (Spring 1990).

of the factor vector. For risk-free statistics, of course, this analysis is relatively easy due to the volumes of data on historical Treasury yield curves which are readily available. For credit spreads, available data must first be "scrubbed" for consistency, and oftentimes holes filled in the series. Even then, spread statistics tend to be more stylistic than risk-free statistics, although still of potential value.

Another extension of the multi-factor framework, but this time beyond the term structure of yields, is to the parameter "yield volatility," or in the more general case, the "volatility term structure." Because of the prevalence of embedded options in fixed-income securities, including liabilities, and because of the dependence of the value of such options on volatility, it is only natural to explicitly model this dependency and seek to manage it, either strategically or tactically.

Recognizing such parameters explicitly as part of the multi-factor structure provides continuity between option management via the "Greeks"(i.e., gamma and delta), and general yield curve management via the notions of "volatility duration" and "volatility convexity." In fact, these latter measures are more convenient in practice for embedded options because they represent measures of the sensitivity of price to changes in the factor directly, in contrast to the "Greeks" which provide option price sensitivities to changes in the underlying security's price, which in turn must be converted to a factor basis. Moreover, even though mathematically equivalent, the volatility duration/convexity analytics are oftentimes far easier to use because in many applications, embedded options can not be easily defined as options on a simple, well-defined underlying security, for which the "Greeks" are easily calculated.

For example, even a callable bond's embedded option has a complicated security underlying it; namely, the callable bond itself. While one can formally perform the decomposition of the embedded option into gamma, etc., it is far more efficient to simply calculate the volatility duration of the bond directly; or better yet, the volatility partial durations.

Chapter 15

Non-Hedgable Risk: Model Risk

Jingxi Liu, Ph.D.
Associate
Capital Market Risk Advisors, Inc.

Biao Lu
Ph.D. Candidate
Department of Economics
Yale University

INTRODUCTION

How confident are you with your derivatives models? As derivative instruments have become increasingly complex, so too have their valuation models, as well as the skills required for their development. Compounding the problem is the fact that much of the financial theory underpinning such models is still in development. In the case of interest rate derivatives, with the academic community still researching and debating the stochastic processes that drive interest rate movements, it is hardly surprising that a market consensus has yet to be reached on the topic, to say nothing of the models used to value derivative instruments based on them.

The past decade is full of examples where undue reliance on faulty models led to losses in some of the major financial institutions throughout the world. Most recently, multi-million dollar losses on the derivative books of NatWest and the Bank of Tokyo Mitsubishi Bank have at least been partially attributed to the use of incorrect models. By some estimates, cumulative publicly disclosed losses due to flawed models have topped $3.82 billion in the past decade.[1] The losses are expected to climb as 1997 has been predicted to be the year of "model risk." With such projections, perhaps it is time for all market participants to take a closer look at the models they are relying on to engage in derivative transactions.

What is model risk? There are a number of analytical methods to price complex securities, such as quantitative formula, simulation, reverse engineering, and scenario analysis. Depending on the structure of the security, personal prefer-

---

[1] Tracked by Capital Market Risk Advisors, Inc.

The authors would like to thank Tanya Styblo Beder, Leslie Rahl, Frank Iacono, and Alan Seater of Capital Market Risk Advisors, Inc. for their valuable suggestions and technical help.

ence, available data, and quantitative engines, each of these methods may be used to evaluate a security. The risk of using a mis-specified model, incorrect inputs, or even misapplying models due to an incomplete understanding of the limitations and assumptions associated with a particular model or a lack of awareness of the differences among models are all examples of model risk.

Are more sophisticated models better than less sophisticated ones? Are more data better than less? Answers to questions such as these, while important in developing models, may not be as obvious as they might seem. Less sophisticated models may make too many simplifying assumptions and provide less flexibility to incorporate market changes. And an inadequate number of data points may not provide statistically significant results. As financial markets become increasingly complex, keeping your model up-to-date is not only good strategy, but essential to competitively participating in the derivatives markets.

While no model is perfect, there is no *right* model without a sufficient understanding of the limitations and the assumptions behind it. No model will give you a right answer if used incorrectly or if the output is not meaningful to its users. In fact, it is probably more dangerous to use a sophisticated model one doesn't fully understand than to use a simpler one that makes intuitive sense. People must be cognizant that the decisions behind model choice and development, strike a balance between being "approximately right" and "precisely wrong."

This chapter uses examples of various models employed to value interest rate derivatives to illustrate the importance of model risk. We will compare three interest rate notes with increasing complexity using three different valuation methods: historical simulation, Monte Carlo simulation, and scenario analysis. In the historical simulation approach, two different mean-reversion models are used, under different time periods to demonstrate the potential impact of data choice when historical data are used to estimate valuation parameters.

EVALUATING THE SECURITIES

The three securities we are going to evaluate are (1) a fixed-rate issue (FRI), (2) a floating-rate note (FRN), and (3) what is commonly referred to as a one-way-floater (OWF), which is a floating-rate note with both a path-dependent floor and cap. All are 10-year instruments issued by the same company, on the same date (April 30, 1997) to alleviate the impact of credit risk and tenor on valuation. The differences in relative cost of these securities can then be attributed to the differences in their structure, and the interest rate path over their life. Exhibit 1 provides a summary of terms for these three securities.

We evaluate the relative costs of each instrument when used as funding tools as a means of comparison. For simplicity, instead of actually pricing the individual instruments, we calculate the internal rates-of-return to estimate the relative costs of each of the three vehicles. While the first two are benchmark borrowings and relatively easy to value, the one-way-floater must be evaluated using simulation, scenario analysis, or reverse engineering. As we will demonstrate in the following sections, different approaches produce quite different results. The *internal-rate-of-return* (*IRR*) of the FRI is 6.35%, independent of the future paths of 6-month Libor. Thus, the following analysis will concentrate on the FRN and the OWF.

Scenario Analysis

Scenario analysis for security pricing is appealing for its simplicity and wide applicability. However, its results depend heavily on the assumed future paths of the underlying variable (in this case, Libor). In general, the projected paths will depict relatively few, and simple possible paths for the underlying. For example, the five scenarios we use here assume only 25 and 35 basis point changes in 6-month Libor, with the underlying changing direction at most once. The actual paths of most underlying variables are often much more complex.

Exhibit 1: Summary of Terms for Three Illustrative Securities
Benchmark Borrowings

	Floating-Rate Note	Fixed-Rate Issue
Borrower:	XYZ company	XYZ company
Size:	$100 million	$100 million
Price:	100	100
Coupon:	6-month Libor	6.35% semiannually
Payment:	Semiannually Actual/360	Semiannually Actual/Actual
Maturity:	10 years	10 years

One-Way Floater

Issuer:	XYZ company
Size:	$100 million
Maturity:	10 years
Index:	6-month Libor
Initial Coupon:	6-month Libor plus 25 bps
Subsequent Coupon:	The higher of 6-month Libor plus 25 bps or previous period's coupon
Reset Frequency:	Semiannually
Payment Basis:	Semiannually, Actual/360
Effective Floor:	The higher of the initial coupon, previous period's coupon or 6-month Libor plus 25 bps
Effective Cap:	Previous period's coupon plus 25 bps

The five scenarios are:

- *Scenario #1-Bull Market:* Libor rates fall at a rate of 25 basis points per semiannual period for 15 out of 20 semiannual periods, and then remain at 0.25%.
- *Scenario #2-Bear Market:* Libor rates rise at a rate of 35 basis points per semiannual period throughout the 10-year period.
- *Scenario #3-Static:* Libor remains constant at the starting Libor rate for the duration of the 10-year period.
- *Scenario #4-Bear Market followed by Bull Market:* Libor rises by 35 basis points per semiannual period for 10 semiannual periods and then falls by 35 basis points per semiannual period for 10 semiannual periods.
- *Scenario #5-Bull Market followed by Bear Market:* Libor falls by 25 basis points per semiannual period for 10 semiannual periods and then rises by 35 basis points per semiannual period for 10 semiannual periods.

No analytical models are required for scenario analysis, and the future paths of the underlying can be chosen arbitrarily. Thus the method is severely dependent on the scenarios selected and is most effective as a tool for stress testing market conditions on a case-by-case basis. While we can improve our confidence in the analysis by arbitrarily increasing the number of scenarios to capture more possible market conditions, the results would approach those of simulation, in which case simulation would be preferred due to its efficiency. Additionally, scenario analysis requires making subjective decisions regarding the probabilities of the various paths for the underlying variable.

Exhibit 2 shows the results for the five scenarios used in this analysis. As one can see, the results are substantially different. In general, the OWF performs better than the FRN in an environment of rising Libor rates (bear market) because of the cap, and performs worse in an environment of falling Libor rates (bull market) due to the floor. In scenarios where Libor both rises and falls, the result depends on the trade-offs between the effects of the two options.

Exhibit 2 also shows weighted IRRs for the FRN and the OWF under several probability distributions. Notice that *prob5* and *prob6* differ slightly with respect to the likelihood of a bear market — in one case the OWF has a distinctive advantage over the FRN (the OWF gives 7.28% IRR while the FRN gives 8.21% IRR), in another, they have the same cost (both give 8.08% IRR).

As stated before, the IRR for the FRI will be 6.35%, independent of the future interest rate path. The FRI is shown in Exhibit 2 for comparison. When we compare all the three securities, in cases of *prob1*, *prob2*, and *prob4*, an issuer would choose the FRN as it produces a lower cost of funds under the assumed interest rate scenarios. In the other three cases we have assumed, we will choose the FRI.

Exhibit 2: Results for the Five Scenarios

Scenarios	FRN	OWF	FRI	prob1	prob2	prob3	prob4	prob5	prob6
#1 Bull	3.28	6.34	6.35	0.2	0.6	0.1	0.1	0.05	0.072
#2 Bear	9.29	8.65	6.35	0.2	0.1	0.6	0.1	0.7	0.678
#3 Static	6.09	6.34	6.35	0.2	0.1	0.1	0.6	0.1	0.1
#4 Bear then Bull	7.88	8.26	6.35	0.2	0.1	0.1	0.1	0.1	0.1
#5 Bull then Bear	3.03	5.90	6.35	0.2	0.1	0.1	0.1	0.05	0.05
prob1	5.91	7.10	6.35						
prob2	4.60	6.72	6.35						
prob3	7.60	7.88	6.35						
prob4	6.00	6.72	6.35						
prob5	8.21	7.28	6.35						
prob6	8.08	8.08	6.35						

Simulation Analysis

Most financial variables follow certain stochastic processes. If the process is known, we can simulate the occurrence of future paths of the variable. If we simulate a large enough number of paths, probability theory tells us that on average, our result will be approximate reality and is the basis of simulation analysis. In most cases, it is a dramatic improvement to scenario analysis. However, in addition to its computational intensity, there is a risk that the results derived from thousands of simulations may nevertheless be "precisely wrong." The reason is that most of the stochastic processes are unknown and very often models for the underlying require statistical parameters to be estimated based on current or historical market data. If "bad" estimates of parameters are used, the results will be misleading. In the NatWest case, it was reported that a critical parameter, volatility, was purportedly incorrectly estimated in pricing interest rate options (interest rate caps), resulting in a loss of more than $120 million.

In our example, three popular interest rate models are used for the simulation. The first two assume mean reversion processes (a process where the underlying variable converts to its long-run mean) for the underlying index (6-month Libor) and uses historical data to estimate the model parameters. The two differ in modeling the conditional variances (the stochastic part of the process) of the instruments — one assumes that the variance depends on the current level of the underlying variable while the other assumes the variance depends on the previous variance. The third assumes a lognormal distribution for the index and uses the forward curve to generate the periodic drift (or the rate of return). We can easily see that the results differ dramatically between the two approaches. Even within the historical simulation approach, depending on which data period is chosen, we will have different answers.

Using Historical Data

The first simulation using historical data assumes that 6-month Libor follows a mean reversion process. The parameters of the process, including the long-run mean, reversion speed, and conditional variance, are estimated using historical data. Let x_t denote the 6-month Libor rate at time t, and assume x_t follows a process that is widely used in the literature to model the interest rate movement:[2]

$$x_t - x_{t-1} = k(\theta - x_{t-1}) + \sigma x_{t-1}^{\alpha} \varepsilon_t$$

where

$\varepsilon_t \sim$ i.i.d. $N(0, 1/12)$
$\theta =$ the long-run mean to which x_t converts over time
$k =$ the mean-reversion speed
$\alpha =$ the conditional variance

The second process is a GARCH$(1,1)$[3] model which uses a similar mean-reversion process, but has a "variance clustering" feature that models the conditional variance of the process. Specifically,

$$h_t = \alpha_0 + \alpha_1 \cdot h_{t-1} + \beta_1 \varepsilon_{t-1}^2$$

$$x_t - x_{t-1} = k(\theta - x_{t-1}) + \sqrt{h_t} \varepsilon_t$$

where

$\varepsilon_t \sim$ i.i.d. $N(0, 1/12)$
$\theta =$ the long-run mean to which x_t converts over time
$k =$ the mean-reversion speed
$h_t =$ the process governing the conditional variance

One drawback of historical simulation is that historical data can include unique episodes that may not repeat in the future. A second drawback is that historical data may not repeat itself in the future. To illustrate data risk, two experiments were done for each process — one used weekly 6-month Libor from 1/8/75 to 4/30/97, the other used the same data but for a shorter period from 1/1/86 to 4/30/97. All other aspects of the simulation are the same. Exhibit 3 displays Libor for the whole period. The estimation results for the long-run mean and the reversion speed from the four simulations are shown in Exhibit 4. The four simulations are referred as mean-reversion (long), mean-reversion (short), GARCH (long), and GARCH (short).

From the estimation results we can easily see that the same model will give different estimations when data from different time periods are used; and different models may provide different answers even when the same data are used. The differences between the two models are much larger when data from the

[2] J. C. Cox, J. E. Ingersoll, and S. A. Ross, "A Theory of the Term Structure of Interest Rates," *Econometrica* (1985).
[3] James Hamilton, *Time Series Analysis* (Princeton, NJ: Princeton University Press, 1994).

longer period is used. Notice that the period of early 1980 observations has unusually high rates coupled with high volatility, which explains the relatively high estimate of the long-run mean when using the data from the longer period in both the general mean-reversion model and the GARCH model.

For the general mean-reversion model, the estimated long-run mean is as high as 7.91%. The initial Libor rate is only 6% for the one-way-floater. Therefore, the Libor rate is statistically reverting/increasing relative to the long-run mean over the 10-year life of the instrument, meaning that we expect Libor to rise in a typical path in this simulation. Thus, more paths in our simulation will resemble the bear market scenario more than those generated from the scenario analysis. When the data of the early 1980s are excluded, the same model gives a long-run mean of only 5.43%, which is substantially lower. This lower long-run mean will imply that a typical simulated path for 6-month Libor will have a lower tendency to rise, and a higher tendency to fall because the long-run mean is lower than the starting rate.

Exhibits 5 and 6 show the histograms for the IRRs for the FRN and OWF from the simulations using the longer period of data and the general mean reversion model. The distribution of the OWF IRRs is apparently more compact because of the collar We can comfortably conclude the OWF performs better because of the lower mean and standard deviation for its IRR. Remember that OWF is a better financing choice in an environment of rising rates, and as we explained above, Libor tends to rise during the 10-year life of the trades. This is exactly what happened here. Exhibits 7 and 8 provide the summary statistics for all four simulations.

Exhibit 3: 6-Month Libor for Historical Simulation Period

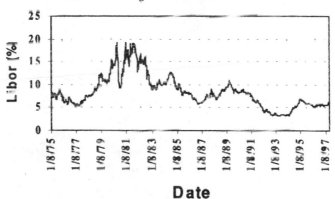

Exhibit 4: Four Historical Simulation Results

	Mean-Reversion (long)	Mean-Reversion (short)	GARCH (long)	GARCH (short)
Long-run Mean	7.91	5.43	5.61	5.42
Reversion Speed	0.002	0.004	0.002	0.004

Exhibit 5: Histogram of Simulated IRR for the FRN
(Mean-Reversion Model, 1/8/75-4/30/97)

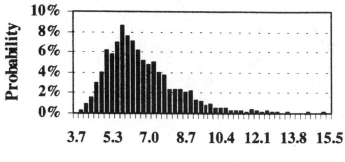

Exhibit 6: Histogram of Simulated IRR for the OWF
(Mean-Reversion Model, 1/8/75-4/30/97)

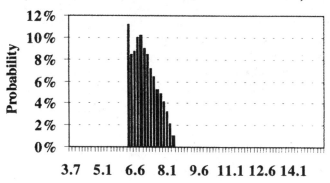

Exhibit 7: Summary of Four Simulations for Long and Short Mean Reversions

	Mean-Reversion (Long)		Mean-Reversion (Short)	
	FRN	OWF	FRN	OWF
Mean	6.61	7.03	5.70	6.76
Median	6.23	6.96	5.63	6.69
Standard Deviation	1.69	0.55	0.90	0.42
Minimum	3.65	6.24	3.55	6.24
Maximum	15.45	8.29	9.88	8.29

Exhibit 8: Summary of Four Simulations for Long and Short GARCH (1,1)

	Garch(1,1) (Long)		Garch(1,1) (Short)	
	FRN	OWF	FRN	OWF
Mean	5.93	7.06	5.67	6.79
Median	5.87	7.00	5.68	6.72
Standard Deviation	2.31	0.59	0.93	0.41
Minimum	0.55	6.24	2.32	6.24
Maximum	13.10	8.29	8.70	8.10

When we compare the cost of the FRI (6.35%) and the simulation results for the FRN and the OWF, we can see that if we use the general mean reversion model and the longer period of data, an issuer will choose the FRI; however, if we use the other three simulation results, an issuer will choose the FRN.

Simulation Using Forward Rate Curve

Another method to price securities that forecasts future cash flows uses the forward curve to drive the index. This simulation is done by first building a 6-month Libor forward curve, and then using the forward rates to simulate future spot rates by assuming that 6-month Libor follows a lognormal distribution. There are several ways to build forward curves, each yielding results slightly different from the others. Here, the 6-month Libor forward curve is built by using Libor rates and swap rates on the issue date of April 30, 1997.

Suppose the forward rates at periods t and $t-1$ are f_t and f_{t-1}, respectively. The drift during period t will be

$$d_t = \ln(f_{t+1})/\ln(f_t)$$

Let L_t be the simulated spot Libor at period t, then L_{t+1} can be simulated by

$$L_{t+1} = L_t \exp\left(d_t - \frac{\sigma_t^2}{2}\Delta t + RAND \cdot \sigma_t \cdot \sqrt{\Delta t}\right)$$

where

σ_t = the volatility during period t
Δt = the length of period t in years
$RAND$ = a random variable with standard normal distribution

In this case, based on the volatility level for interest rate caps at the time when the securities were issued, we choose a fixed volatility of 16%. Exhibit 9 shows the forward curve. Exhibit 10 summarizes the statistical results. Exhibits 11 and 12 are the histograms of the internal rate of returns from the one-way floater and the floating-rate notes.

Exhibit 9: 6-Month Libor Forward Curve on 4/30/97

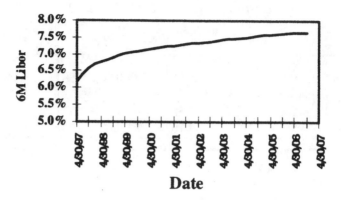

Exhibit 10: Summary Statistics for the Forward Curve Simulation

	OWF	FRN
Mean	7.51	7.24
Median	7.51	7.24
Standard Deviation	0.14	0.18
Minimum	7.05	6.68
Maximum	7.90	7.86

Exhibit 11: Histogram of IRR for the FRN (Forward Rate Curve Simulation)

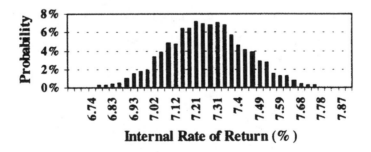

Exhibit 12: Histogram of IRR for the OWF (Forward Curve Simulation)

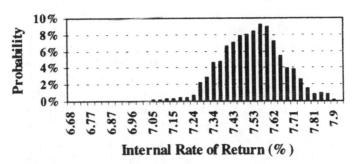

Internal Rate of Return (%)

From the summary statistics of Exhibits 7 and 10, we can see that the general mean-reversion model using the longer period of data gives a much wider range of IRRs for the FRN than the forward curve simulation does. The histogram of the OWF IRRs is much more truncated in the mean-reversion simulation than in the forward curve simulation; that is, the OWF looks much better when compared to the FRN using the historical simulation than when using the forward curve simulation.

From the results of the forward curve simulation, the FRI (IRR = 6.35%) is cheaper than both the OWF (IRR = 7.51%) and the FRN (IRR = 7.24%).

LESSONS LEARNED

From the above analyses we can see how much our answer depends on the model we are using. Here we have only examined three different simulations. There are many interest rate models in the literature. Even within the mean reversion regime, different models exist. Also, there are many data periods we can choose from to estimate the model parameters. To avoid using an inappropriate historical time frame, a more appropriate way to estimate the parameters in the mean reversion model is to use current market data (like prices of swaps, swaptions, caps and floors, etc.). This procedure involves trial and error pricing of these instruments, and thus more intensive computation and modeling. Depending on how much the market has changed, results from using the market data will be different from results of the historical simulation.

Similarly, there are many ways to build forward curves. The different forward curves will have slightly different slopes and thus different drift rates. As indicated by the different simulations we have performed, these differences from modeling will not necessarily be canceled by increasing the number of simulation runs. An important lesson learned here is that we need to be aware of the "model risk" we have assumed and make sure that we have stress tested the impact of the model risk and are comfortable with the results.

This simple example tells us that the risk of derivatives does not come solely from market direction. Markets can certainly follow trends, but are also stochastic. A trader relying on a wrong model runs the risk of losing more often than not. The danger is that we usually do not suspect our model until something dramatic happens. To discover this non-market "hidden" risk, firms should independently check whether their valuations are in line with those in the market.

For many, it is more likely that valuation models are too simplified or outdated. Whether models are developed in-house or bought from vendors, it is critical to understand the assumptions behind them. Because of the various limitations, assumptions are inevitable. The most important thing is to make sure you are aware of the potential impact of those assumptions and are comfortable with them. It is also important to understand how sensitive your answer is to your assumptions. If the potential impact of changing models and/or assumptions is small, then you can sleep well at night. If valuations and/or risk parameters are very sensitive to the choice of model and the selection of assumptions, then rigorous stress testing of both models and assumptions should be regularly performed.

Chapter 16

Measuring and Forecasting Yield Volatility

Frank J. Fabozzi, Ph.D., CFA
Adjunct Professor of Finance
School of Management
Yale University

Wai Lee
Assistant Vice President
J.P. Morgan Investment Management Inc.

INTRODUCTION

There are two critical components to an interest rate risk management system The first component is an estimate of the price sensitivity of each fixed income security and derivative position to changes in interest rates. This estimate is typically obtained by changing rates by a small number of basis points and calculating based on a valuation model how the price changes. The result is an effective or option-adjusted duration measure. If the valuation model employed is poor, the resulting duration measure will not be a good estimate of the price sensitivity of an instrument to rate changes. A critical input to valuation models for cash market instruments with embedded options and option-like derivatives is the estimated yield volatility. The second component of an interest rate risk management system is the estimated yield volatility to assess the potential loss exposure. Consequently, yield volatility estimate play a dual role in an interest rate risk management system.

The previous chapters in this book discussed the measurement of interest rate exposure and the implementation of interest rate risk control strategies based on some expected yield volatility. The focus of the earlier chapters was not on the measurement of yield volatility. In this chapter, we look at how to measure and forecast yield volatility. Volatility is measured in terms of the standard deviation or variance. We begin this chapter with an explanation of how yield volatility as measured by the daily percentage change in yields is calculated from historical yields. We will see that there are several issues confronting a trader or investor in measuring historical yield volatility. Next we turn to modeling and forecasting yield volatility, looking at the state-of-the-art statistical techniques that can be employed.

We are grateful for the many constructive comments of George Chacko of the Harvard Business School.

CALCULATING THE STANDARD DEVIATION
FROM HISTORICAL DATA

The variance of a random variable using historical data is calculated using the following formula:

$$\text{Variance} = \sum_{t=1}^{T} \frac{(X_t - \bar{X})^2}{T-1} \qquad (1)$$

and then

$$\text{Standard deviation} = \sqrt{\text{Variance}}$$

where

X_t = observation t on variable X
X = the sample mean for variable X
T = the number of observations in the sample

Our focus in this chapter is on yield volatility. More specifically, we are interested in the percentage change in daily yields. So, X_t will denote the percentage change in yield from day t and the prior day, $t-1$. If we let y_t denote the yield on day t and y_{t-1} denote the yield on day $t-1$, then X_t which is the natural logarithm of percentage change in yield between two days, can be expressed as:

$$X_t = 100[\text{Ln}(y_t / y_{t-1})]$$

For example, on 10/18/95 the Treasury 30-year zero rate was 6.56% and on 10/19/95 it was 6.59%. Therefore, the natural logarithm of X for 10/19/95 is:

$$X = 100[\text{Ln}(6.593/6.555)] = 0.5780$$

To illustrate how to calculate a daily standard deviation from historical data, consider the data in Exhibit 1 which shows the yield on Treasury 30-year zeros from 10/8/95 to 11/12/95 in the second column. From the 26 observations, 25 days of daily percentage yield changes are calculated in the third column. The fourth column shows the square of the deviations of the observations from the mean. The bottom of Exhibit 1 shows the calculation of the daily mean for the 25 observations, the variance, and the standard deviation. The daily standard deviation is 0.6360%.

The daily standard deviation will vary depending on the 25 days selected. For example, the daily yields from 8/20/95 to 9/24/95 were used to generate 25 daily percentage yield changes. The computed daily standard deviation was 0.8453%.

Exhibit 1: Calculation of Daily Standard Deviation Based on 25 Daily Observations for 30-Year Treasury Zero (October 9, 1995 to November 12, 1995)

t	Date	y_t	$X_t = 100[Ln(y_t/y_{t-1})]$	$(X_t - \bar{X})^2$
0	08-Oct-95	6.694		
1	09-Oct-95	6.699	0.06720	0.02599
2	10-Oct-95	6.710	0.16407	0.06660
3	11-Oct-95	6.675	−0.52297	0.18401
4	12-Oct-95	6.555	−1.81311	2.95875
5	15-Oct-95	6.583	0.42625	0.27066
6	16-Oct-95	6.569	−0.21290	0.01413
7	17-Oct-95	6.583	0.21290	0.09419
8	18-Oct-95	6.555	−0.42625	0.11038
9	19-Oct-95	6.593	0.57804	0.45164
10	22-Oct-95	6.620	0.40869	0.25270
11	23-Oct-95	6.568	−0.78860	0.48246
12	24-Oct-95	6.575	0.10652	0.04021
13	25-Oct-95	6.646	1.07406	1.36438
14	26-Oct-95	6.607	−0.58855	0.24457
15	29-Oct-95	6.612	0.07565	0.02878
16	30-Oct-95	6.575	−0.56116	0.21823
17	31-Oct-95	6.552	−0.35042	0.06575
18	01-Nov-95	6.515	−0.56631	0.22307
19	02-Nov-95	6.533	0.27590	0.13684
20	05-Nov-95	6.543	0.15295	0.06099
21	06-Nov-95	6.559	0.24424	0.11441
22	07-Nov-95	6.500	−0.90360	0.65543
23	08-Nov-95	6.546	0.70520	0.63873
24	09-Nov-95	6.589	0.65474	0.56063
25	12-Nov-95	6.539	−0.76173	0.44586
		Total	−2.35020	9.7094094

Sample mean $= \bar{X} = \dfrac{-2.35020}{25} = -0.09401\%$

Variance $= \dfrac{9.7094094}{25-1} = 0.4045587$

Std $= \sqrt{0.4045587} = 0.6360\%$

Exhibit 2: Comparison of Daily and Annual Volatility for a Different Number of Observations (Ending Date November 12, 1995) for Various Instruments

Number of observations	Daily standard deviation (%)	Annualized standard deviation (%)		
		250 days	260 days	365 days
Treasury 30-Year Zero				
683	0.4902	7.75	7.90	9.36
60	0.6283	9.93	10.13	12.00
25	0.6360	10.06	10.26	12.15
10	0.6242	9.87	10.06	11.93
Treasury 10-Year Zero				
683	0.7498	11.86	12.09	14.32
60	0.7408	11.71	11.95	14.15
25	0.7092	11.21	11.44	13.55
10	0.7459	11.79	12.03	14.25
Treasury 5-Year Zero				
683	1.0413	16.46	16.79	19.89
60	0.8267	13.07	13.33	15.79
25	0.7224	11.42	11.65	13.80
10	0.8346	13.20	13.46	15.94
3-Month LIBOR				
683	0.7496	11.85	12.09	14.32
60	0.2994	4.73	4.83	5.72
25	0.1465	2.32	2.36	2.80
10	0.2366	3.74	3.82	4.52

Determining the Number of Observations

In our illustration, we used 25 observations for the daily percentage change in yield. The appropriate number depends on the situation at hand. For example, traders concerned with overnight positions might use the 10 most recent days (i.e., two weeks). A bond portfolio manager who is concerned with longer term volatility might use 25 days (about one month).

The selection of the number of observations can have a significant effect on the calculated daily standard deviation. This can be seen in Exhibit 2 which shows the daily standard deviation for the Treasury 30-year zero, Treasury 10-year zero, Treasury 5-year zero, and 3-month LIBOR for 60 days, 25 days, 10 days, and 683 days ending 11/12/95.

Annualizing the Standard Deviation

If serial correlation is not significant, the daily standard deviation can be annualized by multiplying it by the square root of the number of days in a year. That is,

Daily standard deviation $\times \sqrt{\text{Number of days in a year}}$

Market practice varies with respect to the number of days in the year that should be used in the annualizing formula above. Typically, either 250 days, 260 days, or 365 days are used.

Exhibit 3: Comparison of Daily Standard Deviation Calculated for Two 25 Day Periods for Various Instruments

Dates		Daily standard deviation(%)	Annualized standard deviation(%)		
From	To		250 days	260 days	365 days
Treasury 30-Year Zero					
10/8/95	11/12/95	0.6360	10.06	10.26	12.15
8/20/95	9/24/95	0.8453	13.36	13.63	16.15
Treasury 10-Year Zero					
10/8/95	11/12/95	0.7092	11.21	11.44	13.55
8/20/95	9/24/95	0.9045	14.30	14.58	17.28
Treasury 5-Year Zero					
10/8/95	11/12/95	0.7224	11.42	11.65	13.80
8/20/95	9/24/95	0.8145	12.88	13.13	15.56
3-Month LIBOR					
10/8/95	11/12/95	0.1465	2.32	2.36	2.80
8/20/95	9/24/95	0.2523	3.99	4.07	4.82

Thus, in calculating an annual standard deviation, the manager must decide on:

1. the number of daily observations to use
2. the number of days in the year to use to annualize the daily standard deviation.

Exhibit 2 shows the difference in the annual standard deviation for the daily standard deviation based on the different number of observations and using 250 days, 260 days, and 365 days to annualize. Exhibit 3 compares the 25-day annual standard deviation for two different time periods for the 30-year zero, 10-year zero, 5-year zero, and 3-month LIBOR.

Reexamination of the Mean

Let's address the question of what mean should be used in the calculation of the forecasted standard deviation. Suppose at the end of 10/24/95 a trader is interested in a forecast for volatility using the 10 most recent days of trading and updating that forecast at the end of each trading day. What mean value should be used?

The trader can calculate a 10-day moving average of the daily percentage yield change. Exhibit 1 shows the daily percentage change in yield for the Treasury 30-year zero from 10/9/95 to 11/12/95. To calculate a moving average of the daily percentage yield change on 10/24/95, the trader would use the 10 trading days from 10/11/95 to 10/24/95. At the end of 10/25/95, the trader will calculate the 10-day average by using the percentage yield change on 11/25/95 and would exclude the percentage yield change on 10/11/95. That is, the trader will use the 10 trading days from 10/12/95 to 10/25/95.

Exhibit 4: 10-Day Moving Daily Average for Treasury 30-Year Zero

10-Trading Days Ending	Daily Average (%)
24-Oct-95	−0.203
25-Oct-95	−0.044
26-Oct-95	0.079
29-Oct-95	0.044
30-Oct-95	0.009
31-Oct-95	−0.047
01-Nov-95	−0.061
02-Nov-95	−0.091
05-Nov-95	−0.117
06-Nov-95	−0.014
07-Nov-95	−0.115
08-Nov-95	−0.152
09-Nov-95	−0.027
12-Nov-95	−0.111

Exhibit 4 shows the 10-day moving average calculated from 10/24/95 to 11/12/95. Notice the considerable variation over this period. The 10-day moving average ranges from −0.203% to 0.079%. For the period from 4/15/93 to 11/12/95, the 10-day moving average ranged from −0.617% to 0.603%.

Rather than using a moving average, it is more appropriate to use an expectation of the average. Longerstacey and Zangari argue that it would be more appropriate to use a mean value of zero.[1] In that case, the variance as given by equation (1) simplifies to:

$$\text{Variance} = \sum_{t=1}^{T} \frac{X_t^2}{T-1} \tag{2}$$

Weighting of Observations

The daily standard deviation given by equations (1) and (2) assigns an equal weight to all observations. So, if a trader is calculating volatility based on the most recent 10 days of trading, each day is given a weight of 10%.

For example, suppose that a trader is interested in the daily volatility of the Treasury 30-year zero yield and decides to use the 10 most recent trading days. Exhibit 5 reports the 10-day volatility for various days using the data in Exhibit 1 and the formula for the variance given by equation (2). For the period 4/15/93 to 11/12/95, the 10-day volatility ranged from 0.164% to 1.330%.

---

[1] Jacques Longerstacey and Peter Zangari, *Five Questions about RiskMetrics*[TM], JP Morgan Research Publication 1995.

Exhibit 5: Moving Daily Standard Deviation Based on 10-Days of Observations

10-Trading Days Ending	Daily Standard Deviation (%)
24-Oct-95	0.757
25-Oct-95	0.819
26-Oct-95	0.586
29-Oct-95	0.569
30-Oct-95	0.595
31-Oct-95	0.602
01-Nov-95	0.615
02-Nov-95	0.591
05-Nov-95	0.577
06-Nov-95	0.520
07-Nov-95	0.600
08-Nov-95	0.536
09-Nov-95	0.544
12-Nov-95	0.600

In April 1995, the Basle Committee on Banking Supervision at the Bank for International Settlements proposed that volatility (as measured by the standard deviation) be calculated based on an equal weighting of daily historical observations [2] Moreover, the committee proposed that volatility estimates should be updated at least quarterly.[3]

However, there is reason to suspect that market participants give greater weight to recent movements in yield when determining volatility. Moreover, what has been observed in several studies of the stock market is that high periods of volatility are followed by high periods of volatility.

To give greater importance to more recent information, observations further in the past should be given less weight. This can be done by revising the variance as given by equation (2) as follows:

$$\text{Variance} = \sum_{t=1}^{T} \frac{W_t X_t^2}{T-1} \tag{3}$$

where W_t is the weight assigned to observation t such that the sum of the weights is equal to 1 (i.e., $\Sigma\ W_t = 1$) and the further the observation from today, the lower the weight.

The weights should be assigned so that the forecasted volatility reacts faster to a recent major market movements and declines gradually as we move

---

[2] The proposal, entitled "The Supervisory Treatment of Market Risks," is an amendment to the *1988 Basle Capital Accord.*

[3] RiskMetrics[TM] has a "Special Regulatory Dataset" that incorporates the 1-year moving average proposed by the Basle Committee. Rather than updating at least quarterly as proposed by the Basle Committee, the dataset is updated daily.

away from any major market movement. The approach by JP Morgan in RiskMetrics[TM] is to use an *exponential moving average*. The formula for the weight W_t in an exponential moving average is:

$$W_t = (1 - \beta)\beta^t$$

where β is a value between 0 and 1. The observations are arrayed so that the closest observation is $t = 1$, the second closest is $t = 2$, etc.

For example, if β is 0.90, then the weight for the closest observation ($t = 1$) is:

$$W_1 = (1 - 0.90)(0.90)^1 = 0.09$$

For $t = 5$ and β equal to 0.90, the weight is:

$$W_5 = (1 - 0.90)(0.90)^5 = 0.05905$$

The parameter β is measuring how quickly the information contained in past observations is "decaying" and hence is referred to as the "decay factor." The smaller the β, the faster the decay. What decay factor to use depends on how fast the mean value for the random variable X changes over time. A random variable whose mean value changes slowly over time will have a decay factor close to 1. A discussion of how the decay factor should be selected is beyond the scope of this chapter.[4]

MODELING AND FORECASTING YIELD VOLATILITY

Generally speaking, there are two ways to model yield volatility. The first way is by estimating historical yield volatility by some time series model. The resulting volatility is called *historical volatility*. The second way is to estimate yield volatility based on the observed prices of interest rate derivatives. Yield volatility calculated using this approach is called *implied volatility*. In this section, we discuss these two approaches, with more emphasis on historical volatility. As will be explained later, computing implied volatility from interest rate derivatives is not as simple and straight forward as from derivatives of other asset classes such as equity. Apart from assuming that a particular option pricing model is correct, we also need to model the time evolution of the complete term structure and volatilities of yields of different maturities. This relies on state-of-the-art modeling technique as well as superior computing power.

Historical Volatility

We begin the discussion with a general stochastic process of which yield, or interest rate, is assumed to follow:

---

[4] A technical description is provided in *RiskMetrics[TM]—Technical Document*, pp. 77-79.

$$dy = \mu(y, t)dt + \sigma(y, t)dW \tag{4}$$

where y is the yield, μ is the expected instantaneous change (or drift) of yield, σ is the instantaneous standard deviation (volatility), and W is a standard Brownian motion such that the change in W (dW) is normally distributed with mean zero and variance of dt. Both μ and σ are functions of the current yield y and time t.

Since we focus on volatility in this chapter, we leave the drift term in its current general form. It can be shown that many of the volatility models are special cases of this general form. For example, assuming that the functional form of volatility is

$$\sigma(y, t) = \sigma_0 y \tag{5}$$

such that the yield volatility is equal to the product of a constant, σ_0, and the current yield level, we can rewrite equation (4) as[5]

$$d\ln y = \mu'(y, t)dt + \sigma_0 dW \tag{6}$$

The discrete time version of this process will be

$$\ln y_{t+1} = \ln y_t + \mu' + \sigma_0(W_{t+1} - W_t) \tag{7}$$

Thus, when we calculate yield volatility by looking at the natural logarithm of percentage change in yield between two days as in the earlier section, we are assuming that yield follows a log-normal distribution, or, the natural logarithm of yield follows a normal distribution. σ_0, in this case, can be interpreted as the *proportional yield volatility*, as the yield volatility is obtained by multiplying σ_0 with the current yield. In this case, yield volatility is proportional to the level of the yield. We call the above model the *Constant Proportional Yield Volatility Model (CP)*.

This simple assumption offers many advantages. Since the natural logarithm of a negative number is meaningless, a log-normal distribution assumption for yield guarantees that yield is always non-negative. Evidence also suggests that volatility of yield increases with the level of yield. A simple intuition is for scale reasons. Thus, while the volatility of changes in yield is unstable over time since the level of yield changes, the volatility of changes in natural logarithm of yield is relatively stable, as it already incorporates the changes in yield level. As a result, the natural logarithm of yield can be a more useful process to examine.[6]

A potential drawback of the CP model is that it assumes that the proportional yield volatility itself is constant, which does not depend on time nor on the yield level. In fact, there exists a rich class of yield volatility models that includes the CP model as a special case. We call this group the *Power Function Model.*[7]

---

[5] Equation (6) is obtained by application of Ito's Lemma. We omit the details here.

[6] See Thomas S. Coleman, Lawrence Fisher, and Roger G. Ibbotson, "A Note on Interest Rate Volatility," *Journal of Fixed Income* (March 1993), pp 97-101, for a similar conclusion.

[7] In the finance literature, this is also known as the *Constant Elasticity of Variance Model.*

Power Function Model

For simplicity of exposition, we write the yield volatility as σ_t, which is understood to be a function of time and level of yield. For example, consider the following representation of yield volatility:

$$\sigma_t = \sigma_0 y_{t-1}^\gamma \tag{8}$$

In this way, yield volatility is proportional to a power function of yield. The following are examples of the volatility models assumed in some well known interest rate models, which can be represented as special cases of equation (8):

1. $\gamma = 0$:   Vasicek,[8] Ho-Lee[9]
2. $\gamma = 0.5$:   Cox-Ingersoll-Ross (CIR)[10]
3. $\gamma = 1$:   Black,[11] Brennan-Schwartz[12]

The Vasicek model and Ho-Lee model maintain an assumption of a normally distributed interest rate process. Simply speaking, yield volatility is assumed to be constant, independent of time, and independent of yield level. Theoretically, when the interest rate is low enough while yield volatility remains constant, this model allows the interest rate to go below zero.

The CIR model assumes that yield volatility is a constant multiple of the square root of yield. Its volatility specification is thus also known as the *Square Root Model*. Since the square root of a negative number is meaningless, the CIR model does not allow yield to become negative. Strictly speaking, the functional form of equation (8) only applies to the instantaneous interest rate, but not to any yield of longer maturities within the CIR framework. To be specific, when applied to, say, the 10-year yield, yield volatility is obtained from the stochastic process of the 10-year yield, which can be derived from the closed-form solution for the bond price. To simplify the discussion, we go with the current simple form instead.

The volatility assumption in the Black model and Brennan-Schwartz model is equivalent to the previous CP model. In other words, yield is assumed to be log-normally distributed with constant proportional yield volatility.

Many of these functional forms for yield volatility are adopted primarily because they lead to closed-form solutions for pricing of bonds, bond options, and

---

[8] Oldrich Vasicek, "An Equilibrium Characterization of the Term Structure," *Journal of Financial Economics* (1977), pp. 177-188.

[9] Thomas S.Y. Ho and Sang-Bin Lee, "Term Structure Movements and Pricing Interest Rate Contingent Claims," *Journal of Finance* (1986), pp. 1011-1029.

[10] John C. Cox, Jonathan E. Ingersoll, and Stephen A. Ross, "A Theory of the Term Structure of Interest Rates," *Econometrica* (1985), pp. 385-407.

[11] Fischer Black, "The Pricing of Commodity Contracts," *Journal of Financial Economics* (1976), pp. 167-179.

[12] Michael Brennan and Eduardo Schwartz, "A Continuous Time Approach to the Pricing of Bonds," *Journal of Banking and Finance* (1979), pp. 133-155.

other interest rate derivatives, as well as for simplicity and convenience. There is no simple answer for which form is the best. However, it is generally thought that $\gamma = 0$, or a normal distribution with constant yield volatility, is an inappropriate description of an interest rate process, even though the occasions of observing negative interest rate in the model is found to be rare. As a result, many practitioners adopt the CP model, as it is straight forward enough, while it eliminates the drawback of the normal distribution.

One way to determine which yield volatility functional form to use is to empirically estimate the model with historical data. To illustrate, we use the 3-month, 10-year, and 30-year spot yields as examples. These yields are obtained by spline fitting the yield curve of Treasury strips every day within the sample period. We use the daily data from January 1, 1986 to July 31, 1997. To be consistent with the previous section, we assume that the average daily yield change is zero. Thus, the model to be estimated is:

$$y_t - y_{t-1} = \varepsilon_t$$
$$E[\varepsilon_t^2] = \sigma_t^2 = \sigma_0^2 y_{t-1}^{2\gamma} \qquad (9)$$

where E[.] denotes the statistical expectation operator. The econometric technique employed is the Maximum Likelihood Estimation (MLE).[13] We assume a conditional normal distribution for changes in yield, after the dependence of volatility on level of yield has been incorporated. The details of this technique are beyond the scope of this chapter.[14] The results are reported in Exhibit 6, where an 8.00% yield is written as 0.08, for example.

Exhibit 6: Estimation of Power Function Models*

	3-month Treasury bill	10-year Treasury zero	30-year Treasury zero
σ_0	0.0019	0.0027	0.0161
	(12.31)	(11.00)	(5.58)
γ	0.2463	0.5744	1.2708
	(8.88)	(15.71)	(18.03)

* t-statistics are reported in parentheses.

[13] The model can also be estimated by Generalized Method of Moments (GMM), which does not impose any distributional assumption. We use MLE here in order to be consistent with the estimation of GARCH models to be discussed later. See K.C. Chan, G. Andrew Karolyi, Francis A. Longstaff, and Anthony B. Sanders, "An Empirical Comparison of Alternative Models of the Short-Term Interest Rate," *Journal of Finance* (July 1992), pp. 1209-1227, for a similar treatment. Also see Timothy G. Conley, Lars Peter Hansen, Erzo G.J. Luttmer, and José A. Scheinkman, "Short-Term Interest Rates as Subordinated Diffusions," *Review of Financial Studies* (Fall 1997), pp. 525-577, for a more rigorous treatment.

[14] Readers can consult James Hamilton, *Time Series Analysis* (Princeton, NJ: Princeton University Press, 1994). Also, there is some evidence that a conditional t-distribution is more appropriate for interest rate data. For simplicity, we maintain the conditional normal here.

Volatility of yields of all three maturities are found to increase with the level of yield, but to a different extent. As the results suggest, assuming the same value of γ for yields of all maturities can be inappropriate. For the 3-month spot yield, γ is found to be about 0.25, significantly below the 0.5 assumed in the CIR model. For the 10-year spot yield, γ is about 0.57, closed to CIR's assumption. Finally, for the 30-year spot yield, γ is about 1.27, significantly above the value of 1 assumed in the CP model. Furthermore, as the previous section mentioned, using different time periods can lead to different estimates. For instance, the behavior of interest rates in the late 1970s and the early 1980s were very different from those in the last decade. As a result, one should not be surprised that the dependence of volatility on the yield level might appear to be different from the last decade.

To illustrate the use of the Power Function Model, Exhibit 7 plots the forecasted volatility of the 30-year spot yield based on the estimates in Exhibit 6. For comparison purposes, we also plot the forecasted volatility when we impose the restriction of $\gamma = 1$. In the latter case, we are actually estimating the constant proportional yield volatility, σ_0, using the whole sample period. The value denotes the yield volatility on each day, annualized by 250 days.

As shown in Exhibit 7, using the CP model with constant proportional yield volatility ($\gamma = 1$) does not significantly differ from using the estimated value of $\gamma = 1.27$.

Exhibit 7: 250-day Annualized Yield Volatility of 30-year Spot Yield: Power Function Model

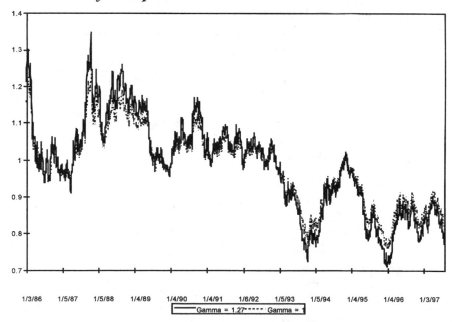

One critique of the Power Function Model is the fact that while it allows volatility to depend on the yield level, it does not incorporate the observation that a volatile period tends to be followed by another volatile period, a phenomenon known as *volatility clustering*. Nor does it allow past yield shocks to affect current and future volatility. To tackle these problems, we introduce a very different class of volatility modeling and forecasting tool.

Generalized Autoregressive Conditional Heteroskedasticity Model

Generalized Autoregressive Conditional Heteroskedasticity (GARCH) Model is probably the most extensively applied family of volatility models in empirical finance. It is well known that statistical distributions of many financial prices and returns series exhibit fatter tails than a normal distribution. These characteristics can be captured with a GARCH model. In fact, some well-known interest rate models, such as the Longstaff-Schwartz model, adopt GARCH to model yield volatility, which is allowed to be stochastic.[15] The term "conditional" means that the value of the variance depends on or is conditional on the information available, typically by means of the realized values of other random variables. The term "heteroskedasticity" means that the variance is not the same for all values of the random variable at different time periods.

If we maintain the assumption that the average daily yield change is zero, as before, the standard GARCH(1,1) model can be written as:

$$y_t - y_{t-1} = \varepsilon_t$$
$$E[\varepsilon_t^2] = \sigma_t^2 = a_0 + a_1\varepsilon_{t-1}^2 + a_2\sigma_{t-1}^2 \tag{10}$$

where ε_t is just the daily yield change, interpreted as yield shock, $E[.]$ denotes the statistical expectation operator, a_0, a_1, and a_2 are parameters to be estimated. In this way, yield volatility this period depends on yield shock as well as yield volatility in the last period. The GARCH model also estimates the long-run equilibrium variance, ω, as

$$E[\varepsilon_t^2] = \overline{\omega} = \frac{a_0}{1 - a_1 - a_2} \tag{11}$$

The GARCH model is popular not only for its simplicity in specification and its parsimonious nature in capturing time series properties of volatilities, but also because it is a generalization of some other measures of volatility. For exam-

---

[15] Francis A. Longstaff and Eduardo S. Schwartz, "Interest Rate Volatility and the Term Structure: A Two-Factor General Equilibrium Model," *Journal of Finance* (1992), pp. 1259-1282. Also see Francis A. Longstaff and Eduardo S. Schwartz, "Implementation of the Longstaff-Schwartz Interest Rate Model," *Journal of Fixed Income* (1993), pp. 7-14 for practical implementation of the model and how yield volatility is modeled by GARCH.

ple, it has been shown that equal-weighted rolling sample measure of variance and exponential smoothing scheme of volatility measure are both special cases of GARCH, but with different restrictions on the parameters. Other technical details of GARCH are beyond the scope of this chapter.[16]

Experience has shown that a GARCH(1,1) specification generally fits the volatility of most financial time series well, and is quite robust. The unknown parameters can again be estimated using MLE. The estimated models for the yields on 3-month Treasury bills and the 10-year and 30-year Treasury zeros are reported in Exhibit 8. Again, we plot the forecasted yield volatility, annualized by 250 days, of the 30-year spot rate in Exhibit 9 as an example.

One can immediately see that GARCH volatility is very different from the previous Power Function volatility. The reason is that GARCH incorporates the random and often erratic yield shocks as well as serial dependence in yield volatility into the volatility model; in contrast, the Power Function model only allows yield volatility to depend on the *level* of yield, without considering how past yield shocks and volatilities may affect the future volatility. The phenomenon of volatility clustering is well captured by GARCH, as revealed in Exhibit 9. On the other hand, the above GARCH(1,1) model does not consider the possible dependence of yield volatility on the level of yield. Thus, theoretically, GARCH volatilities do allow yields to become negative, which is an undesirable feature.

Power Function - GARCH Models

To capture the strength of both classes of models, one may consider combining the two into a more general form, at the expense of more complicated modeling and estimation, however. One way is to adopt the functional form of the Power Function model, while allowing the proportional yield volatility to follow a GARCH process. For example:

Exhibit 8: Estimation of GARCH(1,1) Models

	3-month Treasury bill	10-year Treasury zero	30-year Treasury zero
a_0	1.6467×10^{-8}	3.0204×10^{-8}	1.6313×10^{-8}
	(17.85)	(1.59)	(8.65)
a_1	0.0878	0.0896	0.0583
	(15.74)	(12.19)	(12.44)
a_2	0.8951	0.8441	0.9011
	(211.36)	(122.12)	(123.43)

[16] See, for example, Robert F. Engle, "Statistical Models for Financial Volatility," *Financial Analysts Journal* (1993), pp. 72-78; and Wai Lee and John Yin, "Modeling and Forecasting Interest Rate Volatility with GARCH," Chapter 20 in Frank J. Fabozzi (ed.), *Advances in Fixed Income Valuation Modeling and Risk Management* (New Hope, PA: FJF Associates, Pennsylvania, 1997), for an extensive discussion of GARCH as well as many other extensions.

Exhibit 9: 250-day Annualized Yield Volatility of 30-Year Spot Yield: GARCH(1,1) Model

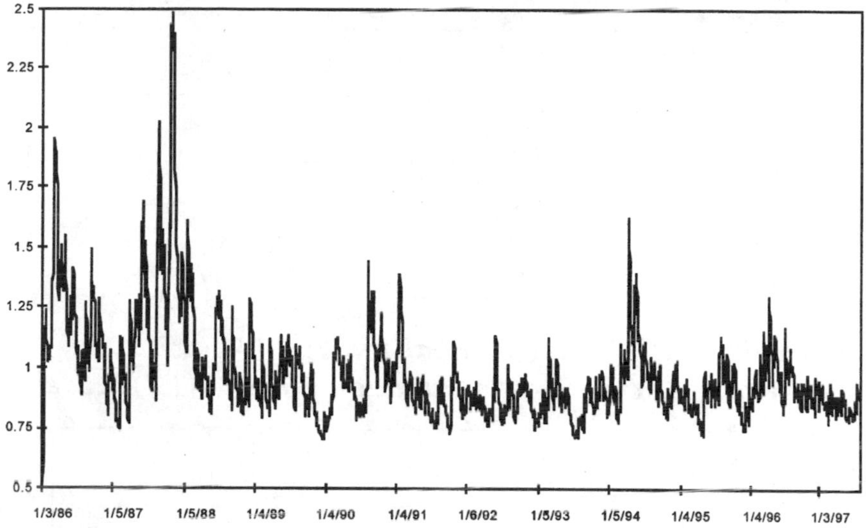

$$y_t - y_{t-1} = \varepsilon_t$$

$$\sigma_t = \sigma_{0,t} y_{t-1}^{\gamma}$$ (12)

$$\sigma_{0,t}^2 = a_0 + a_1 \varepsilon_{t-1}^2 + a_2 \sigma_{0,t-1}^2$$

With the above specification, yield volatility still depends on the level of yield, while past shocks and volatility affect current and future volatility through the proportional yield volatility, σ_0, which is now time varying instead of being a constant.[17] The estimation results are reported in Exhibit 10.

A noticeable difference between Exhibit 6 and Exhibit 10 is the fact that once the proportional yield volatility is modeled as a GARCH(1,1), γ assumes a smaller value than when yield volatility is only modeled as a power function of yield. In fact, γ for all maturities are all below 0.5, as assumed by the CIR model. This suggests that it is important to incorporate the dependence of current yield volatility on past information, or the sensitivity of yield volatility on level of yield may be overstated. For comparison purposes, Exhibit 11 plots the 250-day annualized yield volatility of the 30-year spot rate based on the estimated model in Exhibit 10.

---

[17] See Robin J. Brenner, Richard H. Harjes, and Kenneth F. Kroner, "Another Look at Models of the Short-Term Interest Rate," *Journal of Financial and Quantitative Analysis* (March 1996), pp. 85-107, for a similar treatment and extensions.

Exhibit 10: Estimation of Power Function - GARCH(1,1) Models

	3-month Treasury bill	10-year Treasury zero	30-year Treasury zero
a_0	$8.6802 \times 10\text{-}7$	$3.6185 \times 10\text{-}7$	$3.8821 \times 10\text{-}7$
	(1.59)	(1.23)	(1.37)
a_1	0.1836	0.0556	0.0717
	(12.73)	(11.07)	(14.20)
a_2	0.6424	0.8920	0.8015
	(34.53)	(48.52)	(5.40)
γ	0.2094	0.3578	0.3331
	(10.33)	(28.20)	(6.94)

Exhibit 11: 250-day Annualized Yield Volatility of 30-Year Spot Yield: Power Function - GARCH(1,1) Model

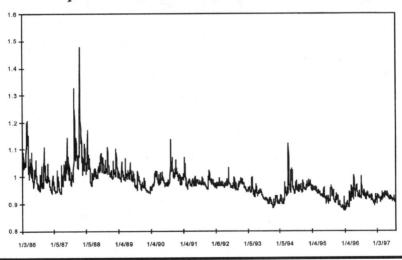

Implied Volatility

The second way to estimate yield volatility is based on the observed prices of interest rate derivatives, such as options on bond futures, or interest rate caps and floors. Yield volatility calculated using this approach is called *implied volatility.*

The implied volatility is based on some option pricing model. One of the inputs to any option pricing model in which the underlying is a Treasury security or Treasury futures contract is expected yield volatility. If the observed price of an option is assumed to be the fair price and the option pricing model is assumed to be the model that would generate that fair price, then the implied yield volatility is the yield volatility that when used as an input into the option pricing model would produce the observed option price. Because of their liquidity, options on

Treasury futures, Eurodollar futures, and caps and floors on LIBOR are typically used to extract implied volatilities.

Computing implied volatilities of yield from interest rate derivatives is not as straight forward as from derivatives of, say, stock. Later in this section, we will explain that these implied volatilities are not only model-dependent, but in some occasions they are also difficult to interpret, and can be misleading as well. For the time being, we follow the common practice in the industry of using the Black option pricing model for futures.[18]

Although the Black model has many limitations and inconsistent assumptions, it has been widely adopted. Traders often quote the exchange-traded options on Treasury or Eurodollar futures in terms of implied volatilities based on the Black model. These implied volatilities are also published by some investment houses, and are available through data vendors. For illustration purpose, we use the data of CBOT traded call options on 30-year Treasury bond futures as of April 30, 1997. The contract details, as well as the extracted implied volatilities based on the Black model, are listed in Exhibit 12.

Since the options are written on futures prices, the implied volatilities computed directly from the Black model are thus the implied price volatilities of the underlying futures contract. To convert the implied price volatilities to implied yield volatilities, we need the duration of the corresponding cheapest-to-deliver Treasury bond. The conversion is based on the simple standard relationship between percentage change in bond price and change in yield:

$$\frac{\Delta P}{P} \approx -\text{Duration} \times \Delta y \tag{13}$$

which implies that the same relationship also holds for price volatility and yield volatility.

Looking at the implied yield volatilities of the options with the same delivery month, one can immediately notice the "volatility smile." For example, for the options with a delivery month in June 1997, the implied yield volatility starts at a value of 0.98% for the deep in-the-money option with a strike price of 105, steadily drops to a minimum of 0.84% for the out-of-money option with a strike price of 113, and rises back to a maximum of 3.45% for the deep out-of-money option with a strike price of 130. Since all the options with the same delivery month are written on the same underlying bond futures, the only difference is their strike prices. The question is, which implied volatility is correct? While the answer to this question largely depends on how we accommodate the volatility smile,[19] standard practice suggests that we use the implied volatility of the at-the-money, or the nearest-the money option. In this case, the implied yield volatility of 0.91% of the option with a strike price of 109 should be used.

---

[18] Black, "The Pricing of Commodity Contracts."

[19] Current research typically uses either a jump diffusion process, a stochastic volatility model, or a combination of both to explain volatility smile. The details are beyond the scope of this chapter.

Exhibit 12: Call Options on 30-year Treasury Bond Futures on April 30, 1997

Delivery Month	Futures Price	Strike Price	Option Price	Implied Price Volatility	Duration	Implied Yield Volatility
1997:6	109.281	105	4.297	9.334	9.57	0.975
1997:6	109.281	106	3.328	9.072	9.57	0.948
1997:6	109.281	107	2.406	8.811	9.57	0.921
1997:6	109.281	108	1.594	8.742	9.57	0.913
1997:6	109.281	109	0.938	8.665	9.57	0.905
1997:6	109.281	110	0.469	8.462	9.57	0.884
1997:6	109.281	111	0.188	8.205	9.57	0.857
1997:6	109.281	112	0.062	8.129	9.57	0.849
1997:6	109.281	113	0.016	7.993	9.57	0.835
1997:6	109.281	114	0.016	9.726	9.57	1.016
1997:6	109.281	116	0.016	13.047	9.57	1.363
1997:6	109.281	118	0.016	16.239	9.57	1.697
1997:6	109.281	120	0.016	19.235	9.57	2.010
1997:6	109.281	122	0.016	22.168	9.57	2.316
1997:6	109.281	124	0.016	25.033	9.57	2.616
1997:6	109.281	126	0.016	27.734	9.57	2.898
1997:6	109.281	128	0.016	30.392	9.57	3.176
1997:6	109.281	130	0.016	33.01	9.57	3.449
1997:9	108.844	100	8.922	8.617	9.54	0.903
1997:9	108.844	102	7.062	8.750	9.54	0.917
1997:9	108.844	104	5.375	8.999	9.54	0.943
1997:9	108.844	106	3.875	9.039	9.54	0.947
1997:9	108.844	108	2.625	9.008	9.54	0.944
1997:9	108.844	110	1.656	8.953	9.54	0.938
1997:9	108.844	112	0.969	8.913	9.54	0.934
1997:9	108.844	114	0.516	8.844	9.54	0.927
1997:9	108.844	116	0.250	8.763	9.54	0.919
1997:9	108.844	118	0.109	8.679	9.54	0.910
1997:9	108.844	120	0.047	8.733	9.54	0.915
1997:9	108.844	122	0.016	8.581	9.54	0.899
1997:9	108.844	124	0.016	9.625	9.54	1.009
1997:9	108.844	126	0.016	10.646	9.54	1.116
1997:9	108.844	128	0.016	11.65	9.54	1.221
1997:12	108.469	98	10.562	7.861	9.51	0.827
1997:12	108.469	106	4.250	9.036	9.51	0.950
1997:12	108.469	108	3.125	9.070	9.51	0.954
1997:12	108.469	110	2.188	9.006	9.51	0.947
1997:12	108.469	112	1.469	8.953	9.51	0.941
1997:12	108.469	114	0.938	8.881	9.51	0.934
1997:12	108.469	116	0.594	8.949	9.51	0.941
1997:12	108.469	118	0.359	8.973	9.51	0.944
1997:12	108.469	120	0.234	9.232	9.51	0.971
1997:12	108.469	122	0.141	9.340	9.51	0.982
1997:12	108.469	128	0.031	9.793	9.51	1.030

What is the meaning of an "implied yield volatility of 0.91%"? To interpret this number, one needs to be aware that this number is extracted from the observed option price based on the Black model. As a result, the meaning of this number not only depends on the assumption that the market correctly prices the option, but also the fact that the market prices the option in accordance with the Black model. Neither of these assumptions need to hold. In fact, most probably, both assumptions are unrealistic. Given these assumptions, one may interpret that the option market expects a *constant* annualized yield volatility of 0.91% for 30-year Treasury from April 30, 1997 to the maturity date of the option. Caps and floors can also be priced by the Black model, when they are interpreted as portfolios of options written on forward interest rates. Accordingly, implied volatilities can be extracted from cap prices and floor prices, but subjected to the same limitations of the Black model.

Limitations of the Black Model

There are two major assumptions of the Black model that makes it unrealistic. First, interest rates are assumed to be constant. Yet, the assumption is used to derive the pricing formula for the option which derives its payoff precisely from the fact that future interest rates (forward rates) are stochastic. It has been shown that the Black model implies a time evolution path for the term structure that leads to arbitrage opportunities. In other words, the model itself implicitly violates the no-arbitrage spirit in derivatives pricing.

Second, volatilities of futures prices, or forward interest rates, are assumed to be constant over the life of the contract. This assumption is in sharp contrary to empirical evidence as well as intuition. It is well understood that a forward contract with one month to maturity is more sensitive to changes in the current term structure than a forward contract with one year to maturity. Thus, the volatility of the forward rate is inversely related to the time to maturity.

Finally, on the average, implied volatilities from the Black model are found to be higher than the realized volatilities during the same period of time.[20] A plausible explanation is that the difference in the two volatilities represents the fee for the financial service provided by the option writers, while the exact dynamics of the relationship between implied and realized volatilities remains unclear.

Practical Uses of Implied Volatilities from Black Model

Typically, implied volatilities from exchange-traded options with sufficient liquidity are used to price over-the-counter interest rate derivatives such as caps, floors, and swaptions. Apart from the limitations as discussed above, another difficulty in practice is the fact that only options with some fixed maturities are

---

[20] See Laurie Goodman and Jeffrey Ho, "Are Investors Rewarded for Shorting Volatility?" *Journal of Fixed Income* (June 1997), pp. 38-42, for a comparison of implied versus realized volatility.

traded. For example, in Exhibit 12, the *constant* implied volatilities only apply to the time periods from April 30, 1997 to the delivery dates in June, September, and December 1997, respectively. For instance, on May 1, 1997, we need a volatility input to price a 3-month cap on LIBOR. In this case, traders will either use the implied volatility from options with a maturity closest to three months, or make an adjustment/judgment based on the implied volatilities of options with a maturity just shorter than three months, and options with maturity just longer than three months.

Recent Development in Implied Volatilities

The finance industry is not unaware of the limitations of the Black model and its implied volatilities. Due to its simplicity and its early introduction to the market, it has become the standard in computing implied volatilities. However, there has been a tremendous amount of rigorous research going on in interest rate and interest rate derivatives models, especially since the mid 1980s. While a comprehensive review of this research is not provided here, it is useful to highlight the broad classes of models which can help us understand where implied volatilities related research is going.

Broadly speaking, there are two classes of models. The first class is known as the *Equilibrium Model*. Some noticeable examples include the Vasciek model, CIR model, Brennan-Schwartz model, and Longstaff-Schwartz model, as mentioned earlier in this chapter. This class of models attempts to specify the equilibrium conditions by assuming that some state variables drive the evolution of the term structure. By imposing other structure and restrictions, closed-form solutions for equilibrium prices of bonds and other interest rate derivatives are then derived. Many of these models impose a functional form to interest rate volatility, such as the power function as discussed and estimated earlier, or assume that volatility follows certain dynamics. In addition, the models also specify a particular dynamics on how interest rate drifts up or down over time. To implement these models, one needs to estimate the parameters of the interest rate process, including the parameters of the volatility function, based on some advanced econometric technique applied to historical data.

There are two major shortcomings of this class of models. First, these models are not preference-free, which means that we need to specify the utility function in dictating how investors make choices? Second, since only historical data are used in calibrating the models, these models do not rule out arbitrage opportunities in the current term structure. Due to the nature of the models, volatility is an important input to these models rather than an output that we can extract from observed prices. In addition, it has been shown that the term structure of spot yield volatilities can differ across one-factor versions of these models despite the fact that all produce the same term structure of cap prices.[21]

---

[21] Eduardo Canabarro, "Where Do One-Factor Interest Rate Models Fail?" *Journal of Fixed Income* (September 1995), pp. 31-52.

The second class of models is known as the *No-Arbitrage Model*. The *Ho-Lee Model* is considered as the first model of this class. Other examples include the *Black-Derman-Toy Model*,[22] *Black-Karasinski Model*,[23] and the *Heath-Jarrow-Morton Model (HJM)*.[24] In contrast to the equilibrium models which attempt to model equilibrium, these no-arbitrage models are less ambitious. They take the current term structure as given, and assume that no arbitrage opportunities are allowed during the evolution of the entire term structure. All interest rate sensitive securities are assumed to be correctly priced at the time of calibrating the model. In this way, the models, together with the current term structure and the no-arbitrage assumption, impose some restrictions on how interest rates of different maturities will evolve over time. Some restrictions on the volatility structure may be imposed in order to allow interest rates to mean-revert, or to restrict interest rates to be positive under all circumstances. However, since these models take the current bond prices as given, more frequent recalibration of the models is required once bond prices change.

The HJM model, in particular, has received considerable attention in the industry as well as in the finance literature. Many other no-arbitrage models are shown to be special cases of HJM. In spirit, the HJM model is similar to the well-celebrated Black-Scholes model in the sense that the model does not require assumptions about investor preferences.[25] Much like the Black-Scholes model that requires volatility instead of expected stock return as an input to price a stock option, the HJM model only requires a description of the volatility structure of forward interest rates, instead of the expected interest rate movements in pricing interest rate derivatives. It is this feature of the model that, given current prices of interest rate derivatives, make extraction of implied volatilities possible.

Amin and Morton[26] and Amin and Ng[27] use this approach to extract a term structure of implied volatilities. Several points are noteworthy. Since the no-arbitrage assumption is incorporated into the model, the extracted implied volatilities are more meaningful than those from the Black model. Moreover, interest rates are all stochastic instead of being assumed constant. On the other hand, these implied volatilities are those of forward interest rates, instead of spot interest rates. Furthermore, interest rate derivatives with different maturities and suffi-

---

[22] Fischer Black, Emanuel Dorman, and William Toy, "A One-Factor Model of Interest Rates and its Applications to Treasury Bond Options," *Financial Analysts Journal* (January-February 1990), pp. 33-39.

[23] Fischer Black and Piotr Karasinski, "Bond and Option Pricing when Short Rates are Lognormal," *Financial Analysts Journal* (1991), pp. 52-59.

[24] David Heath, Robert Jarrow, and Andrew Morton, "Bond Pricing and the Term-Structure of Interest Rates: A New Methodology," *Econometrica* (1992), pp. 77-105.

[25] This by no means implies that the Black-Scholes model is a no-arbitrage model. Although no-arbitrage condition is enforced, the Black-Scholes model does require equilibrium settings and market clearing conditions. Further details are beyond the scope of this chapter.

[26] Kaushik I. Amin and Andrew J. Morton, "Implied Volatility Functions in Arbitrage Free Term Structure Models," *Journal of Financial Economics* (1994), pp. 141-180.

[27] Kaushik I. Amin and Victor K. Ng, "Inferring Future Volatility from the Information in Implied Volatility in Eurodollar Options: A New Approach," *Review of Financial Studies* (1997), pp 333-367.

cient liquidity are required to calibrate the model. Finally, the HJM model is often criticized as too complicated for practitioners, and is too slow for real time practical applications.[28]

SUMMARY

Yield volatility estimates play a critical role in the measurement and control of interest rate risk. In this chapter we have discussed how historical yield volatility is calculated and the issues associated with its estimate. These issues include the number of observations and the time period to be used, the number of days that should be used to annualize the daily standard deviation, the expected value that should be used, and the weighting of observations. We then looked at modeling and forecasting yield volatility. The two approaches we discussed are historical volatility and implied volatility. For the historical volatility approach, we discussed various models, their underlying assumptions, and their limitations. These models include the Power Function Models and GARCH Models. While many market participants talk about implied volatility, we explained that unlike the derivation of this measure in equity markets, deriving this volatility estimate from interest rate derivatives is not as simple and straight forward. The implied volatility estimate depends not only on the particular option pricing model employed, but also a model of the time evolution of the complete term structure and volatilities of yields of different maturities.

---

[28] See David Heath, Robert Jarrow, Andrew Morton, and Mark Spindel, "Easier Done than Said," *Risk* (October 1992), pp. 77-80 for a response to this critique.

Index

The BARRA Cosmos System™

We are pleased to announce the most comprehensive suite of fixed income management tools in the financial industry—The BARRA Cosmos System™. This completely Windows™-based suite addresses the most crucial tasks facing today's fixed income professional: managing domestic portfolios, controlling risk, managing global portfolios and analyzing structured products.

DECISION
MANAGE PORTFOLIOS

GLOBAL RISK MANAGER
MANAGE GLOBAL PORTFOLIOS

RISK MANAGER—U.S.
CONTROL RISK

PRECISION
ANALYZE STRUCTURED PRODUCTS

Challenge

"How can I understand the full range of exposures for my fixed income portfolio? How can I make informed decisions regarding portfolio management?"

Action

The DECISION module within the Cosmos System provides a complete palette of fixed income portfolio management tools for taxable and tax-exempt bonds and derivatives. Building on the strengths of GAT's Integrative Bond System and Precision, Decision lets you:

- View Key Rate Durations (KRD), effective duration, convexity and OAS for any security or portfolio.

- Evaluate the effects of changes in interest rates, spreads and specific trades on your portfolio.

- Monitor compliance and optimize a portfolio based on your criteria.

Decision provides an easy-to-use workspace and Key Rate Duration profiles for any security or portfolio.

2100 MILVIA STREET • BERKELEY CA 94704-1113 • 510.548.5442 • www.barra.com

The BARRA Cosmos System™

We are pleased to announce the most comprehensive suite of fixed income management tools in the financial industry—The BARRA Cosmos System™. This completely Windows™-based suite addresses the most crucial tasks facing today's fixed income professional: managing domestic portfolios, controlling risk, managing global portfolios and analyzing structured products.

DECISION
MANAGE PORTFOLIOS

GLOBAL RISK MANAGER
MANAGE GLOBAL PORTFOLIOS

RISK MANAGER–U.S.
CONTROL RISK

PRECISION
ANALYZE STRUCTURED PRODUCTS

Challenge

"How can I quickly assess tracking error relative to my benchmark and identify the key areas of risk? How can I control multiple dimensions of risk for numerous portfolios?"

Action

The Cosmos System's RISK MANAGER–U.S. provides a comprehensive risk management workspace on your PC. You can:

- Obtain insight into your interest rate and spread risk, and selectively explore in greater detail the dimensions critical to your management strategy.

- Quantify portfolio volatility, both absolute (Value at Risk) and relative to your benchmark (tracking error), by leveraging BARRA's assessment of the volatility and correlations of those risk factors.

- Compare the dimensions of risk across multiple portfolios.

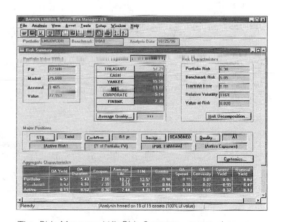

The Risk Manager–U.S. Risk Summary screen gives you a snapshot of many dimensions of risk as well as the overall tracking error versus your benchmark.

⑨ BARRA

2100 MILVIA STREET • BERKELEY CA 94704-1113 • 510.548.5442 • www.barra.com

The BARRA Cosmos System™

We are pleased to announce the most comprehensive suite of fixed income management tools in the financial industry—The BARRA Cosmos System™. This completely Windows™-based suite addresses the most crucial tasks facing today's fixed income professional: managing domestic portfolios, controlling risk, managing global portfolios and analyzing structured products.

DECISION
MANAGE PORTFOLIOS

GLOBAL RISK MANAGER
MANAGE GLOBAL PORTFOLIOS

RISK MANAGER–U.S.
CONTROL RISK

PRECISION
ANALYZE STRUCTURED PRODUCTS

Challenge

"How do I control risk and enhance returns in a multi-country portfolio? How can I create structured portfolios reflecting my expectations?"

Action

The Cosmos System's GLOBAL RISK MANAGER and GLOBAL OPTIMIZER offer a complete desktop solution to your international portfolio risk management needs. You can:

- Obtain an overview of global risk arising from region, country, currency and yield curve bets and concentrate on those components of risk which concern you the most.

- Create optimal portfolios reflecting risk, transactions costs, user-provided constraints and your own return expectations.

- Incorporate your own scenarios for interest rate, spread and currency movements, and construct your portfolio accordingly.

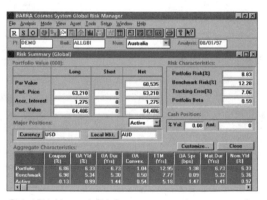

Global Risk Manager's Risk Summary screen gives you a concise overview of your global portfolio's risk characteristics.

2100 MILVIA STREET • BERKELEY CA 94704-1113 • 510.548.5442 • www.barra.com

he BARRA Cosmos System™

We are pleased to announce the most comprehensive suite of fixed income management tools in the financial industry—The BARRA Cosmos System™. This completely Windows™-based suite addresses the most crucial tasks facing today's fixed income professional: managing domestic portfolios, controlling risk, managing global portfolios and analyzing structured products.

DECISION
MANAGE PORTFOLIOS

GLOBAL RISK MANAGER
MANAGE GLOBAL PORTFOLIOS

RISK MANAGER—U.S.
CONTROL RISK

PRECISION
ANALYZE STRUCTURED PRODUCTS

Challenge

"How can I assess the prepayment risk and cashflow distribution of my CMO and MBS portfolios?"

Action

Within the Cosmos framework, BARRA provides a Windows-based analytical module—PRECISION—that includes an extensive database of CMOs, REMIC, RE-REMIC, ABS and MBS deals. You can:

- Assess the relative value and total return profiles of various tranches by running vector analysis and contrasting existing tranches with combination trades and/or collateral.

- Conduct regulatory reporting on the portfolio including FFIEC, NAIC FLUX scores, NYS Regulation 126, FAS91, S&P and A.M. Best reporting.

- Project the future cashflow behavior of the portfolio under user-defined prepayment or interest rate scenarios.

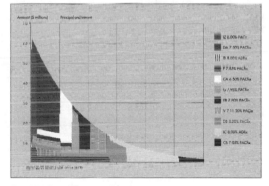

Precision's cashflow graphics help you visualize the projected behavior of any structured product.

# BARRA

2100 MILVIA STREET • BERKELEY CA 94704-1113 • 510.548.5442 • www.barra.com

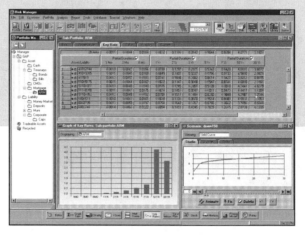